FORCES AND THEMES IN
ULSTER FICTION

John Wilson Foster

FORCES AND THEMES
IN
ULSTER FICTION

ROWMAN AND LITTLEFIELD
TOTOWA, NEW JERSEY

First published in the United States 1974

by Rowman and Littlefield, Totowa, N.J.

© John Wilson Foster, 1974

Library of Congress Cataloging in Publication Data

Foster, John Wilson.
  Forces and themes in Ulster fiction.

  Bibliography: p.
  1. English fiction — Irish authors — History and
criticism. 2. English fiction — 20th century — History
and criticism. 3. Northern Ireland in literature.
I. Title.
PR8803.F6   823 .9 109   73-21870

ISBN 0-87471-494-X

Printed in Northern Ireland by
W. & G. Baird Ltd.

For Jocelyn and my Mother
and to the memory of
my Father—first mentor

ACKNOWLEDGEMENTS

My first and deepest acknowledgement is to my wife Jocelyn who aided me through all stages of the manuscript and made me a gift of time.

My thanks also go to Benedict Kiely who first suggested in Cortland, New York that I undertake a study of Ulster fiction and later guided me through Carleton country where it all began. When the project was in the pilot stage, I received constructive criticism from the anonymous scholar who read my typescript at the request of Gill and Macmillan, and to him I owe my thanks.

Lastly, acknowledgement is due to the Arts Council of Northern Ireland, whose grant made possible this publication of my book.

NOTE ON REFERENCES

Editions of primary sources from which I have quoted in the text are indicated by bold type in the bibliography; the absence of bold type when more than one edition of a quoted source is listed means that pagination in the editions is identical.

CONTENTS

In the life of every man there are periods that are both departures and reunions, separations and reconciliations. Each of these phases is an attempt to transcend our solitude, and is followed by an immersion in strange environments.

Octavio Paz

FOREWORD

THE bulk of this study of Ulster fiction has been written without benefit of previous criticism on the subject or on individual authors, and for the most part I have relied upon the techniques of literary criticism much as a pilot, flying blind, relies upon his instruments. The dangers in this have been offset by the freedom from preconception. Using this freedom, I have tried to explore through the fiction (even, on occasions, at the risk of inflating the fiction's value) aspects of what we might loosely and a little sententiously call the Ulster Experience.

From the beginning I envisaged the book as a topographical scenario, with the chapters arranged by location. This arrangement has given me a cross-section of fictional settings and is an attempt to represent how the Ulster experience relates to environment. It also works chronologically, for the progression of the scenario—the land, the city, suburbia, the overseas cosmopolis—re-enacts the historical and current Irish processes of the drift from the land, of urbanisation and of emigration.

The topographical scenario is also what Mircea Eliade in *Myth and Reality* calls 'an initiatory scenario'—that social, ritual and mythic movement whose chief stages are separation, trial and return. This movement is most familiar to us in the form of adolescent trial that separates the adolescent from childhood and incorporates him into manhood. In fact, my early chapters do tend to deal with childhood, a middle chapter with adolescence and later chapters with middle age, roughly corresponding to the shifts in setting from the land to the heart of the city and to suburbia. This way I have tried through the fiction to show the recent historical traumas and motions of the Ulster people.

Within the scenario, the heart of the study remains close analyses of individual novels and stories. But there is a relationship of sorts between setting and initiatory theme on the one hand and fictional mode and genre on the other, and so my chapters tend to be concerned with different styles and modes of Ulster fiction, ranging from the 'childlike' folk allegory of the first chapter, through the realism of the middle chapters, to the 'decadence' of the later chapters.

In many of these respects, the last chapter functions to make the scenario circular. Working across it, in a kind of counterpoint, are dichotomous traditions and subcultures—Protestant and Catholic, nationalist and unionist, Irish and Scots-Irish, peasant and middle-class. Unless satirised, these aspire to ideal and even to myth. We shall encounter, for example, different versions of the Paradise myth in Ulster fiction. Few of the writers—even the best, among them Joyce Cary, Forrest Reid, Brian Moore, Patrick Boyle and Benedict Kiely—manage to straddle many of the various traditions available to the Ulsterman; in this sense, as well as in the sense of achievement, none of them approach the nineteenth-century fiction writer, William Carleton. Carleton, subject of my introductory chapter, can be said to have fathered Ulster fiction in the process of fathering important strains in Irish fiction generally.

I have called the book a study of 'Ulster' fiction rather than of 'Northern Ireland' fiction because several of the writers discussed were born in the Republican part of Ulster but have set their work freely on either side of the border—e.g. Anthony C. West from Cavan and Patrick MacGill from Donegal. Other writers born in Northern Ireland have with equal freedom and unself-consciousness set their work in the Republic —e.g. Benedict Kiely, Brian Friel and Patrick Boyle. It seemed best, therefore, to disregard the border as a precise cultural divide. On the other hand, I have not tried to be exhaustive in the other direction and have tended to disregard Ulster writers who have not had strong connections, through birth, fictional setting or cultural association, with what is now Northern Ireland. In effect, my book orientates rather than compartmentalises, orientates towards the North-east and, within that, towards Belfast. I have not sought the differentia of fictional Northern-ness, and I am sure that some of what I say could be said equally about fiction in the South. That there is in Ireland a cultural continuity, if neither cultural nor political unity, is self-evident, and a search for vivid lines of demarcation would be fruitless.

Belfast 1971—Dublin 1973

INTRODUCTION

BLACK PROPHET

WILLIAM CARLETON (1794–1869), first and foremost novelist of the Irish peasantry, wrote often and with reckless intimacy about his youth in the Clogher valley, Co. Tyrone. In his sprawling and uneven canon can be found the chief thematic motifs and styles we will presently discover in modern Ulster fiction set close to the land. Ulster writers may not always have been conscious of Carleton's ghost over their shoulders (nothing being easier, as Walter Allen has remarked, than to construe affinities as influences), but a continuity from Carleton to the present exists in Ulster fiction because many of the shaping forces of Northern Irish society have not startlingly altered since his day. Rural fiction is still mightily dependent for its material upon country mores (customs, games, songs, tales, beliefs) and the radical social and community forces that make life outside the city what it is. The relative stability of these folk ways and forces is evidenced in E. Estyn Evans's repeated use of adjectives such as 'immemorial', 'medieval', 'simple' and 'ancient' when characterising rural Irish life of a quarter-century ago.[1] Consequently, much of the social texture and even plots of twentieth-century rural Ulster fiction would be quite familiar to Carleton were he to pay us a visit today.

Some social realities of the mid-nineteenth century have, of course, completely changed, for example the role of England and the Ascendancy in Irish affairs. Carleton could list quite specifically, as he did in the pages of *The Emigrants of Ahadarra* (1847), the grievances of the Irish people,[2] and indeed these gave him his involved but formulaic plots (e.g. evictions, terrorist response, designs on land-holdings, tactical marriages, emigration) and his well-drawn but stock characters (the usurer, the

1. E. Estyn Evans, *Irish Folk Ways*, London 1957, ch. 1.
2. These included: absentee landlordism, subletting, the whole iniquitous middleman system that gave land-agents, gaugers and the like immense powers, enforced subdivision of holdings, the forty-shilling franchise, the use of the truck system in the payment of the labouring classes.

unscrupulous land-agent, the neglectful landlord, the terrorist, the wronged hero). Rural Ulster fiction, as I suggest in Chapter One, now operates with different formulae, of necessity because the social system and the nature of government in Ireland have changed.

Whereas oppression in modern rural fiction in Ulster is obscure and symptomatic, social injustice in Carleton can be swift and terrible, condemning a peasant family to destitution by one flourish of the agent's quill or one thrust of the bailiff's battering-ram. But it can also be slow and impersonal—a landlord's neglect of his estates or the disinclination of families to improve their holdings while the threat of summary eviction hangs over them.[3] Meanwhile the land decays, and we have vivid images of this ruination in Carleton's portrait of the Colonel's Big House in 'The Poor Scholar' and the farms of the Sullivans and Daltons in *The Black Prophet* (1847). The imagery of land-decline is equally common in modern Ulster fiction and occurs in Michael McLaverty, Benedict Kiely, Brian Friel and —in evidence against Catholic farmers—in Shan F. Bullock. Carleton normally used the picture of land-decline to try to shame negligent landlords, and if this connection has disappeared in modern fiction, McLaverty still manages to associate inability to exploit the land's potential with blurred forms of social oppression. Carleton, at the same time, frequently complained of peasant idleness and of the 'abundance and slovenly neglect which is, unfortunately, almost peculiar to our country' (*The Emigrants of Ahadarra*, 1). In modern fiction this suggestion is kept alive that the farmers and peasants themselves are somehow to blame, that they have been inadequate custodians of the green land.

Yet even when a firm and wise hand is kept on the plough, uncontrollable factors conspire against the tiller of the soil, factors which do not discriminate between the meadows of the Catholics and those of the Protestants. 'The climate of Ireland is so unsettled,' bemoaned Carleton, 'the soil so various in quality, and the potato so liable to injury from excess of

3. Both situations play important roles in *The Black Prophet*, even though the novel is set in Tyrone where it was the custom (known as Ulster Tenant Right, but only a custom and not a law) for tenants to receive compensation from incoming tenants for improvements.

either drought or moisture.' (*The Black Prophet,* 175)[4] When rain and warmth—normally conditions of good growth—combine in excess, they lead to a diseased fertility that precedes and accompanies famine. 'Look about you,' the Black Prophet commands a neighbour, 'and say what it is you see that doesn't foretell famine—famine—famine! Doesn't the dark wet day an' the rain, rain, rain foretell it? Doesn't the rottin' crops, the unhealthy air, an' the green damp foretell it?' (*The Black Prophet,* 15) It is no wonder that 'the sweltering and deluged country' is such a powerful image in the work of a man who witnessed successive famines from 1817 and knew like everyone else that heat and moisture were the conditions in which blight and disease prospered.[5] Abundance and neglect, fertility and ruin: this is the hideous paradox that lies at the heart of Carleton's portrait of the land and is a mocking conspiracy of God, the Ascendancy and, did they but know it, the peasants' own inadequacies. The paradox endures, and the imagery of rain and water and of reckless fertility is crucial in twentieth-century writers such as Bullock, Patrick MacGill, McLaverty, Friel and John O'Connor.

Bad government, poverty and the vicissitudes of the soil and climate combine to produce one of the major thematic motifs in Ulster fiction, that of *the blighted land.* The motif has lost some of its passionate force in modern rural fiction because the extreme social conditions of Carleton's time have mostly disappeared. Carleton could summon up images of widespread dearth and hunger and lived through the Great Famine, that horrific conjunction of all the Irish peasant's disabilities. It would be difficult for a modern writer to match the apocalyptic vision of *The Black Prophet* with its terrifying evocations of the soup-kitchens, cadaverous beggars and endless funeral processions under a brooding sky. Yet so traumatic was the Famine for the Irish people that it lingers yet in the folk memory. The Victorian and post-Victorian workhouses in Shan Bullock, Patrick

4. Cf. E. Estyn Evans: 'Here in the hilly fringes of Europe, towards the ocean, even moderately fertile land is limited in extent: soils derived from barren rocks and heavily leached by excessive rains are subject to water-logging, acidity and the accumulation of peat. Spring is the only season without excessive rain.' (*Irish Folk Ways,* 33.)

5. Cecil Woodham-Smith, *The Great Hunger,* London 1968, 93.

MacGill and Michael McLaverty have, even when offstage, inherited some of the emotive currency of the soup-kitchens, and MacGill's Donegal mendicants still bear the haunted and ravaged look of Carleton's famine-struck peasants.

It is easy to understand how decades of bad luck, poverty and decline could breed the notion that somehow the land is cursed. It is a short step from this to the idea that the people themselves, in such intimate traffic with the land, labour under a malign star. The idea of an accursed people can be associated with the high degree of superstition among the rural Irish, particularly superstition surrounding evil, and features in rural Ulster fiction not merely as a background but in the very conception of character and plot-causation.[6] Evil forces are aroused principally by *bad blood,* another major thematic motif in Ulster fiction. This motif is intimately associated with that of the blighted land, because bad blood within families, among neighbours and between the two sects is frequently caused by those personality traits rooted in the poverty and overpopulation of the land— the penchant for scandal, gossip, intrigue, snobbery, fecklessness and avarice. These are chief causes of dissension in Carleton's fiction and remain so in the work of modern rural writers. At its most intense, dissension in family and community escalates into that internecine feuding Carleton called 'factionalism'. 'The Party Fight and Funeral' contains a humorous treatment of this, but in 'Wildgoose Lodge' and in *Fardorougha the Miser* (1839), Carleton grimly portrayed murderous attacks by Ribbonmen on Catholic families. Factionalism has since been watered down in Ulster fiction, but its spirit has lingered, providing the dramatic pulse to much of the plot-work in Bullock, MacGill and McLaverty.

Carleton in 'The Party Fight and Funeral' distinguishes factionalism (feuding among members of the same sect) from party-fighting (or what we nowadays call sectarian strife). His evocations of Ribbonmen, Whiteboys, Orangemen and other 'secret confederacies' acting violently in the service of the Cause, 'that ideal monster', is depressingly familiar. For Carleton, prejudice was arational and self-perpetuating and for those reasons

6. Carleton devoted a novel to the Irish superstition of the evil eye (*The Evil Eye,* Dublin 1860), a belief he characteristically condemned while equally characteristically exploiting.

impossible to eradicate: 'If you hate a man for an obvious and palpable injury, it is likely that when he cancels that injury by an act of subsequent kindness, accompanied by an exhibition of sincere sorrow, you will cease to look upon him as your enemy; but where the hatred is such that, while feeling it, you cannot, on a sober examination of your heart, account for it, there is little hope that you will ever be able to stifle the enmity which you entertain against him.'[7] Perhaps it was depression as much as the melodramatic and farcical streak in him that led Carleton so often to portray sectarianism in a tragicomic light. It is a reaction that has been imitated by subsequent writers, such as Lynn Doyle, as though it were the only viable alternative to the shy evasion of sectarianism or the passive regret for its existence we find in most Ulster fiction writers after Carleton.

Through kinship and ancestral possession, the blood and the land are bound into a near-mystical union. The union depends upon the concord of kin and neighbour ('good blood') and the proper and cordial exploitation of the land's fertility. When the blood is 'bad' or the land is 'blighted', the blood-land nexus is broken and the people's ties with the land severed. Accordingly, there is a vast amount of migration and emigration in Carleton's fiction, usually enforced: sudden evictions (like that of the M'Evoys in 'The Poor Scholar'), sequestrations (such as the banishment of Connor Donovan in *Fardorougha the Miser*), the gradual throttling of willing farmers by unscrupulous agents (as in *The Emigrants of Ahadarra*). Emigration from Ireland, of course, because of oppression and poverty, became torrential during Carleton's lifetime,[8] but in any case his is a fluid social universe. His novels are bustling narratives whose *dénouements* frequently involve all manner of wandering tattlers—mendicants, tinkers, prophecy-men, poor scholars, hedge-schoolmasters. Fewer peripatetics make their appearance in modern Ulster fiction, though they crop up in Kiely, Friel and John O'Connor, and are principals in the novels of MacGill who writes of seasonal migration and life 'on the road'. The modern Irish

7. 'The Party Fight and Funeral', *Traits and Stories of the Irish Peasantry*, London 1893, 152.
8. See W. F. Adams, *Ireland and Irish Emigration to the New World from 1815 to the Famine*, New Haven, Conn., 1932.

themselves are a much less mobile population, although for some there is still periodic navvy-work in England and at home the absurdly glamourised 'travelling people'; post-Famine Ireland, with half of its pre-Famine population sheared off, has lost the random, sporadic movement of Carleton's time and settled into a more patterned movement (with its own post-Famine causes) known as 'the drift from the land' and paralleled by a process of urbanisation. The scenario of this study of Ulster fiction, the land—the town— the city—the overseas cosmopolis, is a model of this patterned movement.

The individual can, of course, reverse the scenario at any time, returning to the fields from which he has been separated. Return is an everyday word in the vocabulary of an emigrant people; the 'returned American', for example, is a veritable character-type in Bullock, St John Ervine, Friel, Kiely, Brian Moore and Maurice Leitch, so common indeed that it is normally meant to convey instantly either comic pomposity or pathetic disenchantment. Return is often anticlimactic or disappointing; sometimes too in the fiction the returning exile discovers to his cost, as I demonstrate in Chapters One and Eight, that the land, in a refractory and even hostile sense, endures; to borrow the title of a little Hubert Quinn novel in dubbing a chief motif in rural Ulster fiction : *the land remains.*

(2)

Lost fields—a major thematic motif which I have used as the title of my first chapter—is at once the beginning and the essence of the scenario, referring as it does not only to the physical loss of the land through blight and bad blood but also to the delayed psychic and spiritual effects of that loss upon the city-dwellers of McLaverty, Moore, Ervine and others. It is primarily, but by no means exclusively, a Catholic motif. Protestants over the centuries have been involved in emigration and the drift from the land; they suffer too from bad blood and bad land. Nonetheless, we would not distort the fictional or historical picture by seeing the trauma of land-loss etched more deeply upon the Catholic than the Protestant psyche which is perhaps why Catholics, with their greater sense of grievance and deprivation in this matter, have contributed the bulk of the writers dealt with in my first five chapters.

Whereas Carleton occasionally showed Protestants suffering equally under the curse of incompetent landlords and ruthless agents (for instance, the Wallace family in *The Emigrants of Ahadarra*), the Northern Dissenters were at other times held to be co-authors with the Ascendancy of the misery of their Catholic fellow-Ulstermen. The memory of the Ulster Plantation, already two hundred years old, still rankled in the minds of Carleton's peasants and is a wound re-opened in the passage that begins 'The Poor Scholar' :

One day about the middle of November in the year 18—, Dominick M'Evoy and his son Jemmy were digging potatoes on the side of a hard, barren hill, called Esker Dhu. The day was bitter and wintry, the men were thinly clad, and as the keen blast swept across the hill with considerable violence, the sleet-like rain which bore it along pelted into their garments with pitiless severity . . .

The father paused to take breath, and, supported by his spade, looked down upon the sheltered inland, which, inhabited chiefly by Protestants and Presbyterians, lay rich and warm-looking under him.

'Why, thin,' he exclaimed to the son, a lad about fifteen, 'sure I know well I oughtn't to curse yees, anyway, you black set; and yit, the Lord forgive me my sins, I'm almost timpted to give yees a volley, an' that from my heart out! Look at thim, Jimmy agra—only look at the black thieves! how warm an' wealthy they sit there in our ould possessions, an' here we must toil, till our fingers are worn to the stumps, upon this thievin' bent.' (*Traits and Stories,* 492)

The grievance over planter dispossession was given a personal sting in Carleton's work because of his pride in belonging, not to the peasantry (as many critics have mistakenly believed) but to a dispossessed yeomanry, a term he used in conscious parallel to that English class; many of Carleton's most autobiographical heroes, such as Jemmy M'Evoy, are sons of 'honest but reduced parents'.

Planter dispossession of the native Irish remains after all these centuries a viable motif in Catholic rural fiction, perhaps because even today hill farmers tend to be Catholic and lowland farmers Protestant,[9] but how this sectarian distribution of land came about, though to a degree historically ascertainable, is almost a matter of two contradictory folk myths upon which fiction writers have drawn. For instance, W. F. Marshall in his historical novel, *Planted by a River* (1948), has his narrator account for 'why so many of the Irish are in the hills and mountains' as if in rebuttal of the claims of Catholic writers from Carleton to McLaverty:

The bulk of them were not driven thither, as they now erroneously assert, and as some of our own people credulously believe. The greater part of them migrated thither, after some years of profitless farming in the lowlands.

For the Planting of Ulster, which was indeed a woeful thing for the Irish gentry, was also a high State policy which caused little disturbance to natives resident on the soil. It is true that newcomers occupied and farmed good land. But it is also true that there was enough good land for all, both for the newcomers and the native born . . .

But as time went on, the settlers on the good land began to multiply, both by a natural increase, and as the result of immigration. On the other hand, the native born in the same kind of areas diminished. For what reason? Because they had not been farmers, day in and day out, as our people had been for generations, and they knew not how to farm land to advantage, as we did. Again, they were not only deficient in habits of industry, but also in such foresight as was evidenced in the gathering of stones, the clearing of scrub, the levelling and fencing of fields, and a general carefulness of tillage.

Because of these deficiencies, for which their history and way of previous living provide explanation and excuse, their holdings became at length unprofitable to them. They were unable to pay even the easy rents demanded in the early years. . . By the natural pressure of events, they had to give way, and remove to the hill country, where rents were trifling, and cheap land abundant. (pp. 208–9)

These have been fertile folk myths, even accounting for the supposed physical differences between rural Protestants and Catholics. Carleton, describing the confrontation between

9. See Rosemary Harris, *Prejudice and Tolerance in Ulster*, Manchester 1972.

Ribbonmen and Orangemen in 'The Party Fight and Funeral', soberly informs us that

In the district where the scene of this fight is laid, the Catholics generally inhabit the mountainous part of the country, to which, when the civil feuds of worse times prevailed, they had been driven at the point of the bayonet; the Protestants and Presbyterians, on the other hand, who came in upon their possessions, occupy the richer and more fertile tracts of the land, living, of course, more wealthily, with less labour, and on better food. The characteristic features produced by these causes are such as might be expected— the Catholic being, like his soil, hardy, thin, and capable of bearing all weathers; and the Protestants, larger, softer, and more inactive. (*Traits and Stories*, 175)

Seventy years later, this was scotched (as it were) by Shan Bullock who was naturally more disposed to think of the lowland Protestants as the tougher of the two : 'They are better clothed and better fed, bolder of eye and bearing; bigger, harder, coarser, tighter of lip, stronger in hand and body.' (*The Squireen*, 4)

Since Carleton, these two folk myths have in the fiction generated versions of the Paradise myth. The Protestant version, adumbrated in Marshall, is a myth of origination and consists of the notion that a kind of Eden was perfected by the planters out of the rough paradise which already existed before their advent and which has ever since been imperilled by the Catholics, fallen angels from their own paradise. It is a hubristic notion, and Bullock and Jack Wilson have tended to the idea that in the presumption of trying to perfect Eden (by what John Montague calls 'an alien discipline') was the paradise lost. In any event, perhaps because the idea of paradise springs out of a sense of loss, the Protestant version is not nearly as potent as the Catholic version which is a story of a Fall in which the Protestant planters play rather a devilish role. In this version, paradise—fleetingly regained only in childhood and fantasy—is that of the green land before the English occupations and the Ulster Plantation, but it has also expanded to include an image of Ireland's oneness, an indivisible nation of passionate men and women. As I try to show in my second chapter, the short story, admirably suited for the exploration of childhood and of fantasy, has been the vehicle for McLaverty, Kiely and Friel to evoke the departure from this paradise and the roundabout return journey. The recovery of paradise is a mythic equivalent to the fictional motif of return which I described above, and we can deem it, after Mircea Eliade, *the eternal return.*[10]

It seems that Carleton was too close to a bustling and mobile pre-Famine population to elevate separation and return into mythic motifs. It is true that planter dispossession does in his work suggest something of a Fall and that there is in his fiction the suggestion of an eschatology, with hell represented in the heinous deeds of the Ribbonmen (see 'Wildgoose Lodge' and the account of the affair in his autobiography with their satanic imagery) and interim judgement visited upon the unjust and the oppressor. But there is no counterbalancing wish for paradise, and the nostalgia of his autobiography, for example, is continually torpedoed by his cautionary regrets and his vital sense of the present. The suggestion of a Paradise myth in Ulster fiction, then, is a post-Famine motif, perhaps even a post-Partition motif, for the search for paradise might seem more urgent and germane to a Catholic population whom the Irish revolution passed by and for whom, in addition, the planter invasion still burns fiercely in the folk memory. It may also be related to the paucity rather than the plenitude of actual grievances in the sense that the more likely appears the achievement of social justice here and now, the more remote and mythic becomes the concept of an ideal Ireland. Perhaps, more simply, the Paradise myth reflects the passive dreams of a people debilitated by hunger and hardship.

(3)

For all the deprivation suffered by Carleton's people, they are a rich and lively assortment; even in the throes of hunger and sickness they have a feverish energy. The bustling activity of Carleton's Ireland contrasts sharply with the slow motion of a great deal of subsequent rural Irish fiction, the kind of work I discuss in Chapters One and Two. If we assume that the contrast is not wholly one of genre or one involving Carleton's uniqueness, we might cast around for tentative social reasons

10. Mircea Eliade, *The Myth of the Eternal Return,* London 1955.

for the passive image of rural Ireland in much post-Famine fiction. In particular, the peculiarly passive image of sex in modern rural fiction ought to be accounted for, since in this regard Carleton's fiction is altogether livelier and healthier.

A possible explanation might lie in the increase in the moral as well as spiritual power of the churches—especially the Catholic Church—that accompanied the decline of medieval and pagan aspects of pre-Famine Ireland. This increase seems to have brought with it a greater puritanism in the sexual habits of the Irish. By contrast, the interference of the priest in the private lives of Carleton's peasants seems slight. When he is feeling anti-clerical, Carleton points to priestly meddling in politics (for instance, in *The Emigrants of Ahadarra*) or to priestly gluttony (in 'Denis O'Shaughnessy Going to Maynooth') rather than to Church interference in day-to-day morality. The clash between Church and private conscience, a topic that looms large in modern Irish fiction from Joyce to Brian Moore, does not loom large in Carleton. In addition, Carleton felt free to make sport of celibacy and sexual passivity, for they seem neither issue nor ideal among his people. The celibate priestly scholar is a character-type in his stories, of course, but when the scholar chooses flesh over spirit, as Denis O'Shaughnessy does, it is the obvious thing for him to do rather than the tortuously philosophical choice it is in later fiction. In any event, it remains true that the Catholic Church, more than any other institution, has helped to create a sexually puritanical and repressed nation. A lot of fiction after Carleton expresses, consciously or unconsciously, that repression.

Many medieval and pagan aspects of Ireland can be said to have disappeared with the Famine and subsequent land reforms, perhaps creating something of a vacuum which the Church helped to fill. E. Estyn Evans has called the Famine 'a grim watershed in social and economic history' that obliterated so many folk ways 'that it might be regarded as the end of prehistoric times in Ireland'.[11] Even at a glance, the rural Ireland of modern fiction seems a tired and sparse countryside from which half of Carleton's busy pre-Famine population has vanished. Those who remained after the Famine experienced a

11. Evans, 10.

change not only in the customs and folk ways of the land, but
in the psychic realities that produce them. For example, Carleton
lamented the high incidence of early marriage in rural Ireland :
'There is not a country in Europe where so many rash and un-
reflecting marriages are made as in Ireland; the habit has been
the curse of the country.'[12] He goes on to discuss the frequency
and methods of elopement and abduction, information he freely
used in his plots. In startling contrast is the notorious reluctance
of the modern rural Irish to enter into marriage (confirmed in
statistics) and to initiate themselves into sexuality, the protraction
of engagements between rural couples often into middle age,
and the passionless manner in which courtship is conducted,
all of which have been exploited by writers such as Patrick
Kavanagh, Kiely, Friel and Bullock. True, Carleton also wrote
of the tedious and passion-killing middleman system of courtship (comically in 'Phelim O'Toole's Courtship'), but the impression of greater impulse, passion and sexuality in Carleton's Ireland
sticks. In Chapter One of this study I examine the intimate
connection between changes in sexual mores after the Famine
and changes in the distribution and inheritance of land.

Exceptions to the depiction of post-Famine rural Ireland as a
passive and fatigued place suggest themselves in the works of
Lynn Doyle, Benedict Kiely and Patrick Boyle, which I discuss
in Chapter Three. The fiction of these men is often possessed of
feverish vitality and, in the case of the latter two, sexual liveli-
ness. Indeed, sexuality and violence in Boyle and Kiely are
frequently geared to a manic pitch in extreme reaction to the
other side of their fiction, its pathos and sentimentality. Lack
of centre—expressed stylistically in the sharp swing between
tones and a lack of genuine realism, and psychologically in the
characters' swing between energy and depression—tends to
characterise rural and Catholic fiction, certainly in Ulster. It is
evident in Carleton. Thomas Flanagan speaks of 'two streams'
in Carleton, one flowing with love, affection and sacrifice, the
other with violence, savagery and superstition.[13] Elsewhere in
his book Flanagan speaks of two kinds of music in Carleton, that

12. David J. O'Donoghue, *The Life of William Carleton*, London 1896,
I, 94.
13. Thomas Flanagan, *The Irish Novelists 1800–1850*, New York, 1959,
291–2.

of the fiddle which accompanies dancing and mirth and that of
the harp which accompanies heroism, sacrifice and death.[14] Most
of Carleton's fiction veers between the passive modes of pathos
and sentimentality and the active modes of grotesque and
macabre comedy, between the themes of victimisation and murderous violence, and, in psychological tone, between depression
and mania.

This oscillation, in terms of mood, seems part of the Irish
character itself. Carleton recognised this when he wrote of pathos
and humour as 'the two levers by which the Irish character is
raised or depressed; and these are blended in a manner too
anomalous to be ever properly described'.[15] 'Blended' is hardly
the word. Carleton goes on to describe the reaction of congregations to sermons, swinging between 'grotesque and clamor-
ous grief' and 'that rough, blunt satire and mirth so keenly re-
lished by the peasantry'. It is true that the congregations, ever
ready to please, take their cues from the priests' manner, but elsewhere Carleton commonly remarks on the spontaneity of Irish
grief and joy. Other writers have acknowledged the emotional
alternation of the Irish character. Joyce summarised it with one
portmanteau word : *funferall.* Speaking of the primacy of
imagination in the Celtic character, Sean O'Faolain describes
the Celts as 'struggling, through century after century, with this
imaginative domination, seeking for a synthesis between dream
and reality, aspiration and experience, a shrewd knowledge of
the world and a strange reluctance to cope with it, and tending
always to find the balance not in an intellectual synthesis but in
the rhythm of a perpetual emotional oscillation'.[16]

Dream and fantasy accompany both ends of the emotional
oscillation. This is evident when we consider how Ulster fiction
—as a species of Irish literature—treats death and sex, the two
subjects which set the emotional pendulum swinging most amply.
When sex and death are turned into pleasant fantasy they become, respectively, sentimental romance and self-indulgent
pathos, and Irish literature in general and Ulster fiction in
particular have numerous examples of these modes. When sex
and death are turned into unpleasant fantasy they become,

14. Flanagan, 305.
15. 'The Poor Scholar', *Traits and Stories*, 499.
16. Sean O'Faolain, *The Irish*, Harmondsworth 1969, 22.

respectively, grotesque and macabre. Vivian Mercier has demonstrated the archaism of the macabre and the grotesque in
Gaelic and Anglo-Irish literature.[17] In Carleton, a writer to
whom Mercier makes only passing reference, death is matter
either for pathos or for the macabre, both responses reflecting
generic conventions. But they surely reflect also psychological
reaction. Through hyperbole and self-indulgence in the direction either of pathos or of the macabre, the Irishman seeks to
purge his fear of death. In fiction as in life, however, pathos and
the macabre can become their own ends : the Irish, for all their
attempts at purgation, remain greatly preoccupied with death
(a preoccupation which their Catholicism does not help to
diminish) and the fiction writers obsessively so, witness the
countless death-scenes, wakes and funerals.

If many of Carleton's weakest scenes are pathetic, many of
his most powerful images and scenes are violent and macabre—
the references to the bleeding of bullocks and calves by peasants
staving off hunger in 'The Poor Scholar', the descriptions of
the ravages of typhus and cholera during famine in *The Black
Prophet,* the account of the attack by Ribbonmen on Wildgoose
Lodge in the story of the same name. This last is a potent piece
indeed (as Carleton modestly acknowledged), but so macabre is
its description of the Lodge children being spitted on bayonets
and tossed back into the flaming house that it is almost comic.
A macabre and menacing comedy skirts, too, Carleton's personal account of the aftermath of the Wildgoose Lodge affair.[18]
In arguably the most horrific and resonant scene in modern
Irish literature, Carleton in his autobiography recalls encounter-
ing on his way south from Co. Tyrone the gibbeted body of the
Ribbon leader, Paddy Devaun, disintegrating in putrescence and
autumn heat, a mere sack swinging in the breeze with 'long
ropes of slime shining in the light, and dangling from the bottom'.
The gibbet was erected so close to Devaun's mother's house that
she could not fail to overlook the nauseating remains of her
son as she went about her daily tasks. 'The greater part of the
county of Louth,' Carleton discovered, 'was studded with
gibbets. . . Every sack was literally covered with flies, which

17. Vivian Mercier, *The Irish Comic Tradition,* Oxford 1962, ch. 3.
18. O'Donoghue, *The Life of William Carleton,* I, 129-35.

having enjoyed their feast, passed away in millions throughout the country.' 'During that autumn,' adds Carleton biblically, 'fruit in the county of Louth was avoided, as something which could not be eaten.' For all its horror, Carleton's recital of these dark happenings has a blackly comic edge, establishing a mid-point between realism and caricature, revulsion and risibility which is the hallmark of the macabre.

Sex in Irish fiction tends similarly to be either sentimental or else grotesque, and as in the treatment of death the lack of serious centre suggests a deep-lying fear or embarrassment. Of course, in Carleton's case one must also take into account literary genre and motivation. If his treatment of love and sex errs on the side of sentimental romance, it is partly because this was a popular mode in the nineteenth century. It also suited his propaganda purposes. For example, all his heroines, as Darrell Figgis pointed out, are beautiful and unsullied as befitted the ideal Irish peasant girl being presented to the English reader.[19] On the other hand, there is much less grotesquerie in his fiction —offstage profligacy, abductions and rapes—than macabre humour. No less than the macabre, grotesquerie is a species of fantasy and one which in Irish literature has often been associated with giantism (frequently involving gluttony in pursuit of food, drink or sex). Mercier traces giantry through Irish literature from Finn to Finnegan, though without mentioning Carleton in this context. Billy Carleton the celebrated river-leaper, weight-thrower and champion athlete of several town-lands almost fills the role of giant himself, and he put his athletic enthusiasm to good fictional account, for instance in the comic-epic battle between Grimes and Kelly in 'The Party Fight and Funeral'.

If we choose to see the inclination towards giantism and heroic legendry (even when given mock treatment) as in one sense the Irish reaction to the oppression and deprivation they have suffered, we might choose to see explicitly sexual grotes-querie as a reaction to puritanism and repression in sexual matters. The archaism and continuity of grotesquerie in Irish literature, demonstrated by Mercier, would suggest that it is as much a racial tropism as a literary device. The most talented

19. Darrell Figgis, ed., *Carleton's Stories of Irish Life,* London 1918, xxix.

practitioners of the grotesque in contemporary Irish fiction are perhaps the Ulster writers, Patrick Boyle and Benedict Kiely, whose comic fiction corroborates Mercier's contention that 'evocations . . . of the sexual act in Irish literature are almost uniformly ugly'.[20] Both writers, particularly Boyle, have also exploited giantism in their fiction.

Superficially the lack of centre and synthesis is not impoverishing, for the pendulum can swing widely without coming to rest in the contemplative centre of apprehension. But in the end it militates against the fiction's ability to liberate the reader and writer by precluding realism and, ultimately, tragedy. Commenting on the primacy of the senses over intellect in Irish writing, O'Faolain adds: 'It is . . . a curious thing about modern Irish literature that it has produced so few feet-on-the-ground realistic novels. . . We Irish do not, so far, ponder deeply or write realistically.'[21] Of any Ulster writer writing about the land, Carleton has the most elaborate and effective disguise for the absence of deep thought and a realistic vision. This disguise takes the form of generic and stylistic richness, of an amazing medley of farce, burlesque, gothic, romance, melodrama, fitful realism, satire; of the fictional, the polemical and the documentary. His views on any topic of moment to nineteenth-century Ireland (and, perforce, contemporary Ireland) are as various as his styles, seducing his critics into accusing him of flippancy, insincerity and the prostitution of his talents. Aware of such charges when he changed tack once again in *Valentine M'Clutchy* (1845), Carleton prefaced his novel with a tacit admission of his inconsistency but a denial of his mendacity: 'I have written many works upon Irish life, and up to the present day the man has never lived who could lay his finger upon any passage of my writing, and say "that is false".' This is one line of defence. Another, and better, would be to show how his contradictions and asymmetries operate *fictionally* within his canon and within his individual works. It does seem to me, especially in the light of contemporary fiction criticism, that most Carleton criticism has been misdirected by an insistence on treating Carleton as an autobiographer or social historian

20. Mercier, 49.
21. O'Faolain, 130–1.

or political polemicist rather than as a fiction writer with his own lively theories of fiction writing.[22] I have erred in this direction myself but only because I am here engaged not in Carleton criticism *per se* but in trawling through Carleton's turbulent waters for forces, themes and styles that have been fertile for subsequent Ulster writers. In any event, no critic is seeing Carleton whole while he simply praises what he likes (Carleton's celebration of peasant Ireland and espousal of the cause of reform) and damns what he dislikes (Carleton's conservative acceptance of the overall social system in nineteenth-century Ireland and his conversion to Protestantism). Carleton has paid the critical price in Ireland for straddling more often than any other writer the deep divisions that lie like geological faults across the Irish, and particularly the Ulster, psychic landscape : those between nationalist and unionist, between Little Irelander and West Briton, between Protestant and Catholic, between North and South, between countryman and townsman. His very career has the monstrous improba-

22. As a first, tentative contribution to a redirected critique of Carleton, I would suggest that he ought to be studied first and foremost as a comic writer; the crowded canvas, static characters, the curve of the protagonists' careers from low to high fortune, the just distribution of deserts in the *dénouements*: all these suggest the genre of comedy. Furthermore, all those prefaces, affadavits, footnotes, supporting evidence, didactic interruptions of the narrative belong to a fiction in which the distinction between fact and fiction is blurred: if his fiction aspires to fact, so too does his fact aspire to fiction, a fiction in which irony and the manipulation of viewpoint are highly important. Just how fact and fiction, genre and matter intermingle can be seen if we translate Carleton's comic elements into the social realities of nineteenth-century Ireland, and vice versa. The intrigues and conspiracies of his plots are the machinery of comedy but also the desperate struggle for survival of a hungry and oppressed people; the dissimulations of his characters are the familiar comic element of mistaken identity but also belong to a Darwinian world of greedy agents and scheming landgrabbers; in milking his numerous departure scenes of their pathos he is also reflecting a world of incessant emigration; his sentimental dock scenes and death scenes similarly represent everyday occurrences; his comic device of sesqui-pedalianism operates against a social background of widespread illiteracy and ignorance in which any kind of learning is absurdly reverenced; even the fits and swoons that climactically punctuate his narratives with the familiarity of romantic comedy or Victorian melodrama can be seen as particularly appropriate in a peasant population debilitated through starvation and disease. It is time now to restore the balance in Carleton criticism by de-emphasising the social and emphasising the generic. This might obviate Walter Allen's kind of dismissive and misguided remark that Carleton tried and failed to write tragedy; see *The English Novel*, Harmondsworth 1958, 131.

bility the feat seems to require : he was the peasant (in early lifestyle if not in breeding) who became a celebrated Irishman, the Tyroneman who journeyed to Dublin across a hungry and gibbeted landscape, the poor scholar whose novels were addressed to the drawing-rooms and cabinet-chambers of England, the Roman Catholic who became a Protestant without a deathbed reconversion to the faith of his fathers. Incredible as it may seem, he is the writer, a hundred years dead, whose work best illuminates Ulster's present agony, a testament doubtless to the unchanging nature of Ulster politics as well as to the modesty of subsequent Ulster fiction, but a testament also to a writer whose courage and forthrightness have yet to be acknowledged.

(4)

In one important respect, however, Carleton's relevance to modern Ulster fiction is limited. Carleton is in the main a rural writer whereas a good deal of twentieth-century Ulster fiction has been set in Belfast. Because much of this fiction has been written by Protestants and has not tended to illustrate the kind of emotional and stylistic oscillation I have been discussing, it is tempting to see this oscillation as a Catholic rather than a Protestant characteristic. This view has a superficial attractiveness. The Catholic religion, the atavism of the native Irish expressed through myth, tale and song, the Celtic mind and imagination— all play a part in the make-up of the Catholic writers I have mentioned including Carleton, and the Irish people who served as models. If the stereotype is to be believed, Protestants exhibit a narrower emotional range and a greater, more careful and on the whole less imaginative stability, a stability that owes itself to their Protestant religion, the mythless recency of their Irishness, and their Scottish patrimony.

To some extent the fiction bears this out. The search for a psychological mean is, for example, a major theme in the work of Shan Bullock, St John Ervine and Jack Wilson. Moreover, the fragmentary myth of a rural paradise which I mentioned in a Protestant context does not inspire pathos and nostalgia so much as crankiness, in the case of Bullock, and anger, in the case of Wilson. There is a group of Belfast writers whose fiction does express a nostalgia for a kind of lost social paradise, but these writers—discussed below in Chapters Six and Seven—

belong to the middle class (a social class dedicated, by definition, to equilibrium) and in their fiction supply some of the serious psychological centre missing in Carleton and other Catholic writers. The price they pay is their lack of generic spread and verbal texture that characterise so much Catholic fiction.

To make too clear a distinction on this score between Protestant and Catholic writers would be foolhardy, first of all because the Scots-Irish have been emotionally and spiritually hibernicised more than they care to realise, and secondly because Ulster Protestant and Catholic writers to some extent share the same literary heritage, and literary heritage is always in part independent of social and racial reality. In the end, perhaps it is intimacy, or lack of intimacy, with the land that is more important than race or religion in determining the nature of fictional vision in Ulster. Ervine and Bullock, primarily rural writers, may seek a psychological mean but they do so with more allegory than psychology at their command. Leitch and Wilson, two young contemporary Protestant writers who set their work on the land, have a good deal of the macabre and the grotesque in their fiction. Significantly, middle-class Protestant writers such as Forrest Reid and Janet McNeill who eschew the grotesque and the sentimental, the pathetic and the macabre are urban writers whose links with the land are tenuous. Brian Moore, an Ulster Catholic born in Belfast (and to whom I devote Chapter Five), shares their separation from the land and their urban, middle-class background. Perhaps in oblique consequence, Moore has been able to write maturely and realistically, though the attempted tragedy in *Judith Hearne* does threaten to relapse into pathos.

Despite the importance of Belfast in the imagination of many Northern writers, it would yet be untrue to say that Carleton's fertile vein of influence and precedence has been worked out. The land may tend to simplify and polarise the Irish psyche, but younger writers, convinced that there is an essentially tragic vision embedded there, have begun to return to the land. Perhaps the most interesting contribution to date of Jack Wilson, Maurice Leitch and John Montague—who, along with Anthony C. West, preoccupy me in Chapter Eight— has been their deepening of Bullock's exploration of the Protestant psyche beyond caricature. These writers have also been courageous enough to tackle sectarianism frontally and to trace its wellsprings in racial psychology. Finally, such writers will only approach real insight, real liberation and the possibilities of tragedy if they can truly leap the rivers of contention and separation that Carleton leaped. And it is likely to be Carleton's boisterous, unsettling and distractingly comic ghost that they will encounter somewhere along the way.

I

LOST FIELDS

(1)

T H E loss of the land is traumatic, even for those who leave of their own volition. All of those who leave do so because, one way or another, the land cannot satisfy or fully sustain. The incapacity of the land for sustaining life in Carleton's fiction is easily explained. Oppressive or negligent authority—an incompetent landlord, an unscrupulous agent, a crooked lawyer—dispossesses a family, wrongly banishes the young hero, or else does nothing to help reverse the land's tendency to barrenness or decay. Or the peasants themselves are neglectful or inadequate. Or the climate is too unsettled, the soil bad—any number of acts (or omissions) of God. Considered together, rural writers after Carleton present more complex and intractable reasons why people become separated from the ancestral land. The acts of God remain, of course, as do the inadequacies of the farmers, but if oppression remains a divisive force, it is no longer oppression by the Ascendancy but by industry and the city drawing off the land's manpower.

Industry as a destructive force is first recorded by Shan Bullock and Patrick MacGill, both of whom published before or around the First World War. Bullock writes of an essentially pre-industrial Fermanagh, but in *Dan the Dollar* (1906) the factory system and modern business methods are shadowy contributors to dissension. Patrick MacGill has a more socialistic concern for the injustices of employment, particularly industrial employment, whether in wild Donegal or the grey towns of Scotland, a concern expressed in such novels as *Children of the Dead End* (1914) and *The Rat-Pit* (1915). It is with Michael McLaverty, however, that the depletion of rural manpower and industrial oppression in Ulster become forces almost as important as landlordism in Carleton. McLaverty sets his fiction during the inter-war years in or around Belfast and shows a countryside

vulnerable to the parasitic needs of that city but fortunate
(unlike MacGill's impoverished Donegal) in at least having a
catalyst for its passive energies. McLaverty's fiction makes the
crucial transition in our scenario from the land to the city. It
is not an easy transition. If McLaverty's people stay on the
land they endure hardship and poverty. If they move to the
city they find equal hardship in the ghettoes, a hardship even
more punishing because there is not even the salve of beauty
provided by a decayed landscape. This dilemma is central to
McLaverty.

The city of Belfast, the North's major industrial area, burgeons
as the land is depopulated, a process which has an irreversibility
such as land-loss in Carleton (even when it entailed emigration)
never had. But whereas the growth of Belfast as an industrial
city and major port began fairly recently,[1] the trek from the
land, particularly from the West and uplands, is an ancient
process. Only slightly abated, it goes on today and is still a
constant theme in rural Irish fiction.[2] With each age it is the
product of a different set of causes operating upon the short-
comings in soil and climate. T. P. Coogan, writing as recently
as 1966, adduces a contemporary and international cause, but
the end-result and the emotions it arouses are very old :

The decline of the small farmer is a world-wide phenomenon and
the trend is probably irreversible. But when an Irishman stands
on a mountain in Connemara or Kerry or Donegal and looks
down at the anguished beauty of a valley in which formerly there
were hundreds of cottages and now are only half-a-dozen, he gets
a kind of heart sickness. When he considers that in the few
cottages still visible along the valley families averaging eight or

1. An account of the rise of the city can be found in *Belfast: The Origin
and Growth of an Industrial City,* ed. J. C. Beckett and R. E. Glasscock,
London 1967.
2. Census returns from the Republic of Ireland for 1966–71 showed a
pattern of continuing urbanisation and rural depopulation, with the
Connacht counties of Leitrim, Mayo, Roscommon and Sligo and the Ulster
counties of Donegal and Cavan all suffering falling populations (*The Irish
Times,* 29 Jul. 1972); Northern Ireland figures for 1961–66 showed net
movements into Counties Antrim, Armagh, Down and Londonderry and net
movements out of Counties Fermanagh and Tyrone, also a high number of
migrants to the eastern counties of Antrim and Down from the western
counties of Fermanagh, Tyrone and Londonderry (Government of Northern
Ireland, *Census of Population, 1966: General Report*).

nine children were reared for the cities of the world, he feels inclined to shake his fist at God and government. And still the drift from the land is going on—to the bigger Irish towns and to England and America.[3]

Coogan's pessimism is less relevant to contemporary Northern Ireland, but his sentiments nevertheless echo those with which writers such as McLaverty and Kiely lament the suffering of their characters on bad or neglected land in the pre-war North.

The penchant of the rural Irish for squabbling and feuding does not (at least in the fiction) make for easy relations on the land, and sometimes drives victims away. In rural fiction after Carleton this continues to be an important source of dramatic tension, although sectarianism is muted, perhaps because in normal times it does not cause friction or violence.[4] A new cause of bad blood, instrumental in driving people off the land does, however, make its appearance. 'A hundred years ago,' wrote Conrad Arensberg in 1937, 'before famine, clearances and land reform, all the sons and daughters could hope to be provided for on the land. Such a situation is still an ideal, but little more. One cannot subdivide one's holding any longer, and new farms are hard to get. Today the farmer looks forward, ordinarily, to "settling" only one son "on the land".'[5] Because of this and because 'rural Ireland knows neither primogeniture nor junior right',[6] there have been two crucial and divisive post-Famine developments in family relations on the land which rural writers have exploited. Firstly, children often vie with one another for inheritance of the land, and from McLaverty to Jack Wilson sibling rivalry has been a boon to novelists.

3. T. P. Coogan, *Ireland Since the Rising*, London 1966, 152.

4. On the contrary, if my reading of Harris's *Prejudice and Tolerance in Ulster* is correct, sectarianism promotes a formalisation of human and social relationships on the land; we shall see in this chapter and in Chapter Eight what happens when an individual disrupts the fragile equilibrium.

5. Conrad M. Arensberg, *The Irish Countryman*, London 1937, 73.

6. Arensberg, 57; if Carleton is to be believed, this did not hold for pre-Famine Ireland; he remarks that 'among the peasantry the youngest usually gets the landed property—the elder children being obliged to provide for themselves according to their ability, or otherwise a population would multiply upon a portion of land inadequate to their support' ('The Party Fight and Funeral', *Traits and Stories*, 153); this would imply that sibling rivalry is a post-Famine family problem, but it does not accord with Arensberg's contention that before the Famine all the children could be settled on the land through subdivision.

Secondly, the father frequently holds on to the land so long that bad blood is created between parents and children. This dramatic tension between the generations is built into a system of kinship and inheritance which Arensberg calls 'partriarchal familism', and which has been exploited by Shan Bullock, Michael McLaverty, Anne Crone and several other rural novelists. The result is that power on the land resides with the old, and the land can suffer because of this. 'In Ireland', remarks Coogan sadly, 'eleven out of every 100 people are over the age of seventy, and an uncomputed but significantly large number of its aged population are small farmers. With the pitiful tenacity of age, they hold on to their land while their children slowly grow past innovation.'[7] The unlucky sibling unable to inherit the land and the chosen son unwilling to wait often choose to move into the town or city, and so for them and their issue the land is lost, perhaps for ever.

All of these divisive social forces that draw or drive people off the land provide the plots and dramatic tension in a good deal of rural fiction after Carleton. I am thinking particularly of writers we can roughly call naturalists because they dramatise social forces without humour, fantasy, melodrama, propaganda and the other enlivening agencies that Carleton pressed into service. Novelists such as Shan F. Bullock, Michael McLaverty, John O'Connor, Joseph Tomelty, Sam Hanna Bell and the several really minor figures (e.g. Hubert Quinn) are in a sense depressing because they write truthfully of a people who have suffered psychic as well as material deprivation. In particular, there is a deadening impression of sexual inactivity and lack of passion. Assuming that this does more than reflect the authors' prudery, there are social reasons for such a passive view of rural sex. Love and marriage are bound up with the availability and inheritance of land. According to Arensberg. the high incidence of rural bachelorhood and prolonged celibacy (which Harris confirmed in the North in the 1950s) dates from the cessation of subdivision in the mid-nineteenth century. Children are forced to wait, unmarried, for their parents to die or become infirm. Young people sufficiently alive to be impatient or bored migrate, leaving behind, more often than not, the celibate and

7. Coogan, 153.

lonely. And those who do inherit the land are often too old, too set in their ways, or too poor to marry one of the few available women in the area. The result is that 'the country people are the ones among whom marriage is latest in Ireland, bachelorhood and spinsterhood most common, fecundity greatest'.[8] Things are changing on the land, of course, but it is the pre-Second World War Ulster countryside with which I am concerned in this chapter. If the naturalists write truthfully about a slow-blooded and passionless people (however dutifully fecund) whose piety is like a tourniquet upon the soul, it is no wonder that these novelists do not lift the reader's spirit.

I would prefer to call most of the novelists I have mentioned 'local' or 'rural' naturalists rather than simply 'naturalists', in order to convey their modest stature and their strongly regional flavour. Only two of the novelists, Bullock and McLaverty, are of importance and, conveniently, one of these is a Protestant, the other a Catholic. Both novelists, like the other minor ones, take great pains to describe, after Carleton, local folk ways and habits surrounding fishing, eating, farming and particularly courtship and death. This is in part a matter of local colour and of the writers' regionalism. However, there is a third reason why I prefer to call these novelists local or rural naturalists, with the emphasis on the qualifiers. These writers use folk ways in order to re-create a world very different from that in which most of us live, a rather primitive, ritualistic and insulated world. In so far as they do not judge this world by our standards and in so far as they tend to be basically pessimistic in their recognition that the land is always finally lost and their people unhappy, the local naturalists are not really moralists. What Walter Allen says of Hardy could be applied equally to Bullock and McLaverty: 'Hardy was scarcely a moralist at all, because in his universe morals were beside the point: between the forces of nature, including therein the forces of his own nature, and man's aspirations there could be no reconciliation; they were eternally opposed, and from the human view the workings of nature must appear hostile and malign.'[9] There is, in this superficial sense, a tendency towards a kind of Greek tragedy

8. Conrad M. Arensberg and Solon T. Kimball, *Family and Community in Ireland*, London 1968, 195.

9. Walter Allen, *The English Novel*, 246.

in the naturalists, particularly Bullock.[10] Nevertheless, the special morality of the world created by these novelists, a morality so very different from our own, is important in explaining what goes on inside the novels. The local naturalists, in fact, do not write tragedies so much as folk allegories.

As well as being morally insular, these allegories tend to preclude all but the crude, typological psychology reflected in the character types—the miserly father, the ungrateful son, the interfering mother *et al.* It is because in novels such as *Bridie Steen* (1948), *This Pleasant Lea* (1951) and *My Heart and I* (1955) she employs a more perceptive psychology that I hesitate to call Anne Crone a rural naturalist. In several ways she fits the category—in her use of familistic rivalries and tensions as plot (usually viewed through the eyes of the chief female character), in her seriousness, in her use of Fermanagh folk ways as texture, in her sense of the conflict between the land and the city. But she does have this slightly mannered, Jane Austen-ish psychological perception as well as a tendency towards popular romance. If I call her a middle-class writer, it is by no means in disparagement, since she is a fine writer, but in order to distinguish her from the classless, regionalist style and world of the rural naturalists.

Local naturalism as folk allegory explains, in moral as well as social terms, how the land can be lost. Moral transgressions on the land are also social transgressions—holding on to the land too long before passing it on, willing possessions to the wrong person, being unneighbourly, avaricious or scandalous. But there are two opposing extremes of moral transgression which, as well as relating to social conditions on the land, have quasi-mythic significance. One way of losing the land is by neglecting it, by conspiring in its natural tendency to decline or run to seed. This is a transgression which Carleton frequently detected among his peasantry; in Bullock it becomes a betrayal of the land and one most often committed by Catholics. The other transgression is wilful self-alienation from the land and community through pride, solitariness, arrogance. Most of the novels of local

10. On the other hand, Carleton's comic restoration of his protagonists' rights and the comic defeat of the unjust are in one sense the fulfilment of a wish to see a hardworking peasantry supervised by benevolent landlords, and in another sense the response of a moralist to a tragic situation .

naturalism involve a chief character who fails to submit to community will and who violates the spirit of the land by criticising rural conditions and the ancestral lifestyle, by importing alien ways and notions, and by acting above his station. In the city, pride, ambition and stubborn self-reliance are virtues, but these are qualities for which the rural Irish, both Catholic and Protestant, have a puritan contempt. At the conclusion of the novels, the character who exhibits them must forfeit his happiness, his money, perhaps even his life. For such a character the land is lost, maybe irrevocably. For the others, those prepared to pay the price of submission (the loss of passion, joy and liberation), the land remains.

(2)

Shan F. Bullock set his work in the Erne country in Co. Fermanagh, a landscape variable enough to afford him imagery both of fertility and of barren failure. Though he recollected this world when he was 'in city pent', office-bound in London like Lamb before him, his novels are not particularly nostalgic or sentimental, partly because of their curious edge of irony, partly because his characters are not, as John Boyd has rightly remarked, especially likeable.[11] In company with the other rural naturalists, he packs his narratives with documentary information about local customs. These customs belong to the last century, but Bullock's canon bridges the nineteenth and the twentieth centuries; *The Loughsiders* (1924), for example, his last novel, introduces modern mechanisation into the landscape but at the same time features the Big House. According to Benedict Kiely, 'Bullock was the last Irish writer to see the Big House functioning efficiently.'[12]

Bullock's primary theme, as it is developed in three novels—*The Squireen* (1903), *Dan the Dollar* (1906) and *The Loughsiders* (1924), the last generally accounted his best—has the appearance of tragedy, but the novels are really a combination of romantic melodrama and local naturalism. The theme can be simply stated. The chief character, through arrogance, in-

11. John Boyd, 'Ulster Prose', in *The Arts in Ulster*, ed. Sam Hanna Bell, Nesca A. Robb and John Hewitt, London 1951, 108.
12. Benedict Kiely, 'Orange Lily in a Green Garden', *The Irish Times*, 29 Dec. 1972.

sentience and a penchant for intrigue, manages to alienate the spirit of the land and the people around him. Against the current of what we sense is his hidden, better self, he is guilty of hubris and at the novel's end must be punished for it. The careers of the eponymous heroes of *The Squireen* and *Dan the Dollar* describe therefore a tragic curve, beginning in modesty or difficulty, reaching a high point of good fortune before plummeting to ruin or death. For Bullock, hubris is a tendency in the Protestant character whereas its opposite—idleness and passive endurance—is a Catholic vice; both result in the land's spiritual or material bounty being lost or perverted. However, because Bullock's characters do not rise much above caricature, his work falls far short of tragedy and is at best naturalistic folk allegory.

The Squireen, the weakest and most melodramatic of the three novels, concerns Martin Hynes, a man of social pretensions who, finding himself in debt, jilts the girl he cares for, Kate Trant, in order to marry Jane Fallon whose father is a wealthy farmer. With Jane's dowry he is able to pay off his debts and enjoy temporary prosperity and happiness before the death of their child reverses his fortunes. While husband and wife grow apart, a succession of blows completes the downfall—a disastrous harvest, the death of Martin's mother, Martin's near-death in a bog. Upon partial recovery, Martin ignores advice not to go horse-riding and, in emotional tumult, he falls at a jump and is killed.

Martin Hynes's hubris originates with his cantankerous arrogance and domineering ways. Because he is pure ego and will, he refuses to believe in God or prayer, unlike Jane, nor, as she does, can he see the beauties of nature. His fatal and 'tragic' act, of course, is in rejecting Kate Trant for Jane Fallon, thereby choosing against his better nature the world of will and objects over the world of nature and feeling. That he is killed in a passion, having repudiated feeling, and at the hands of nature, having belittled nature (for instance, during the honeymoon in Donegal), is heavily ironic.

The symbol of Hynes's hubris is Hillside House, acquired by his successful father. The fact that Hynes has 'come into' the house suggests (as does the faintly contemptuous term 'squireen') that Hynes behaves above his station. Community and land take their revenge in a ballad-like progression. The marriage takes place in the spring, Martin and Jane are fleetingly happy during that summer and harvest, but in the winter lose their new-born child and suffer estrangement. The succeeding summer is a deluge. 'It was a wet season, full of mists and floods, the hills sodden to the roots, the lowlands dank and blighted. Men stood forlorn under pitiless skies, waiting by stricken fields for God to stay the rigour of His hand.' (p. 242) The land which Martin would not love and to which he would not pay homage helps to destroy him.

Yet in a sense nature scorns man's love and homage. The Hillside estate, after one summer of spectacular fruitfulness, reverts after Martin's death to a wilderness described in the novel's opening pages before the narrative flashback. By seeking its own rather than man's controlled fertility, the land parodies Hynes's fall from one summer of fertile happiness into a passionate and fatal riot of the blood.

Dan the Dollar is a better novel than *The Squireen,* less melodramatic and with more social texture. The novel opens with the pathetic attempts of the Ruddys to survive on their twenty-six acres of 'bad to middling' land in Fermanagh. The family consists of Sarah Ruddy, her husband Felix, and two adopted children, Phelim and Mary. The return of Dan, the couple's natural son, changes the fortunes of the Ruddys. Dan has made a fortune in Chicago and he returns to lavish his money on his family and the community, in the process acquiring the nickname of the novel's title. As often happens to rich strangers in rural Ireland, especially rich strangers who are also native sons, Dan discovers the family and community perversely reluctant to match the spirit of his magnanimity. In the eyes of the natives, Dan is guilty of a kind of hubris and his subsequent misfortunes can be seen as punishment. Like the squireen he is arrogant and overbearing, criticising rural Irish ways and unfavourably comparing them with Chicago methods, making little of Felix's farm at Shrule. The changes he introduces—up-to-date business methods, industry and social reform—are alien to the loughsiders and are only superficially accepted (in that peasant Irish way) as long as they are to the loughsiders' immediate advantage, like a body temporarily accepting a tissue-graft before the inevitable rejection. Nor does Dan make any progress in befriending Phelim and Mary, and he alienates his mother by refusing to give God credit for his own astounding material success.

Dan's profoundest 'sin' is committed when he prevails upon the family to improve their social status by moving from Shrule to a big house and estate at Springfield, a move which Phelim refuses to make. The family, dwarfed by the lavish surroundings at Springfield, is unhappy and Mary begins to think more of Phelim, to whom she has been tacitly promised, and less of Dan, to the American's chagrin. As though in punishment for uprooting the family, Dan hears from Chicago that he is ruined and decides to return to America to start afresh. He asks Mary to accompany him but she refuses, and when he sets sail the family treks back to Shrule where Phelim awaits them. Whereas the fortunes of the land mock Martin's fortunes in *The Squireen*, in *Dan the Dollar* the fortunes of the Ruddys mock Dan's career, the family returning to the kind of modesty from which Dan himself began and from which he now must begin again. The upshot is the same, though : the land remains, exacting with grim irony eventual payment from those who grow apart from it through hubris.

The Loughsiders, Bullock's last novel, dramatises the tortuous climb of the central character to the height of his modest ambition, but because the novel does not show his downfall it describes only the first half of the 'tragic' curve. Richard Jebb owns twenty acres of poor Fermanagh land from which he ekes out a living by careful husbandry. His neighbours the Nixons have a much larger and richer farm, something which seems to be in Jebb's mind when he asks Henry Nixon for his daughter Rachel's hand. Being a score of years younger than forty-five-year-old Jebb, Rachel turns him down. Providentially for Richard (and as though in payment for Rachel's own little expression of hubris), the Nixons suffer a sharp reversal of fortune when Nixon dies and the two sons, Jim and Sam, are unable to make the farm yield as it did for their father. Jebb hovers close to the family in their distress, an oblique man 'whose understanding always was tempered with policy'. 'Stiff-necked and high nosed', Richard Jebb is liked but not well-liked, partly because—like Dan Ruddy—he learned some scheming ways and some contempt for his slow-witted countrymen while in America. Before the novel is concluded he seems to prove his claim that neither God nor prayer is needed to ensure a man's success. He changes his affections with remarkable ease from Rachel to her newly widowed mother Ruth, manoeuvres Sam into emigrating, plots Rachel's marriage to an ex-policeman, and then by a ploy worthy of Volpone he makes Jim believe he has seriously wounded him with a shotgun blast and had better therefore leave the neighbourhood. The field clear in every sense, Richard marries Ruth and moves in to take possession of the coveted Nixon farm. Given Bullock's universe, however, there is no reason to believe that Jebb's intrigues will go unpunished and that the bad 'luck' which visited the Nixons and had a few practice-shots at Richard himself will not also return to seek the land's revenge.

Egoism and arrogance are Protestant failings because of the Protestant's concern with things of the world rather than the welfare of the soul. In most of his novels Bullock deals exclusively with Protestants, but in *Dan the Dollar* he explores what he sees as the opposing psychologies of planter and native Irish. The novel has, in fact, two interwoven plot-strands, one of which—the return of Dan to Shrule and his alienation of the family and community—I have already discussed. For the purpose of this theme the rest of the Ruddys are grouped together against Dan. But for the purposes of the second theme, there is a clear distinction between Sarah the mother and the other three members of the family, Felix, Phelim and Mary. In the family's struggle to stave off destitution before Dan's return, only Sarah is of any worth, a hardworking Protestant married to a feckless product of a mixed marriage and burdened with two equally unworldly Catholic children. None of the three is concerned with success or prosperity : Phelim plays his fiddle and tells his stories, Mary (aptly named) has her Catholic piety, Felix his rambling idleness. Sarah alone has kept the family's heads above water. Once the family had rented a good farm of thirty-five acres in 'fruitful Gorteen', then another in Garvagh, and now the present small and barren one that thwarts Felix's indifferent efforts to make it fruitful. When Dan returns, he is in sympathy only with his mother (whose Protestant qualities he has inherited with a vengeance), finding his father's idleness foolish, Phelim's nature-worship incomprehensible and Mary's sacrificial bent distasteful.

At the end of the novel, the forces of unworldliness, of the past, of pleasure over work win out, as symbolised in Mary's rejection of Dan. These are conditions to which the spirit reverts if given half a chance. The land mirrors this trait in the human psyche. The wild music Phelim plays and the childlike, artless nature he shares with Mary and Felix accord with the wildness to which Felix's land reverts, a reversion the Ruddys, by moving from poorer to poorer land, imitate. Without the competent hands of Bullock's Protestant farmers, 'The hedges grew wild over ditches choked with bramble. Gaps were deep in mud. Gates hung twisted or broken. Once in old ancient times some fields had been in cultivation; now they lay barren, the rounded lands showing like ribs in a skeleton.' (p. 53)

The notion that Catholics allow their land to go to waste is a folk myth Bullock shares with Marshall in contradiction to the folk myth of planter dispossession used by Carleton and McLaverty. Protestant land is not merely better land but has plainly had human will stamped upon it. The contrast runs through Bullock's fiction. Felix's plot may be bad, but 'in capable [i.e. Protestant] hands, after great labour and constant attention, the farm might at last have grown kindly'. *The Squireen* begins with the contrast made even more explicitly. 'Now Bilboa, Armoy and Drumhill are big and bare, and these regions are Catholic; but Gorteen is small and fruitful, and this is Protestant'. (p. 3) Certainly Gorteen is naturally more fertile, but without Protestant will, the contrast would not be as marked. Entering Gorteen 'You seem to have stepped into a new country. Hedges become trim, lanes and fields orderly, houses neat, offices clean, crops flourishing. You have gardens and lawns, flowers in the windows and curtains behind them, knockers upon the painted doors and steps before them.' (p. 3) The ultimate in the Protestantising of the land is to be found in the Nixon farm in *The Loughsiders,* a model of snugness, tidiness and modest prosperity. A desirable place, adds Bullock after a lengthy description.

The danger remains that the land will revert to its wild state. The wildness of the land lies latent just as the wildness of the native Irish spirit lies dormant under Protestant supremacy. When Henry Nixon dies, the farm relapses. 'Slowly but surely the work of Henry's life was being undone. Fields going back to wild nature, rushes, thistles, weeds, untrimmed hedges,

choked ditches, neglected gaps and fences.' (p. 127) The Protestantising of the land, like the political dominance of the
planters, is a precarious business. To wring success from their
efforts, the Protestants must continually be 'humouring the land
into fruitfulness'. The most that can be expected is a small and
modest fruitfulness, small fruitful Gorteen surrounded by bare
hills like the planters surrounded by the native Irish. To err on
one side is to lose one's grip on the land and see it revert to its
own useless fertility. To err on the other side is to be Protestant
with a vengeance and arrogantly to stamp one's personality
upon the land and community.

The dilemma is not merely one of land-fertility but of moral
and psychological stance. The ideal resolution is to strike a mean
between a worshipful, self-denying love of nature and an ego-
tistical domination of nature, between demanding the land's
material bounty and meekly accepting its spiritual bounty. Both
extremes are, for Bullock's purposes, adequately represented in
his fiction. On the one side we have native Irish, such as Phelim
and Mary, who are self-sacrificial and all but impotent, though
they are in touch with the spiritual forces of nature. Phelim wins
Mary only by waiting passively for her while she in turn is the
model of the fey peasant girl. On the other side we have well-
drawn hubristic characters, such as Dan Ruddy and Martin
Hynes. But the moral and psychological mean is inadequately
represented in Bullock's fiction. It could be an exciting notion,
but we flatter Bullock by summarising it for him : the notion
that time is on the side of the land and of the native Irish, that
Protestants will 'revert' to Irishness (in the way Sarah Ruddy
has 'reverted' by marrying a half-Catholic and adopting two
Catholic children) unless they are eternally vigilant and forceful.
Alas, for vigilant and forceful characters Bullock gives us 'slow-
blooded Loughsiders with their inborn canniness of mind and
nature, their awful reticences implanted deep as their creed
itself' (*The Loughsiders*, 62). If these self-righteous and anal-
retentive characters who populate most of his pages represent
the (essentially Protestant) mean, they are not especially pleasant,
and only marginally more sexually alive than Bullock's Catholics
and spiritually considerably less alive. Characters such as Jane
and Red Hugh Fallon, who might have achieved the mean, are
simply not rounded enough to do the job. The most sympathetic

characters in Bullock's fiction are people like Dan Ruddy and Martin Hynes, if only because they make the other characters seem corpse-like.

It is difficult to gauge Bullock's own attitude towards the hubristic characters, for there is a vein of mockery and irony running through his work. In the case of Richard Jebb, for example, it is hard to know whether emotion (even loneliness) or avarice is his chief motive in asking Rachel for her hand; and are we to find offensive his toadying behaviour with the Master of the Big House? Are Bullock's sympathies with the squireen? And does he realise that Dan Ruddy is the most likeable character in *Dan the Dollar*? Perhaps such confusions reflect Bullock's own kind of 'hubris', for like his hubristic characters he became separated from the land and saw his loughsiders through the eyes of an outsider. But perhaps they are the price local naturalists pay for faithfully creating an allegorical world in which they cannot totally participate and which is not in any case a particularly lovely or pleasant world. The truth is that none of the local naturalists create wholly sympathetic characters, though Bullock's are probably the least likeable.

(3)

Michael McLaverty's love for the north-eastern countryside and its Catholic farmers may not be greater than Bullock's love for the Protestant loughsiders of Fermanagh, but the expression of his love is certainly less problematic. In contrast to Carleton's, McLaverty's is a gentle love, patient in its fidelity and slow to admit judgement. Whereas the emotions of the nineteenth-century writer swing like a weathercock between exasperation and euphoria, pathos and muscular humour, McLaverty's work is more monotonous, in the real sense of that word, always aspiring to the devotional and pathetic. His figures and landscapes aspire to the condition of still life and many of his best fictional moments, such as the MacNeill children's ramble on the hills overlooking Belfast in *Call My Brother Back,* have a painterly quality of composure : fittingly, the ramble ends with the children kneeling in a chapel, 'their whispered prayers sounding as loud as wind in grass'.

Yet such undefiled moments are rare. McLaverty's love for his people does not preclude an acceptance of their manifold short-comings. If their innocence remains curiously intact and is the lasting impression many readers have of McLaverty's work, this is because their faults and blemishes belong not to our world but to their own more primitive world. In their own world they are anything but innocent and their lives anything but composed. In fact, McLaverty has inherited from earlier rural writers the theme of the blighted land. Looking closely, we can see that McLaverty's simple pieties and beauties are furred with a cancer as malign as that which blemishes the beautiful pike in *The Choice.* Odd it is, then, that Benedict Kiely can remark that in McLaverty 'there is no suspicion that the soul behind the lovely face of rural Ireland might be rotten' and that 'McLaverty, simply, poetically, without any reservation, loves the life of rural Ireland for its own sake'.[13] There is indeed a rottenness in McLaverty's world, a blight larger than the sum of its social causes and which atrophies the will of his characters and spreads loneliness and impotence like a virus.

McLaverty in using the 'blighted land' motif follows Carleton's tracks by evoking the undependable climate and grinding poverty some of the rural Irish have suffered. Nor, any more than Carleton's, have his people forgotten that their ancestors were dispossessed of the rich land by the planters and driven to the rocky uplands or soggy littorals. At the same time, McLaverty gives a modern dimension to the motif of the blighted land and in so doing deprives it of its sectarianism. Along with John O'Connor, Sam Hanna Bell, Joseph Tomelty and Hubert Quinn, McLaverty writes of the North in the inter-war years when the decline of the small farmer, rural depopulation and the accompanying growth of the industrial working-class began to accelerate. It is a social no-man's land in which McLaverty's people are trapped. Not that they understand their predicament. Almost never—to Alec's chagrin in *Call My Brother Back*—do McLaverty's people question the premises of the system that seems to oppress them, and their vague dissatisfaction not with their lot in *this* system or in *this* country but in the world at large lends them a social innocence that reminds one of Hardy's peasants.

13. Benedict Kiely, *Modern Irish Fiction—A Critique,* Dublin 1950, 39-40.

D

The blight upon the land and the resulting separation of his chief characters from their ancestral fields is McLaverty's principal theme whether his stories and novels are set on Rathlin Island, on the shores of Strangford Lough or in the damp country rimming Lough Neagh (three of his favourite locales). Driven for one reason or another from the land, his people seek refuge on the grim edge of industrial Belfast where they find, however, that poverty infects both city and countryside, making escape from the blight on the land largely illusory. The Griffin family in *Lost Fields* (1941), for example, finds the penury in Belfast just as grinding as that from which they fled in the countryside, living as they now do beside a river polluted by industrial waste. Johnny Griffin looks at a different river when he revisits his mother's cottage and the fields of his boyhood at Toome on the shores of Lough Neagh, but in the beauty of the landscape is the taint of that ruin and neglect that drove him away in the first place.

He put down the bucket and crushed his way through the hedge into the neighbouring field. It sponged under his feet; it required stubbing; and he recalled how, when his father had worked it, it had yielded crops of corn and potatoes. But all that land had been mortgaged and nothing remained now only the house and the small field with the well. The shape of the land had changed but little in the course of thirty years. Here and there a blown-down tree was honeycombed with holes, hedges had grown taller and wider at the legs, but the fields had not changed.

In his walk he had come to the top of a hill where he saw far away the River Bann scything through flat soggy country spreading itself out in Lough Beg where he saw the tree-covered island and the spire of a ruined church. . . Below him was the demesne, its walls tumbling, and rabbits running wild in its naked fields. (pp. 44–5)

The decay is never specified : there is the hint of too much rain, too much water, the hint too of mismanagement, and beyond these, in the images of the ruined church and the tumbling demesne walls, the hint of larger social forces outside the control of the Griffins and other small farmers. The land was once good, perhaps, but the Griffins seem to have been prevented from exploiting its small potential.

This almost mysterious decline of the land and the seductive growth of Belfast—between which the characters are suspended —is a basic background equation in McLaverty's fiction, but the equation only assumes the complexity of plot through the writer's use of certain social and ritual factors : on the one hand, patriarchal familism and the generational rupture and taboo-violation it entails; and on the other, the lust for scandal that can easily become victimisation.

In This Thy Day (1945) employs the emotionalism invoked by familism, for in this novel the dullness and injustice of a lifestyle fashioned by and for the old threaten to smother Ned Mason, his sweetheart Mary Devlin and the other young people. Father Toner, concerned about the young people leaving for the city or going 'across the water' and hearing that Ned's father did not will his son the family farm, sees the malaise of his parish as socially congenital :

'What blight is coming over this land ! . . . that the only things making life are the animals in the fields and the flies in the dung-heaps !' . . . He took off his hat and let the cool breeze ruffle his thinning hair, and then suddenly he drew up near the hedge when the words of old Mason's will sang through his mind : *I leave all my possessions to my wife for her day.* He had tried to persuade him to leave the small farm to Ned, but the old man was immovable : 'My wife will do all that's good for him. I can set my mind at rest about that.' The priest clicked his tongue as the memory of the old man's death came before him. Why didn't he leave the small farm to Ned and let him marry before he is too old and too cold to have children ! Everything for her day. How often had he seen the same words in the wills of dying men ! It was like a formula in this part of the country or like an old song that had been handed down from one generation to the next. (pp. 19–20)

All the ill-fortune in *In This Thy Day* seems to flow from old Mason's refusal to pass the farm to Ned, so that Mrs Mason, the novel's chief antagonist, appears more as the instrument than the originator of bad blood. As if smitten with her dead husband's lack of charity, she attempts to drive a wedge between Ned and his sweetheart. On the pretext of her husband's body lying at home, she forbids Ned to help fight the fire consuming Luke Devlin's cottage. Adding acrimony to her uncharitableness, she calls Luke, Mary's father, a good-for-nothing and his son John a drunkard. Other antisocial actions follow but they backfire when one of her horses is killed in Hardyesque retribution and her son Ned, despairing of ever getting the farm, emigrates. Through the hardness of this woman's heart (a hardness, it transpires, that permitted her housekeeper to die in the workhouse years before), an only son, custodian of the ancestral land, is driven out to establish roots elsewhere.

Bad blood in this novel originates with the conflict inherent in rural familism, but its instrument is the human heart twisted by pettiness and enmity. In rural fiction, gossip and scandal-mongering are potent dramatic forces and can escalate into community censure and even—as a later McLaverty novel (*The Choice*, 1958) shows—into lethal victimisation. Swift to condemn, McLaverty's people spread gossip like a fungus and assassinate character with prattle. Nor is scandal in 'this country of idle tongues' (as AE called Ireland) ever silenced by a sense of respect, for even in the presence of death—as at the wake for Father Toner's housekeeper—the busy tongues rattle and rumour.

Generational rivalry is implicit in rural familism and the young are most frequently the victims. But when the young are driven to the city, the ruthlessness with which they become infected can sometimes in turn victimise the countryside. Though *Lost Fields* takes place largely in Belfast, it depicts a family recently moved to the city, and thus we can view the rivalry between Johnny Griffin and his son Hugh in terms of rural familism. When Hugh wins, and ousts his parents and sisters from their Belfast home, we feel he is victorious because the struggle is waged under conditions in which he is not at a disadvantage. There is in the city no farm to inherit by laborious socio-ritual means, and no taboos to observe. The subjugation of the young in the countryside has become their victory in the city.

The Griffins are going under in their fight for survival in the bleak back-streets of Belfast, and Johnny and his wife persuade his mother to leave her cottage in Toome to come and live with them and swell their meagre income with her old-age pension. This uprooting of the old woman against her wishes is premonitory of the grief and hardship in the rest of the novel; it is also the primary offence in the novel and, like such offences in Bullock and old Mason's action in *In This Thy Day*, must be answered for. The old woman does not fit into the life of an oppressed industrial family and yearns for the clear water and pure air of the countryside. She becomes an obstacle to Hugh's marital plans by occupying the room he wants to live in with his wife. It is Hugh, growing up in urban congestion that stifles charity, who is the principal agent of bad blood in *Lost Fields*. Whereas in the country the young meekly accept a situation in which they cannot marry until the old vacate the homestead, the urban young show no such meekness, and Hugh suggests his grandmother go into the Union workhouse. His invocation of the spectre of the workhouse, that symbol of a family's shame and disintegration, is a 'sin' against his family and ancestry. Even after the old woman dies, Hugh continues to offend against his rural forebears and the bonds of his family. When Johnny takes his family back to the cottage at Toome (a kind of symbolic dying of the family), leaving Hugh and his bride in Belfast, the son refuses the offer of the caged wild bird (an Irish townsman's traditional link with the countryside), and later demolishes the old goat-shed, thereby severing his blood-bonds with the land. Hugh represents the end of innocence as he cynically prepares to breast his way through the rigours of city life that broke his father. Opportunities are there if he is cunning and forceful, but in losing intimacy with nature he has irrevocably lost part of himself.

(4)

While socially interesting, *Lost Fields* and *In This Thy Day* lack genuine character interaction to supplement the interaction of each character with the *forces* of family, community and society. This gives the novels a stodginess and general lifelessness. Only in one novel—his first and best—has McLaverty been able to rise above the social and community forces that bear down on his people to make a genuinely poetic statement. *Call My Brother Back* (1939) shows a family driven from the impoverished land into the ghettoes of Belfast where they find because of poverty and sectarian strife that they are no better off. In addition, the novel continues the allegorical theme we encountered in Bullock as well as in *Lost Fields* and *In This Thy Day*—the resilient and vaguely mystical power of the land to shape the destinies of those who leave it, and to destroy those who, through hubris, violate its spirit.

The novel has poignancy, too, which the other McLaverty novels lack, the painful beauty of a first novel wrenched from deep feeling. *Call My Brother Back* transcends its allegorical naturalism to become an authentic and poetic novel about the loss of childhood.

Call My Brother Back is in two parts, the first of which ('The Island') paints in primary colours and large brushstrokes the MacNeill family's now happy, now straitened circumstances on Rathlin Island seen mainly through the eyes of Colm MacNeill, a rueful thirteen-year-old. Colm's joy in Rathlin's birds and rocks and tarns is edged with yearning as if he scented the island's slow dying through the growing anachronism of its people's lifestyle (pillaging from shipwrecks, drying kelp, reading news of the outside world in outdated newspapers) and the drain by emigration on its manpower. Upon the death of his father, Daniel, after a night-long drenching at sea, Colm leaves Rathlin for college in Belfast where the rest of his family soon join him.

Call My Brother Back, then, is about the MacNeill family's uprooting from their island home. At the same time, the novel cannot be called a simple lament for the lost land, for the MacNeills are more or less forced to leave Rathlin because the island in its dearth cannot sustain the young and vigorous. Such is the power of the land that leaving, even for the best motives, seems to incur its wrath. The unhappy fate of the MacNeills is in a sense sealed once they leave the island, making the sectarian strife in Belfast an effect rather than cause of that fate. In McLaverty, as in Bullock and the other local naturalists, the land both blesses and curses, offers freedom and holds in thrall.

If the novel's first part presents an islandscape of hazardous and tainted freedom, the much longer second part ('The City')— set amidst the Troubles of the 1920s that preceded and accompanied the setting up of the Northern Ireland state—is overshadowed by symbols of bondage : the college, the hospital, the cramped MacNeill house, and, more obviously, the mills, jail, police 'cages' and curfews. From industrialism, institutions and political affairs, escape is fitful and transient, conveyed in episodes (such as the family excursion on the old Bangor boat and the children's ramble over Black Mountain) that serve to reinforce for reader and character the sense of entrapment in the family's slogan-daubed street.

Call My Brother Back exploits the contrast between island and city, but, as I have hinted, it is no simple contrast between rural delight and urban nightmare. In their part of Belfast, the MacNeills are still close to the countryside despite the grimness of their living conditions :

When they opened the back door they looked out upon a large stretch of waste ground : clothes-lines hung here and there; hens moved about; and boys were playing football, bundles of coats marking the goalposts. . . At the top of the street were the brick-yard and brickfields, and beyond that again more fields straggling up to the foot of a mountain. The mountain was so close they could see a few scattered houses at its foot and cattle in the fields. (p. 99)

Hills are in sight to this day from even downtown Belfast and have been an important safety-valve for the city's industrially oppressed; McLaverty's people are never more than a stroll or a short bus or tram ride away from fields and trees and rivers.

If the MacNeills' new life in Belfast is not all grey and con-crete, neither was their life on Rathlin all green and idyllic, for McLaverty's islanders live uneasily between his vision of summer's yellow stagnation :

The sea lay in a hot calm. On the shore sea-rods whitened with salt; flies bunched around decaying heads of dog-fish; and rotten sea-weed stagnated in the warm air. Fresh tar on the boats bubbled and blistered; and captured flies rotted in the spiders' webs. (p. 57)

and his vision of harsh cold and death :

The corn and barley ripened early; the beans and hay were safely stored; and then blighting mists and black frosts swirled over the land. Daniel's grave had lost its freshness and nothing re-mained on the mound except a circular rusted wire that once held a wreath of flowers. (p. 63)

Island and city seem to interlink in another way. In 'The City' McLaverty skilfully uses as backcloth the political and sectarian events of the Troubles—the 'Belfast Celtic' soccer riot, the setting up of the B Specials, partition, the inauguration of Stormont by the king and queen. By degrees this background becomes fore-ground through Colm's older brother Alec's involvement with the IRA. It could be argued that the increasing impingement of the Troubles on Colm's consciousness and on the plot of the novel is McLaverty's way of concretely redeeming the promises of social discontent in 'The Island', of giving precise political shape to the MacNeill family's hardship and trials first on a bleak island and then in a grim back-street. For Alec, Rathlin means spineless acquiescence and lack of self-respect. The islanders, McLaverty writes, 'never questioned their right to a better land; they loved the fishing and the excitement of finding a box or a log washed up on the shore'. Alec, having bitten the apple of worldly knowledge in Belfast, refuses to accept the opiate of such innocent pleasures or the lifestyle on an island where the people work 'like slaves at the kelp', as Alec remarks, 'and gettin' damn all for it in the end'. 'And look at the land,' he laments, 'the spongy look of it would give you cramps in your belly.' 'And then he'd talk to them about Ireland and how the people long ago were robbed of their lands; or standing on a hill he'd turn towards the mainland and tell how the good land was in the hands of the planters and the old Irish scattered like sheep among the mountains and the rocks.' (p. 64) It is Alec who embodies the novel's social allegory. His choice, once having been to the city, is between certain slow wastage of the body and spirit on Rathlin, and in Belfast the illusory possibility of republican vic-tory and the real possibility of violent death. This is a version of that dilemma which is central to the novels of local naturalism.

But while the city enables Alec, in a way traditional to Irish nationalism, to articulate politically the discontent on the land, the family's life on the island is no inchoate existence waiting to be given shape and dignity by their subsequent experiences in the city. On the contrary, in McLaverty the drift from the land is something of a collapse into chaos. A man's broken relationship with the land causes (not merely prefigures) the dark events that follow. The reason is that the land seems to have its own kind of moral inviolability and exacts its own kind of loyalty; any attempt to violate its spirit and innocence unleashes pain and guilt. And so it is arguable that Alec's condemnation of life on Rathlin goes beyond mere grousing and amounts to something like an insult to the islanders, the island and his ancestors. At college in Belfast, Colm wonders if Alec 'still begrudged the island its existence'. It may even be possible to interpret Alec's murder at the hands of assassins or the security forces as the price exacted by the land for his worldly knowledge (specifically the knowledge of injustice) and for his condemnation of the island. If this seems far-fetched, it must be remembered that McLaverty's moral universe subsists primitively below the everyday world of social and practical morality, and even of Catholic morality. True, the novel is framed by Colm's relation to Catholic liturgy. He begins in an ignorant and vaguely poetic love of the Mass (p. 20) and ends by joyously receiving Holy Communion (p. 255). But fictional frame is all this is; Colm's insight into the meaning of the Mass does not signify release for him from the primary constraints of the novel, though it does signify an aspect of his maturation. In McLaverty's novels, moral crises are created by the violation of ancient taboos which have nothing to do with Catholic religion. To this extent, he is not a particularly 'Catholic' writer.

That McLaverty is not centrally concerned with giving political focus to his people's discontent is confirmed by the fact that Alec's murder does not greatly disturb the novel's flow and that Alec slips quietly from the book leaving Colm the undisputed central figure, a boy pursued by the ghosts of obscure longings and uncertain duties rather than by the army or police. Colm's longings and restlessness are independent not only of a city's civil war but of an island's limping economy. The way Colm's emotional changes span his life in Belfast and Rathlin helps blur even more the contrast between the novel's two settings. Early in the novel Colm watches 'with a sweet yearning sadness' the evening sun on Rathlin shake itself 'from its cage of clouds' and wing slowly across the fields. Island images of captivity and precarious escape recur in the paralysed rabbit Colm releases from a snare, in the fleet of clouds 'moored to the wild hills of Scotland', in the ship 'caught between two pincers of rock'. Accompanying this notion of captivity is fear. One night on the island Colm recites and translates a Latin ode learned from Father Byrne concerning 'a fawn seeking its timid mother on the lonely mountains, not without a groundless fear of the breezes and of the thicket' (p. 15). Colm's fear can in part be identified with the obscure fear of the fawn. In Belfast his fear would be justified enough,

but in fact fear of sectarian violence is never his primary motivation; through the city in its death throes he wanders in a daze
of pubescent half-understanding. His real fear is larger, at once
more personal and less precise than fear of the Troubles, a fear
that combines with sadness in the presence of nature and which
is his foreboding that desire will remain formless and hence
unrealisable, a common adolescent emotion.

Since all that happens in *Call My Brother Back* must finally
be related to Colm, whose changing consciousness governs the
novel, we can see the sporadic natural images of captivity and
tentative escape in 'The Island' as prefiguring the darker scenes
of bondage in 'The City' and hence these scenes in both city and
island as primarily being McLaverty's method of plotting crises
in Colm's emotional development. For McLaverty's portrayal
of Alec and for the novel's social allegory, the values implicit in
nature and in the city are vitally important, but for his portrayal
of Colm and for the novel's theme of adolescence, nature and the
city are merely metaphors. Nature bulks larger than the city in
Colm's consciousness, but this may be so mainly because it permits McLaverty to image the boy's emotions with greater variation in tone than the imagery of the city would permit. The novel
opens in a rainstorm with Colm sheltering under a rock on which
the day before he had carved his name and age. At the novel's
end, Alec dead, his sister Theresa and younger brother Jamesy
about to depart for England, Colm rides a city tram to the end
of the lines and walks in the open country :

The air was clear and cold, the hedges black and ragged and the
bare thorns glistening with drops of melted frost. The road was
black and to his right snow lay in the crevices of the mountain.
He walked aimlessly, not caring, and then he came to the Lagan
and turned along the tow-path.
    An exhausted wintry sun was setting in amber behind him. The
river flowed black and still, carrying a flock of clouds upon its
back. . .
    A chill mist rose from the ground. Two men passed with grey-
hounds on leads. Swans with wings akimbo were moving up to the
quieter reaches for the night, a fan of wavelets widening behind
them. . . The grass on the banks was combed by the water. The
fields were deserted and their grass limp and grey. (pp. 259–60)

Whereas nature at the novel's opening is tense and anticipatory, here it is spent, waiting for uncertain renewal as Colm is himself emotionally wasted, pupa-like before the unimaginable condition of young manhood. When images of Belfast and its troubles float into Colm's tired mind in the novel's closing lines, they merge with memories of Rathlin and the countryside around the city, synthesising the novel's two settings and two parts into the strange and dreamlike currency of adolescence.

Call My Brother Back, then, is not primarily a novel about the Troubles. Rather is it a novel about the price exacted by the deserted and violated land. In addition, McLaverty's first novel is a troubled song of the awakening adolescent heart, a love-story without a beloved.

(5)

Only two or three interesting novels have been thrown up by that veritable wave of minor writers writing about rural Ulster life—Samuel S. McCurry, Agnes Romilly White, Margaret Norris, Lydia M. Foster, W. R. Megaw. Two such interesting first novels were published in the same year (1948): Joseph Tomelty's *Red Is the Port Light* and John O'Connor's *Come Day—Go Day.* Sam Hanna Bell's *December Bride* was published on the heels of these two in 1951. All three are qualified successes only, with stretches of fine writing and lively scenes that almost manage to keep at bay the endangering familiarity of their themes. None of the three writers, alas, proved to have McLaverty's stamina as a novelist and among them only three novels, as far as I know, were subsequently produced, one by Tomelty and two by Bell.

The themes, motifs and style of rural naturalism are reflected in the three first novels, and all are apparently set, like most of McLaverty's novels, in the inter-war years. O'Connor's novel depicts poverty in Co. Armagh, a poverty exacerbated by the rival emotional claims within the extended family. Familistic conflict also provides the plot of Bell's *December Bride,* with the conflict centring on a familiar hubristic character at odds with the community. Tomelty exploits the theme of self-alienation in *Red Is the Port Light* by presenting two hubristic characters whose destinies are fatally intertwined. In all three works the poison that destroys the emotional relationships can be traced back ultimately to the blighted land.

As in the novels of Bullock and McLaverty, the resolution of *Red Is the Port Light* is contained in the premises of character and circumstance that obtain in a folk world of omens and taboos. Both major characters, Winnie Norton and Stephen Durnan, could have stepped off the pages of Bullock or McLaverty. Set mainly in Portaferry, Co. Down, the novel opens with Stephen Durnan burying his mother and in the same scene accepting a job as a lamp-trimmer on a coaster. The coaster is skippered, he discovers, by Captain Norton against whom he had testified at an official inquiry after Norton's previous ship went down. Norton, an alcoholic, was responsible for the ship's sinking and for the deaths of the crew, he himself being saved by Durnan and losing his deep-sea captain's ticket at the inquiry. The voyage of the *Glendry* is equally hapless and, again through Norton's drunkenness, the coaster goes down in Strangford Lough and Norton, after an attempt by Durnan to save him once again, is drowned. Nursed through his convalescence by Norton's widow in her home up the lough, Durnan recovers and later marries her. Soon after the marriage he finds that she is insane and has to kill her in self-defence.

The novel is the story of a blighted love-affair, both Winnie and Stephen being cursed in their separation from their respective communities, Winnie by her own choice and Stephen by being a 'by-blow' or love-child. In a more mundane sense, too, both are strangers, for Winnie was born in another town of a Belgian sailor father, while Stephen's ignorance of the identity of his father (though he suspects him of being an adulterer) promotes in him a sense of not belonging in Portaferry where he has returned after running away to sea at the age of thirteen. As the novel progresses Norton ceases to be the villain of the piece, for we learn that his wife is frigid and given to wandering and eating herbs. Correspondingly we think less of Durnan and are inclined to second his self-reproach for informing on Norton. In a way recalling McLaverty, Durnan's testimony is removed from that moral universe in which we would deem it right and proper (it was like giving evidence at a murder trial, one character says in Stephen's defence) and placed in that more primitive world in which it is seen as a transgression against the spirit of the community.

When two accursed characters come together, the conclusion is inevitable, and Durnan, when he confronts Winnie with her madness, is forced to choke her as she comes for him with a razor. Like motifs in a ballad, the three symbols of heron, ash tree and port light dominate the novel. The port light symbolises warmth—'it was to him the symbol of home, of a real home, with a wife, with children' (p. 27)—but is quenched by the more powerful images of the heron (loneliness) and the ash tree (death).

With some honesty, Tomelty centres Durnan's curse on his bastardy and Winnie's on her sexual frigidity, thereby presenting two extremes of sexuality, adulterous desire and impotence. However, since Durnan's conjectures about his parentage are hazy and fleeting, the impression of the novel, reinforced by the childlessness of Robert and Susie King and the hinted homosexuality of Fenner, is of sexlessness. The novel does not wilt entirely under this impression of infertility, for during the first seventy-five and the last ten or twenty pages there are some vivid scenes and nicely paced writing. The account of the ill-fated voyage of the *Glendry*, with its economic description and taut narrative that might put us in mind of Gore Vidal's *Williwaw*, is splendidly atmospheric :

The land was gone. The dark grey sky and the mist that the sea churned now seemed to be one. There was a silence in the sky for a moment, as if day was begetting night. Then there came a great howl from the wind, gathering darkness about the ship. Now there was only mist, sea and wind tossing the water helter-skelter. Durnan knew that scarcely a mile away there were cows grazing, horses going home, and housewives making ready warm meals for their returning husbands. But here there was just the madness of the sea and the wind, tugging, laughing wildly together in a mad melody.

Looking out he could see the long tower that marked Rock Angus, and he knew they were at the threshold of the bar. Falling on his knees, he crouched into a corner as he lit the port light. A branch of seaweed fell at his feet. He could see its bellied beads shine golden in the gleam of the port light. The wind lifted it, and tapped it fiercely against his boots. Its beads shone with the varnish of the sea, bringing to his mind the colour of his mother's coffin.

The port light recalled the tabernacle lamp. 'She's buried facing south,' the gravedigger had told him, as if the south meant something; and yet he liked it, for there was a promise in it, a promise that he found no words for.

Gripping the rail, he came towards the foc's'le. (pp. 41–2)

Fine too is Durnan's confrontation with Winnie after she has been wandering the loughshore, her mad mouth yellowed with the petals of dandelions. It is a pity that Tomelty could not sustain the asperity and crispness of the opening chapters recounting the voyage, the shipwreck and Durnan's convalescence. Thereafter Durnan's quest for happiness bogs down in the familiar community conflicts of rural Ulster fiction, and the plot into smothering inaction. Despite a resurrection in the last few chapters, we are likely to remember from *Red Is the Port Light* its theme of sexual and psychic privation more vividly than the sporadically fine writing by which such privatiton is conveyed.

Come Day—Go Day is set in Co. Armagh in the neighbourhood of the River Callan and probably, though we are not told, in the provincial city of Armagh. The date of the action is hardly important (the novel appears to take place during the 1920s or 1930s, judging by the Tom Mix movies showing in the cinema), but the setting is important in so far as the background action concerns the closing of the mill on which the characters depend, and the consequent redundancy of most of the community. The degradation familiar to readers of McLaverty dogs the inhabitants of the Row, a street which is the property of the mill and which suffers periodic flooding from the Callan and the enforced idleness of its men. Since the owner of the mill is called Boyd and the town is divided into Protestant and Catholic sections, we are probably meant to infer sectarianism at work in the suffering of these people, but this is not amplified or made explicit.

The novel's middleground concerns the community passion for 'bullets', a bowling game in which a man relays an iron ball down the narrow country roads for a distance of several miles (a game still played in parts of Ireland). Bullets is a diver-

sion for these people from the dullness of their lives, and joins
the pantheon of clandestine or obscure rural sports that in Irish
fiction provide, along with poteen-making, a ready-made platform for comedy, heroics and allegory—greyhound-racing, cockfighting, pigeon-racing and ferreting. Less culturally remote is the
novel's foreground, the baneful influence of Tommy's aged
mother on his marriage to Teasie. Only under pressure from his
wife does Tommy at last leave his mother's house and even then
the old woman works her will from a distance. Against the
suffocations of family and community, comic and pseudo-
romantic relief is provided by Pachy and Kelly, two vagabond-
ish rogues.

Each level of the story has its climax : the mill re-opens, the
community hero Macklin beats the Hammer-man, a bullets
champion from Belfast, in a long-drawn match (or 'score'), and
Tommy's mother dies. The ending of the novel is therefore
meant to be affirmative with the community winning through on
two fronts and Tommy, after the trauma of his mother's death
leads him temporarily to drink, gaining a measure of emancipation in which his love for Teasie might flourish. The mother
is not in herself a villainous woman and Neilly, Tommy's young
nephew who is perhaps closest to being the novel's hero, has a
good relationship with her, but as in McLaverty and Tomelty
the close-knit ties of family and community, so benign in principle, work in practice to the detriment of the individual.
Especially stultifying is the influence of parents, and the 'stubborn
father' who refuses to relinquish the farm to his sons finds his
equivalent in this novel (as in *Red Is the Port Light*) in the figure
of the 'aged mother' who, by coddling her son or simply
dominating him, monopolises his sense of duty and eclipses his
sexuality.

Come Day—Go Day begins and ends tamely, but the scenes
of the bullet 'scores' and the St Patrick's Day celebration are
well-conceived and well-written. The figure of Pachy, too, though
something of a cliché (the wandering and avuncular scholar-fool),
helps save the novel. Pachy expresses in his real or fantastic
career a whole social mythology : he worked in the mill, joined
the British Army like many indigent and discontented Irish,
served in India, returned to a world shrunken in comparison and
took to the open road as a way of maintaining his broader

horizons. At the same time, Pachy is an idler and bletherer; when he and Kelly upon their release from prison after a street brawl go off to England in 'search' of work, we might see them re-enacting the restless motions of a stricken people or else wandering without purpose in a semi-dreamworld of their own concoction.

Pachy is a comic figure, but there is a blacker kind of comedy in the novel. Haunting the Row and its troubles (much as the workhouse haunts the poor in Bullock and McLaverty) is the asylum, a source of both menace and fun. Madness echoes too in young Kelly's fierce mongrel that Neilly helps to drown in a scene of comic horror. Neilly attaches a huge stone to a rope tied around the dog's neck and has his younger brother Shemie edge the stone into the water.

> Then suddenly, Neilly shouted to Shemie, and there came a plumping splash as the rock hit the river. The next instant, with a yelp of bewildered terror, Gyp was snatched awkwardly over the edge of the bank. The three boys rushed forward and peered down into the river. Its smooth surface was shattered and, beneath the twisting frills of water, young Kelly, with starting eyes, thought he could make out the body of the dog in writhing distortion.
>
> 'Oh Gyp! Oh Gyp!' he moaned, over and over. The next moment, as if resurrected from the river bed, by the force and intensity of the young boy's anguish, the dog's head rose above the surface. It was whining and breathing gruffly.
>
> Thunderstruck, the boys stood still. Then Neilly shouted: 'Get back. Get back! The rope's slipped. We're ruined.'
>
> He and Shemie skipped back, but young Kelly was struck motionless. He stood like one in a dream. (p. 159)

Neilly brings the scene of bungling to a close by finally managing to drown the dog after it rises berserk from the river and attacks its young master.

It is fitting that this scene of comic horror should take place at the river, for it is the imagery of water that dominates *Come Day—Go Day*. It occurs in the novel's memorable accounts of the drowning of the mongrel, the horrendous rainstorm that washes out a 'score', Neilly's repeated and symbolic attempts to carry two full buckets of water from the pump to his house without stopping, Shemie's continuous falling in the river. The novel begins with an angry morning rainstorm and ends as young girls emerge after grey evening rain to chant, 'rain, rain go to Spain'. Despite the affirmation of the novel's climaxes, the ending is likely to strike us as pathetically hopeful rather than optimistic. *Come Day—Go Day* is a chronicle of decay in captivity, for the lives of those who choose not to flee like Pachy but to stay are at the mercy of the water that symbolises their plight. In O'Connor's novel ambition, passion and will seem waterlogged, unfloatable.

Though arguably a lesser work of art than his slim volume of folk essays, *Erin's Orange Lily*, Sam Hanna Bell's *December Bride* is a well-recounted story that gives its own twist to the themes to be found in Bullock, McLaverty, Tomelty and O'Connor. The novel is set among a Scots-Irish Presbyterian community of farmers and cottiers around Strangford Lough and probably on the Ards peninsula. It opens with the marriage of a middle-aged couple against the background of a meeting-house graveyard. From among the gravestones one surreptitious witness conveys to another her disgust that the bridegroom has made his own son his best man. '*Whose* son?' asks her companion sarcastically. 'He's as bad as the rest—there's bad blood in the whole bloody tribe.' The rest of the novel is an extended flashback, telling the story of how the middle-aged couple have come to be married and how the bad blood came to be infused.

Sarah Gomartin and her mother come to the Echlin household as female help upon the death of Sarah's father and of Margaret Echlin, and in time they insinuate themselves into the Echlin family. In a boating accident on the lough, old Andrew Echlin apparently lets himself drown so that Sarah and his two sons may be saved, and thereafter Sarah becomes the woman of the house and its virtual head. The two brothers and Sarah form an uneasy *ménage-à-trois*, turning away from Sarah's pious mother and the disapproving community. After her mother's death, Sarah has two children by one or both of the brothers, and since she cannot decide which brother to love she remains unmarried. At the end of the novel, in order to give a respectable start to her own daughter's married life, she consents to marry the surviving brother, Hamilton, in the scene that opens the book.

Sarah Gomartin is the familiar figure (recalling Vera Reilly in McLaverty's *Truth in the Night*, for instance, or Winnie Norton in Tomelty's *Red Is the Port Light*) who is prepared to do her own bidding even at the risk of incurring the wrath of the community and spiting her own face. The story differs slightly in having a degree of sexual realism, for in rural Irish areas such naïve *ménages-à-trois* and *ad hoc* families, such scant regard for the sanctions of city law upon sexual and parental relations are to be found. However, Sarah's virtual bigamy is not the chief reason she is regarded by the community as a villainess; rather is it that strangeness and aloofness that marks all the hubristic characters of local naturalism. Sarah is guilty of disturbing the Echlins' family set-up (perhaps even of indirectly causing the death of Andrew), of turning away from the Church and her own mother, of wanting to establish her dominance in the Echlin household and of extending the Echlin land-holdings, and, most importantly, of whetting the rivalry between the brothers Frank and Hamilton, a rivalry already primed for conflict in the tradition of rural familism. It is Sarah who creates bad blood between the Echlins and their neighbours and who brings upon the Echlins something akin to a curse or blight (which is how the watcher at the wedding uses the phrase 'bad blood').

The role of religion in *December Bride* is of interest in the light of the fact that McLaverty, Tomelty and O'Connor are Catholic writers writing about Catholic communities. In local naturalism, religion tends not to be a significant factor in the fictional crisis and resolution but rather a given, a constant which is not (curiously, we might think) at odds with community morality. Nor is religion as such really significant in Bullock, who is more interested in *racial* distinctions between planter and native Irish. Bell, on the other hand, chooses to make religion a complicating factor in *December Bride* through the figure of the Rev. Edwin Sorleyson, who spearheads the community pressure on Sarah and her mother to return to the Church and to conform, but his influence wanes and reaches its nadir when he puts a fevered hand down Sarah's open dress. Sorleyson is a hypocrite whose spirituality clashes with his carnality, but is perhaps also meant to represent the Protestant clergy ministering with small success to a people who are naturally puritan, innocent and credulous in their Scottish way but without the firm collective faith of the Roman Catholics. 'In a drought', Bell remarks, 'the peasants might flock to church with every mark of fervour to pray for rain, but they knew that when rain did come, it would come fast, rolling, drenching the world from horizon to horizon and not seeking out, with scrupulous justice, the meadows of the pious.' (p. 164) Sarah and the Echlins seem to fall from their faith more precipitously and consciously than the rest of the community, but we cannot really dignify the fall as apostasy, though I think Bell in a confused way would have us do so.

The ambiguous role of religion in *December Bride* is, I think, damaging, perhaps in part because the issues exceed the narrow moral framework of local naturalism as I have defined it. Religion apart, there is nothing essential in *December Bride* that cannot be discussed in terms of themes common to Bullock, McLaverty, Tomelty and O'Connor: land-hunger, sibling rivalry, defiance of community will and morality. It is true that the characters in the Protestant writers, Bell and Bullock, are more prosperous than those in the three Catholic writers, but no sense of material or spiritual well-being seems to result from the greater prosperity and we still have an image of lives lived parsimoniously in every sense of the term. It is true also that Sarah, like Bullock's Richard Jebb, seems to get away with her defiance of the community, but of course her relative freedom carries the penalty of the community accusation of bad blood. She may be a heroine to the reader simply because she represents life amidst death, but in the novel's moral context, it is reasonable to assume that her transgressions will pursue her. The accusation of bad blood will, in the manner of the countryside, survive as long as the family remains in the area. At the novel's end there is in fact a suggestion of the family's drift to the city, for Sarah's daughter plans to live in Belfast after marriage. Awaiting them in Belfast, however, is the boiling sectarianism that simmers in the country, a sectarianism that Bell tersely portrays in his account of Petie Sampson's visit to the city during which he is attacked by Catholics. In *December Bride* there is no escape from the blighted land any more than in the other rural writers. We are unlikely to feel a sense of liberation when we put down Bell's novel, which is unsurprising in a work that begins with a wedding in a graveyard and ends, in a scene shortly before the wedding, with ancient shadows playing about the hearth of a dying fire.

2

THE SHORTEST WAY HOME

(1)

THE local naturalists give us a rather lopsided and pessimistic view of life in rural Ulster. They present lives largely bereft of pleasure; what small pleasures there are usually exist only in memory. McLaverty is a typical case. When Tom Magee in *The Choice* (1958) tries to tell his daughter what draws him back to his native village, his recollections are of fierce joy, but we receive them secondhand not only through Tom's memory but through the pathetic mist of his brokenness :

He told them of a windy October night when branches wrenched off trees and the moon flying through the tatters of the sky he, and his brother that's dead, with a wide net and two quiet dogs bagged thirty rabbits; and if the gamekeeper had come on them that night, so mad were they with excitement they would have flung him into the lake. And the lough too was a storm of wild duck in October : many a night he and a man by the name of O'Hara lay in a flat-bottom boat among the reeds, and with two hammerless guns banging till the barrels were hot. They had a tough job rowing home with their cargo against the stream. (p. 78)

Rarely if ever, to the detriment of his novels, does McLaverty depict such scenes directly. If I described McLaverty's best fictional moments as expressing innocence and composure, his work read *in toto* creates a rather different impression. The reader comes from McLaverty's fiction remembering his characters as frozen in dreamlike passivity and his scenes as daguerrotypes of injured virtue. What makes McLaverty's fiction, and the work of the rural naturalists in general, so depressing is that the meagrest fraction of the human potential is accounted for. Up to a point, this is because the theme of the fiction is the inability

59

of the characters to escape their blighted lives. Such a theme pursued uncompromisingly and with naïve directness restricts the fictional universe to an imaginary rural Ulster almost devoid of energy, happiness and passion. It also presents a technical problem for the writer : how to convey blight without permitting his work to suffer from the contagion. With few exceptions, the novels I discussed in the last chapter are not successful solutions to this problem. In McLaverty's case, *Call My Brother Back* escapes the contagion in its parable-like purity and simplicity. Outside that novel, his successes have been short stories, thirteen of which were collected in *The Game Cock and Other Stories* (1949).

There are two reasons why the social backdrop of hardship and deprivation is not as depressing in McLaverty's best stories as in the novels of local naturalism. To begin with, the backdrop is relieved by humour and fantasy just as, the stories would have us believe, in real life. In my Introduction I hinted at the possible connection between humour and fantasy on the one hand and rural oppression and poverty on the other. I suggested two kinds of humour, one rather wan and pathetic reflecting hardship fairly directly, the other debunking and tending towards burlesque as though in reaction to the forces of oppression. Similarly there are two kinds of fantasy, one sentimental and cheap, a barely concealed wish-fulfilment, the other vital and oblique, a dream of heroic feats. We might venture an hypothesis, that in the fiction of rural Ulster humour and fantasy flourish best in the most deprived settings. McLaverty's comedy is fairly pale and his fantasy restrained, but in Brian Friel, Benedict Kiely and Patrick Boyle—all of whom set their Northern stories in the rough country west of Lough Neagh—humour and fantasy are unbridled.

If there is anything to Frank O'Connor's theory that the short story is a genre of and about 'submerged populations',[1] then it is little wonder that the short story is a Catholic rather than Protestant form in Ulster and that its backdrop is deprivation. Nor in the light of our connection between deprivation and comic fantasy is it any wonder that the Ulster short story is greatly given to this mode. But though comedy and fantasy act to leaven the

1. O'Connor develops the concept of 'submerged population groups' in his Introduction to *The Lonely Voice: A Study of the Short Story*, London 1963.

dull dough of rural poverty and disability, sentimentality and pathos can still result if the comedy and fantasy are too gentle. It is here that the torsion and necessary economy of the short story form come to the rescue. McLaverty's use of the astringencies of the short story form is the second reason his stories escape the flat pessimism of his novels. In stories such as 'Pigeons' and 'The Game Cock' a submerged revelation ironically reverses or undermines the initial illusion or fantasy.

'Pigeons' is a fine story that uses some of the incidents surrounding Alec's death in *Call My Brother Back*. The poverty and brief, simple pleasures of working-class Belfast families are re-created with McLaverty's characteristic poignancy in this story and spiced with delicate observation, as in the young narrator Frankie's memory of being awakened by his older brother Johnny of a morning: 'My eyes would be very gluey and I would rub them with my fists until they would open in the gaslight. For a long while I would see gold needles sticking out of the flame, then they would melt away and the gas become like a pansy leaf with a blue heart.' When Johnny is killed (offstage, unlike Alec) it appears a case of republican martyrdom during the Troubles of the 1920s. However, the effect of Frankie's guileless narration with his blind repetition of 'Johnny died for Ireland' (a phrase he overhears the neighbours repeat during the wake) is to sabotage the notion of martyrdom with a bitter-sweet irony. The last thing these people can afford is the heroic gesture of their young men's deaths. By the story's end, 'Johnny died for Ireland' becomes an incantation, a death-spell, and the narrator's obvious ignorance of the meaning of the words points up the story's governing irony: the disparity between the abstraction 'Ireland' for which Johnny allegedly dies (and to which a fanatical Christian Brother tries to make Frankie and his schoolmates swear love) and Frankie's mundane but life-enhancing concern for the safety of the pigeons he has inherited from his dead brother.

If in 'Pigeons' life subverts death, in 'The Game Cock' death subverts life. Even more explicitly, the latter story works on two levels. The narrator recalls the time when as a boy he accompanied his father from Belfast to Toome for a cockfight, travelling in the early morning with their fighting cock in a potato bag. The cock escapes before they board the train and leads them a merry dance along yard-walls and into a public lavatory before an irate group of disturbed residents finally corners the bird. The cock nevertheless wins the main and proves himself 'a great warrior'. On their return to Belfast they find that the game cock has died. Asked by the boy what he will do with the bird, his father is only momentarily nonplussed. 'What'll I do with him! What'll I do with him! I'll get him stuffed! That's what I'll do!'

'The Game Cock' is a story of comic mishap that ends, upon the death of the cock, with the father's apparently irrepressible ability to turn loss into gain, death into immortality of a kind. But something else is going on in the story. The narrator's family came from the countryside to live in the Falls Road area, a depressed, Catholic section of Belfast still close enough to the countryside for the family to keep a fighting cock without comment from the neighbours. In travelling to the main, the boy and his father are re-acquainting themselves with the land, for the boy's grandmother lives at Toome and the father knows his way around sufficiently to acquire poteen for the cock. After arriving, the boy accompanies his uncle to a 'tumbled demesne' around a ruined Big House. When he asks where the ladies and gentlemen are, the uncle spits and replies: 'They took the land from the people and God cursed them.' In the train back to Belfast, the clacking wheels rattle out the uncle's remark.

The story on this level is not simply the boy's initiation into that sense of deprivation and wrong which began on the land and which will preoccupy him as an adult Catholic. Somehow the story's two levels interconnect, and they do so ironically. The Ascendancy might have gone but only ruin remains because the Irish, having regained the land, have frittered away the beauty of their patrimony in idleness and pointless violence. The uncle shows the boy where he has 'slaughtered' trees for the fire, a verb that would be startlingly misplaced were it not ironic. To the father, the cock simply represents financial gain and can be preserved by taxidermy: he is unable to see the beauty of the bird (just as the father in 'Pigeons' cannot see the beauty of the tumblers), which, being 'a great battler' and 'a great warrior', is the ironic inheritor of encomia some might use to praise those who fought the Ascendancy and fell, among other places, at Toome. Beneath the story's comedy is a great emptiness of spirit, a sense of tragically squandered opportunity, perhaps even the notion of lost paradise.

A use of irony similar to McLaverty's is common to many short stories, of course, certainly to those of Benedict Kiely and Brian Friel that employ comedy or fantasy. Even so, we ought not to expect that in the short story form we will find liberation from the insulated, allegorical world of the rural naturalists. If irony is a blow for realism against dream, nevertheless the short story is not in the last analysis a realistic form; each story establishes— partly through its brevity and partly through the self-referentiality of its parts—a small and idiosyncratic universe. Irony works within the boundaries of this universe without transgressing them. In 'Pigeons' and 'The Game Cock', for example, irony exposes the betrayal of, but does not thereby negate, certain ideals. Indeed, if irony is defined for our purposes as the perverse action of time, then the stories' original fantasies are raised safely above time into myth and ideality. The beauty and freedom of the tumblers in 'Pigeons' become the beauty and freedom of the Irish people, somehow lost or betrayed, now mythically enshrined. The beauty and courage of the bird in 'The Game Cock' become the beauty and courage of an earlier Irishry. It is the refusal of McLaverty, Kiely and Friel to test the health and implications of their mythicised fantasies that renders even their best stories suspect.

All three storywriters, like others before them, are fond of using childhood as a fantasy-world upon which time is shown as having worked its ironic will. Storywriters are attracted to childhood for its microcosmic properties[2] : the child, after all, can be seen as a microcosm of the adult human being. It can also be seen as a microcosm of the race. McLaverty, Friel and Kiely re-create in the fleeting joys of childhood a nostalgic (and ulti- mately mythic) picture of what the native Irish once were— landed, passionate, heroic and independent. The traumas of childhood (a childhood journey, a childhood discovery) recapitu- late the betrayal and loss of the aboriginal paradise, the lost fields of Chapter One. When the author re-creates his childhood or one of his characters remembers childhood, he is attempting a return to this paradise, a return as vulnerable to life's ironies as

2. It may be possible, however, to think of children as one of Frank O'Connor's submerged population groups.

both childhood and the aboriginal paradise were to the vicissitudes of time and history. With luck, the story itself will transcend
time and so prove, in generic terms at least, the shortest way
home.

(2)

Brian Friel's stories are usually set in MacGill country, among the
hard, empty hills and obscure villages of Donegal and Derry,
and demonstrate vividly the connection between social deprivation and sentimental fantasy. As starvation of the body leads to
hallucinations of the mind, so Friel's characters are inveterate
fantasists, and the cheapest, most poignant fantasies are those
that colour the harshest landscape. In 'Mr Sing My Heart's
Delight', the narrator's grandmother, whose husband is wintering
in Scotland earning enough money to tide them over the rest of
the year, moons deliriously over the vulgar coloured wares of the
travelling Indian salesman and, there in a remote Donegal
cottage, listens to his equally cheap chatter about the Garden of
Eden in the distant Punjab. Having chosen such fantasies as his
subject-matter, the author has to walk a thin line if he is to
record them without exposing too ruthlessly their cheapness and
thereby have his stories collapse into mere sentimentality.

In solving this problem, Kiely, as we shall see, takes the bull
by the horns by plunging into mock-heroics, but Friel, on the
other hand, relies somewhat dangerously on the pathetic irony
of such fantasies taking place at all among brooding western hills
and stony fields. Many of his stories concern a character's initiation into the reality behind illusion. Illusion might take the form
of a belief in a golden tomorrow (e.g. 'The Gold in the Sea'), the
memory of a golden yesterday ('Among the Ruins') or the daydreams of exotic places ('Mr Sing My Heart's Delight' and
'Straight from His Colonial Success'). The author pierces such
hopes and memories with humour and compassion but allows his
characters to retain an altered illusion to make life bearable for
them. The whole process is rather formulaic. Initial information
which also establishes the story's tone (exposition) is followed by
the setting up of an illusion (complication), followed by disillusionment (climax) and ending with the reinstatement of a
modified illusion (coda). This formula is imposed on a naturalistic
background of poverty and hardship. The question that comes to

mind when we read story after story is whether Friel (primarily a dramatist) is on a busman's holiday in his short stories, whether he is doing much more than playing deftly with an emotional and structural formula learned from O'Connor, O'Faolain, McLaverty and Kiely. This is not to say that Friel's two volumes of short stories—*The Saucer of Larks* (1962) and *The Gold in the Sea* (1966)[3]—do not in their unevenness (despite the levelling influence of constant publication in *The New Yorker*) throw up some very fine stories which almost manage to transcend their formulism and which stand on the brink of real and liberating insight.

Friel's formulism is perhaps too evident in such a story as 'Straight from His Colonial Success'. Cathy begins in scepticism about her husband Joe's enthusiastic memory of his childhood pal Bryson, newly returned from Kenya. Behind Bryson's bravado and apparent success Cathy discerns loneliness and unhappiness. When Joe comes to share her perception, Cathy at the story's end replaces his earlier enthusiasm with her own wistful and partly sexual daydream. 'I don't know what it is,' she murmurs to her sleeping husband. 'But he has got something.' 'The Potato Gatherers', a better story, also uses counterpoint to modify the dream-fantasy. Philly and Joe, two young brothers, play truant to gather potatoes on a Co. Tyrone farm and earn some pocket-money. Philly, the younger brother and a novice at potato-gathering, begins in lavish energy, enthusing about what he'll buy with the money, a shotgun, no, a bicycle, a gaff, a scout-knife. The sun rises and declines as he grows tired, the work irksome, the fear of tomorrow's school menacing until at last, in the darkness, he is deflated and miserable. The upward curve of Joe's optimism crosses Philly's disillusionment at noon and at the story's end he allows himself, to Philly's descant of despair, a stroke of fantasy at once less accessible and more 'poetic' than Philly's cheap consumerism :

'Do you know what I'm going to buy?' Joe said, speaking more loudly. 'If she gives us something back, that is. Mistah! Mistah

---

3. Many of the stories in these two volumes have been collected into one paperback volume, *The Saucer of Larks*, London 1969; it is from this edition I have chosen stories for discussion.

Philly! Are you listening? I'm going to buy a pair of red silk socks.'

He waited for approval from Philly. When none came, he shook his brother's head. 'Do you hear, mistah? Red silk socks—the kind Jojo Teague wears. What about that, eh? What do you think?'

Philly stirred and half raised his head from his brother's lap. 'I think you're daft,' he said in an exhausted, sullen voice. 'Ma won't give us back enough to buy anything much. Not more than a shilling. You knew it all the time.' He lay down again and in a moment he was fast asleep.

Joe held his brother's head against the motion of the trailer and repeated the words 'red silk socks' to himself again and again, nodding each time at the wisdom of his decision. (pp. 42–3)

Whereas Philly is initiated into a realisation of the poverty and tawdriness of the world into which he has been born, Joe is initiated into fantasy, seduced by a specious poetry that might anaesthetise him against that tawdriness but that might also prove in the end destructive in its unfulfillability. Joe's fantasy (more so than Philly's, for Joe's is born out of tribulation) betrays the social deprivation around him, as Cathy's concluding daydream betrays a flaw in her apparently happy marriage.

A Friel story punctuates one fantasy only to reinstate a new one which serves, unintentionally I believe, to confirm the deprivation in which fantasy flourishes. Because of this the story remains locked within its own universe. Although this is to an extent a feature of the short story, Friel does not convince me that he realises fully the ills of his people—the sexual paralysis, the dearth of passion, the emotional bankruptcy, the violent sublimation. Too often the climactic revelation, masquerading as an emancipating insight, is really the author's own illusion. A comic story, 'The Widowhood System', will illustrate what I mean.

This story is a piece of comic allegory that purports to celebrate sexual fulfilment over abstention. As a typical rural, middle-aged bachelor, it is only on the death of his mother that Harry Quinn can pursue his dream of having a pigeon-loft and breeding the All-Ireland champion. His blue-moulded liaison with a forty-four-year-old spinster, Judith Costigan, who longs for him to propose, is symbolised for us in the 'widowhood' system of pigeon-racing Harry adopts (whereby the cock is allowed to desire but not to mate with a hen before he is sent to the race). On the day

of the All-Ireland championship, Judith takes a hand and lets
the cock into the hen's cage but Harry intervenes; fulfilment,
Judith is trying to say in her own leaden way, is a better entice-
ment than deprivation. Harry defends the system on the grounds
that the cock would not return were the union consummated. As
if to test the system (such being the story's comic allegory), she
leaves Harry that day and sure enough Harry goes in search of
her with rather more enthusiasm than his racer has ever shown
over the hen. At the end of the story Judith and Harry kiss and
embrace for the first time, 'and for that half-hour, for all
the crying, they were the happiest couple in the whole of
Mullaghduff'.

In fact, however, it is not the spirit of the widowhood system
that is vindicated, but of the 'natural' system (whereby the birds
are allowed to mate before the hen is sent to the race). Harry
might go in search of Judith, but it is she who returns to him. In
his arms, Judith tells 'how that afternoon his talk of the widowhood system had given her the idea of going away, going anywhere, with the certainty at first that he would come searching for
her. And then, when she was wandering along the Strabane road,
how that certainty abandoned her, and how she had had to
come back.' And it is she, not Harry, who now whispers : 'Will
you marry me?'

These confusions in columbine strategics to the contrary, 'The
Widowhood System' is, beneath the comedy, an attempted vindi-
cation of the larger life-principle that the natural system invokes
—that fulfilment, and sexual fulfilment in particular, is a better
enricher of human relationships than dream, desire and deferred
promise. The principle seems to be proved, for after the reunion
with Judith, Harry sees his two faithful bachelor pals, Handme
Levy and the Fusilier Lynch, in a new light :

Talk of the cock led him to Handme and the Fusilier—the big long
string and the wee tight keg—sitting in the dusk of the loft, discussing automation, their feet ringed with empty bottles, waiting
for replenishments. The more he talked of them, the funnier they
seemed to be. Never before had they seemed funny. After all, they
were his friends, his best friends. But now, for the first time, he saw
them in another way, and they were ludicrous—two middle-aged
men wasting their lives, waiting for a pigeon to come home. (p. 142)

Harry's new perception implies, surely, that he sees his own wasted life as ludicrous, and the reader is then free to add to this the wasted life of a society that promotes with such singular willingness long years of parent dominance (with which the story opens), bachelorhood, and the sublimation of sexual energies. If this is so, then the idea that Harry can escape through changing is itself an illusion that is true only for the purpose of a story. Even for this purpose I am not sure it works. The story is not only premised on Harry's sexual inadequacy but finally endorses it : Harry the seduced is as ludicrous a figure as Harry the Guinness-swigging sublimator. Because the disinclination or inability of the men to take sexual initiative is part and parcel of the debility and deprivation Harry is supposed to triumph over, his fulfilment and liberation are illusory. If Friel realises this, the ending would be ironic, but I am not convinced that he does realise it.

My analysis possibly seems heavyhanded for a story that is, at least on the surface, comic, but a similar analysis would not be heavyhanded in the case of 'Foundry House', Friel's best story to date and one that ranks with the very best of McLaverty and Kiely. Like the other Friel stories, it uses the formula of illusion in stark contrast to humdrum reality, a climactic revelation to the chief character that it *is* illusion, followed by his half-conscious, half-deluded acceptance of a modified illusion in the coda. But the story is also mythically rich in raising part of its fantasy to the level of ideality. Moreover, the story is beautifully written. My qualms concern Friel's restriction of his moral and philosophical universe of discourse which, since I take it to be unintended, does not disturb the story's finer workings.

On the death of his parents, Joe Brennan applies to succeed them in the gate-lodge to Foundry House, the lodge where Joe grew up while his father worked for Bernard Hogan, the owner of the Big House. Joe remembers the Hogans as grand, 'one of the best Catholic families in the North of Ireland'. The roseate nature of Joe's childhood memories is conveyed in the description of the gate-lodge as having a fairytale appearance and as being out of sight of the Big House, whose location amidst the greenery one could only guess. But as Joe discovers, things have changed. Around the house is a tangle of shrubs and 'decaying trees', and when he is invited to the house with his tape-recorder so that the Hogans can hear a tape from a daughter who is now a nun in

Africa, Joe finds whole rooms unused and Mr and Mrs Hogan
waiting out their days visited only by their son, Father Declan, a
former childhood playmate of Joe's. Mr Hogan himself, whom
Joe recalls as a lively and patriarchal figure, has been altered by
senility but is yet imposing, 'a giant who had grown in height
and swollen in girth instead of shrinking, this huge, monolithic
figure'. After playing Sister Claire's message for them, during
which old Mr Bernard has a seizure, Joe returns to the lodge
and his own chaotic family of wife and nine children. The story
concludes with Joe telling his wife that the Hogans are un-
changed, and chanting into his youngest child's ear : 'The same
as ever. . . A great family. A grand family.' Is it a lament, or a
stroke of self-delusion?

Joe's dream-memory of the Hogans is shattered when he finds
a family suffering from a desuetude of the body and will, just as
the house itself lies largely unused. The parents aged, only son a
priest, only daughter a nun, the overwhelming impression is of
infertility, of a kind of emotional abstentionism. In sharp contrast
are Joe's nine unruly children who swarm over the grounds and
pack into one small gate-lodge while two spent people occupy the
huge house on the hill. 'How many young Brennans are there?'
asks Father Declan. 'Such healthy children, too,' says Mrs Hogan
who has seen them playing in the avenue, 'and so . . . so healthy.'
Later she repeats as if abstracted : 'Such lively children they are,
too, and so healthy, so full of life.' Joe's visit to the house climaxes
with old Mr Bernard's impotent crying of his daughter's name
as her voice unreels from the recorder, a cry more terrible for its
lack of precise meaning though in it we sense the expression of a
great loss and a thwarted will. Joe ends the story surrounded by
the progeny of his own undoubted fertility in a domestic scene
that begins in disharmony on his return from the house and concludes in what seems like a measure of Joe's self-congratulation
and even happiness over his own productive situation.

On another and by no means conflicting level, Joe has clearly
lost something by his discovery that the Hogans are a family
spent in will and destined for imminent extinction. His crooning
into the child's ear is a lament, a requiem, but also a pathetic
desire to keep alive the personal illusion of the house; why else
would he tell his wife Rita that nothing has changed and that
they invited him to stay for tea (which they did not)? We can see

why he needs this personal illusion. His life has moments of domestic happiness, but he could not be described as being content, unsurprisingly considering his place in the kind of world he inhabits. In contrast to Joe's memory of it, the house is now situated 'between the new housing estate and the brassiere factory', twin images of modernity and of the price paid by Joe and his ilk for their liberation from the paternalism of the Foundry Houses of the last century. Although Joe is a radio-and-television mechanic, more than his father could presumably have hoped to be (and a suitably contemporary occupation), his is a dull existence beset by financial woes and a chaos of children. His application to live in the gate-lodge is a move dictated as much by economy as by sentiment, for his eleven-strong family lived until then in three rooms above a launderette.

On this second level, then, 'Foundry House' is an indictment of what Irish (and by extension, Western) society has become since the Victorian middle class declined and the working class was 'emancipated', and so the healthiness and vitality of Joe's family must be balanced against the vicarious grandeur that Joe and his father once knew and which Joe has lost. The huge, monolithic figure of Mr Bernard inching its way across the faded carpet represents the decline of the old order but also, in its lithic endurance, grandeur raised to the power of history, of myth. And so Joe is at once disillusioned and overawed. For somehow the Hogans are partly responsible for their own fate through a profound loss of will : there is 'no one to take over the foundry when the time would come', Joe muses. 'Everything they could want in the world, anything that money could buy, and they turned their backs on it all. Strange, Joe thought. Strange. But right, because they were the Hogans.' Yet the Hogans' betrayal and repudiation of their own social ideal leaves that ideal intact; Joe's disillusionment coincides with his realisation of what the Hogans have stood for. In 'Foundry House', illusion is liberated from the dross of reality and fallible childhood memory and exalted into ideality and myth.

To stop there in our interpretation would be to verify the richness of 'Foundry House' and to suggest the high level on which adverse criticism would have to be made. Yet the story has implications that are disturbing. Neither the 'new' myth of social grandeur nor the 'new' respect for his own situation that

Joe discovers is at all salutary. On the one hand, considerable humility is required of Joe in his keeping alive a myth of social grandeur. He acknowledges *vis-à-vis* the Hogans a 'vague deference to something long ago', but he flatters himself in calling it vague. Throughout the story Joe is cap-in-hand before the Hogans, stammering in confusion when Mrs Hogan calls at the lodge and in general re-enacting his father's servility of a generation ago. The myth of social grandeur that is debunked and then reinstated in the story is in fact the glorified memory of a semi-feudal past of ruling haves and obsequious have-nots.

On the other hand, Joe's private life seems to require a similar humility. That life might be fertile in contrast to the Hogans, but is it not a dutiful fertility encouraged by a church whose own priests (like Father Declan) are issueless? And does not Joe need the myth of the Hogans partly because it provides him with a private corner away from the prying demands of his wife? It is Rita who dictates what Joe will write in his application for the gate-lodge, she who commandeers the conversation when Mrs Hogan calls, she who berates Joe when he returns from the house. Joe is loth to relinquish the myth of the Hogans because that myth is synonymous with his own childhood when he was free from the demands and responsibilities of a wife and family. The image of male passivity is repeated in old Mr Bernard's submissiveness before his wife, and we are given the hint that perhaps Claire became a nun against his weak will. Fittingly, then, the story ends with Joe changing nappies on his youngest child while he talks about the Hogans.

There is a social dilemma in 'Foundry House' analogous to that we found in other rural fiction. Joe is caught between the stagnation of the land with its compensating echoes of a grand past and the philistine impersonalisation of the urban industrial present. Whereas Friel is aware of this dilemma, Joe's nostalgic mythicisation of the rural semi-feudal past unbalances the story by making the Hogan family instead of Joe the tragic focus. Besides, there is also a sexual dilemma of which Friel seems less aware. The alternatives Friel provides in his stories to the sexual debility of the land represented by the Hogans (i.e. Harry's passive seduction in 'The Widowhood System' and Joe's passive fecundity in 'Foundry House') are certainly not alternatives to be cheerful about. Nor are they the only alternatives that need obtain. By unconsciously closing off his options, Friel severely restricts the universality of his work.[4] It seems to me that Friel, by refusing to test or breach the social and moral premises of the rural area in which his stories are set, is in danger of confining his work within a regionalist framework.

(3)

Michael McLaverty and Brian Friel would no doubt disclaim any mythic intent, but it would be hard to imagine Benedict Kiely so doing. Kiely as a man and a writer is a fierce protector of legend and myth, so it is not surprising that he often inserts as a character in his work the privileged custodian of group history and lore : Arthur Broderick in 'The Heroes in the Dark House', Charles Roe in *Dogs Enjoy the Morning,* the Old Master in 'A View from the Treetop'. These characters represent a facet of Kiely's own world-view usually hidden by a flamboyant surface : the curator behind the iconoclast. Kiely's wish to preserve and commemorate is a reaction to an acute sense of time and loss. In many of the stories in his single collection to date (*A Journey to the Seven Streams,* 1963),[5] e.g. 'The Wild Boy', 'The Pilgrims' and 'The Shortest Way Home', the innocence and wonder of a Tyrone boyhood are traumatically, poetically and often comically ended. Against the transient flow of time Kiely erects a small pantheon of legendary figures and small epics of legendary events. Memorable characters frozen in time flit across our vision—the Cowboy Carson, Red Cunningham, Yellow Willy, Packy Noble, Lanty, and Isaac who wanted to grow up to be a German. These characters, while captured with magnificent realism, are frequently cast as emperors, magicians, mythic heroes, clowns and devils, for Kiely makes no bones about his mythic intent. It is the mythic resonance of his best stories that forces us to defer reservations about the basic sentimentality and

---

4. I find Friel's very good play *Philadelphia—Here I Come!* finally lacking liberating insight for this very reason: the America he presents as an alternative to life in Ballybeg is so grotesquely Irish-American (represented by the drunken aunt and the namby-pamby uncle) as to be no real alternative at all and so the dice are loaded before the game begins.

5. A second collection, *A Ball of Malt and Madame Butterfly,* London 1973, has since appeared; these dozen stories confirm Kiely's growing partiality to the extended short story and novella.

passivity of a vision not radically different from that of McLaverty and Friel.

In achieving this resonance, Kiely capitalises on the genius of the time-haunted Irish for creating legend and spinning anecdotes, for the Irish are given hugely to celebrating and enshrining human feats, frailties and eccentricities. But there is a technical reason when the use of story and legend becomes tongue-in-cheek, for it is a way of informing the reader that the writer knows he is fishing in the dangerous waters of nostalgia and sentimentality. This mock-heroic or mock-mythic ploy allows the nostalgic artist to have it both ways, to weep real tears through the glycerine tears of theatricality.

Another way of defeating time is to associate childhood with the childhood of the race, that Better Time before the land and life on it became blighted. The writer uses the magic world in which childhood is lived as a cover for his use of the 'return to paradise' motif. The writer could as easily send an adult on this journey, but there is less chance of coyness and outright fantasy if the journey is seen through the eyes of the narrator as child. The journey to a paradise that is inevitably flawed initiates the boy into the sadness of the adult world but more particularly the sadness of his race, in this case the native Irish. In 'Homes on the Mountain' and 'A Journey to the Seven Streams' the journey is, in the manner of the magical journey of Joseph Campbell's monomythic hero, long and hazardous, but like all mythic journeys it proves the old saying about the longest way round.[6]

Raconteur and local historian, the narrator's father in 'A Journey to the Seven Streams' leads his family on a Sunday expedition in search of a stone fiddle on the shore of Lough Erne. The fiddle is an eighteenth-century monument to the haplessness of a baronet's minstrel who drowned—in whiskey and lake-water—during baronial festivities at the local Big House. The mode of progression chosen for the excursion is Hookey Baxter's motor car, 'the child of his frenzy', a skittish and unprepossessing composite of various factory models. With Hookey at the wheel, daft Peter Keown stoking, the narrator's father navigating, nine of them set off. Everything that could go wrong goes wrong : tyres deflate, the engine overheats, the car

6. See Joseph Campbell, *The Hero with a Thousand Faces*, Cleveland 1970.

shies at the feet of steep hills. Balked in their efforts to reach the monument, the party settles for a picnic where seven streams meet at the Minnieburns.

From the beginning the journey is presented with affected magniloquence. The father brings his family out 'to see in one round trip those most adjacent places of his memories and dreams'. When objections are raised as to the appearance of Hookey's car, he counters hyperbolically :

'Regardless of appearance . . . it'll carry us to the stone fiddle and on the way we'll circumnavigate the globe : Clanabogan, the Cavanacaw, Pigeon Top Mountain and Corraduine, where the barefooted priest said Mass at the Rock in the penal days and Corraheskin where the Muldoons live . . . and the Minnieburns where the seven streams meet to make the head waters of the big river. Hookey and Peter and the machine will take us to all those places.' (pp. 266–7)

'Like a magic carpet,' the narrator's mother adds doubtfully. The fact that the trip is undertaken at a time when it was rare and venturous to ride a motor car reinforces the mock-epic manner. Hookey is dressed like Lindbergh, 'in goggles, leather jacket and helmet; an appropriate costume, possibly, considering Hookey's own height and the altitude of the driver's seat in his machine'.

The mock-epic manner continues. 'At the ready,' roars the narrator's father upon the arrival of Hookey and his machine. 'Prepare to receive cavalry. . . God bless us look at Peter. Aloft with Hookey like a crown prince beside a king.' Departure coincides with the tolling of the church bell which, the narrator thinks, 'could have been a quayside bell ringing farewell to a ship nosing out across the water towards the rim of vision'. They pass through foreign townships ('they're strange people in Gortin') and through the hostile territory of Tattysallagh where a throng of small boys scatters before the car then closes again 'like water divided and rejoining', one of the small boys hurling a half-grown turnip at the noisy and receding intrusion.

The mock-epic manner offsets the mundaneness of the troubles that plague the trippers, the contrast producing the story's comedy. But beneath both the mundaneness and the mock-heroics, one detects a seriousness of purpose that rises to the surface when the narrator describes the landscape they pass through.

The fields, all the colours of all the crops, danced towards us and away from us and around us; and the lambs in the green hills, my father sang, were gazing at me and many a strawberry grows by the salt sea, and many a ship sails the ocean. The roadside trees bowed down and then gracefully swung their arms up and made music over our heads and there were more birds and white cottages and fuchsia hedges in the world than you would readily imagine. (p. 274)

This rhapsodic tone is maintained as a subsong throughout the entire story. When Hookey's car balks at a steep hill, the party abandons the stone fiddle as its destination and journeys instead to where the seven streams meet.

So we came to have tea and sandwiches and lemonade in a meadow by the cross-roads in the exact centre of the wide saucer of land where seven streams from the surrounding hills came down to meet. The grass was polished with sunshine. The perfume of the meadowsweet is with me still. That plain seemed to me then as vast as the prairies, or Siberia. White cottages far away on the lower slopes of Dooish could have been in another country. (pp. 280–1)

The magic of the number 'seven', the symbolism of the cross-roads and of the centre, the lingering 'perfume' of the flowers, the vastness of this other country : all communicate the archetypal nature of the family's journey. When the narrator's father expresses disappointment at not reaching the high hills, his wife responds : 'What matter. The peace of heaven is here.'

The mock-epic departure becomes a mythic return to the Source of Life, the confluence of the river's seven tributaries representing Eliade's Cosmogonic Centre and Edenic paradise.[7] And the troubles that mar the voyage are the trials weathered by Campbell's monomythic hero on his journey perilous. On the other hand, the location of the stone fiddle is somewhat more

7. See Eliade's discussion of the Cosmogonic Centre in *The Myth of the Eternal Return*.

difficult to interpret since it seems to represent a second paradise, a place of dancing and minstrelsy. 'A pity in a way', laments the father, 'we didn't make as far as the stone fiddle. We might have heard good music. It's a curious thing that in the townlands around that place the people have always been famed for music and singing. . . It could be that the magic of the stone fiddle has something to do with it.' And from the fiddle's location, too, all things can be seen : 'The deep lakes of Claramore. The far view of Mount Errigal, the Cock of the North, by the Donegal sea. If you were up on the top of Errigal you could damn' near see, on a clear day, the skyscrapers of New York.' But it is also a place associated by the end of the story with death : not only the death of the fiddler but the silencing of the gaiety and minstrelsy by television and other alien forms of entertainment. The stone fiddle is a headstone over a dead past and of the dying spirit of Irish music-making and mirth (Kiely being seemingly as oblivious to the semi-feudal injustice of that past as Friel is in 'Foundry House'). It signifies too the promise of paradise after death. Thus we can understand why the family fails to reach the fiddle that sunny Sunday morning. No mechanical devices, however ingenious and innovative, can transport us to the paradise that awaits us after death. In believing that Hookey's machine will magically carry him anywhere he wants to go, the narrator's father exhibits the hubris of a newly technological age. He does finally reach the stone fiddle, but only when his funeral cortège leads along the Erne shore. That Sunday trip in search of eighteenth-century ghosts is a premature journey towards death thwarted by Hookey's temperamental machine and the comic sense of life it generates. The family has to settle for a brief, earthly paradise and the magic source of life where seven streams converge.

The same mountainy area in the North-west is the setting for 'Homes on the Mountain', a story first published in *The New Yorker*. Here, too, paradise is re-located after a troubled search, but it is a paradise no longer capable of sustaining life or illusion. The father's nostalgia that remains intact in 'A Journey to the Seven Streams' is shattered in this story when the father encounters the blemished beauty of a childhood haunt. 'Homes on the Mountain' contains three concentric dramatic matrices of increasing importance. It begins and ends with the narrator and his boyhood friend Lanty who used to recite—being no song-sters—exercises in sentimentality from the collection of Irish Fireside Songs they purchased with the half-crowns given them by the narrator's improvident American godmother. 'Perhaps, unknown to ourselves,' ventures the narrator, 'we were affected with the nostalgia that had brought my godmother and her husband back from the comfort of Philadelphia to the bleak side of Dooish Mountain.'

The Ireland of Percy French *et al.*, kept alive in the yellowed pages of the Irish Fireside Songs ('Sure a little bit of Heaven fell . . .') and exploited by Lanty and the narrator to keep the half-crowns flowing, is perpetuated in the addled nostalgia of the expatriate memory which causes the godmother's husband un-wisely to build a house on the rough, wet side of the Tyrone mountain where he had spent his boyhood. The building of the house and the housewarming dinner on Christmas Day are the chief actions of the second dramatic layer of the story that encloses the rich kernel. Before dinner, the narrator and his brother are taken by their father in search of two relatives across the dark hills the old man walked as a youth. It is this quest that constitutes the real return of the story: the motif of the returning Americans has been cleverly used to introduce a more indigenous and at the same time archetypal return.

The walk is hard, down boreens, across streams, up a steep hill in a grey mist, and finally through ankle-deep mud to reach the dilapidated cottage of John and Thady O'Neill. The father's reunion with the old men is muffled, nostalgic, somewhat embar-rassing, it seems, for all concerned. Kiely captures perfectly the laconic good nature and conversational progress of a con-frontation between country Irish people and comparative strangers :

'It's years since we saw you, Tommy,' said John.
'It's years indeed.'
'And all the wild men that had been in the army.'
'All the wild men.'
'Times are changed, Tommy.'
'Times are changed indeed,' said my father.
He backed his chair a little away from the fire. Something unpleasantly odorous fried and sizzled in an unlidded pot-oven.

The flagged floor, like the roof, had sagged. It sloped away from the hearth and into the shadows towards a pyramid of bags of flour and meal and feeding stuffs for cattle.

'But times are good,' said John. 'The land's good, and the crops and cattle.'

'And the money plentiful.'

'The money's plentiful.'

'I'm glad to hear you say it,' said my father. (pp. 172-3)

Despite their comparative wealth, the aged O'Neill brothers are poor : poor in their lack of passion, though Thady in family legend was reputed to have been a 'ladies' man'. 'There was the day, Thady,' [my father] said, 'when Martin Murphy and myself looked over a whin hedge at yourself and Molly Quigley from Crooked Bridge making love in a field. Between you, you ruined a half-acre of turnips.' But Thady's passion has long since gone, if it ever existed, mummified through anecdote in the memory of someone he has not seen for years. John, even poorer, courted Bessy for sixty years ('and nothing in the nature of love transpiring') until she died. They are poor also in their barrenness : unmarried and childless like many mountainy people, they await death without the consolation of knowing that their land will remain in the hands of kin. And they are poor, finally, in their lack of will and spirit; the cottage is coming down around them, doomed and decayed like themselves, and they do nothing to prevent it.

The ironic contrasts between this dramatic core of the story and the other scenes are clear. The decay of the brothers' cottage is a pathetic foil to the building just completed on Dooish Mountain. The barrenness of their lives contrasts with the Americans who revel in community and a wealth of family relationships. Their lack of passion, too, is ironically recalled in the Fireside Songs of swashbuckling Irish gallantry. When the narrator after visiting John and Thady thinks of the fighting men of yore commemorated in those songs, the figures of the aged brothers shrink further into sad paleness.

The Ireland of popular myth (native and expatriate) is given the lie in the depleted lives of John and Thady O'Neill who have money but little else. What is the nature of the blight they endure, and who is responsible? To some extent, the brothers seem victims of social change. The limekilns the narrator and his father pass and which are now fallen into disuse (like the passionless O'Neill brothers themselves) suggest a mountainy way of life made redundant by the lowland factories, just as television dooms the crossroads dancing and minstrelsy in 'A Journey to the Seven Streams'. One senses, in addition, the distant seduction of the towns and cities that draw fertile and energetic manpower from the wet hills. Yet the blight has surely been there since the people chose or were driven to inhabit the hills and mountain valleys. 'It's the rain and mist,' explains the father to his sons. 'And the lack of sunshine and wine. Poor Thady, too, was fond of salmon and women.' But if a harsh climate has conspired with social changes to oppress them, the brothers are also to blame, guilty of spiritual penury and failing courage as they permit reasonably rich land to decay and the cottage, once beautiful, to dilapidate. It is as if they have been somewhat negligent custodians of the land. To understand this better, we might at this point give an archetypal reading of 'Homes on the Mountain'.

Indication that the visit to John and Thady O'Neill's cottage is to be more than a simple debunking of the popular and expatriate illusion about Ireland is given in Kiely's lavish description of the journey. The trio descend through boreens, travel along a widening stream, past a cross-roads and on towards the gapped, stone parapet of a bridge. Before they cross the bridge, the narrator and his father and brother pass disused limekilns 'lining the roadway like ancient monstrous idols with gaping toothless mouths'. Once across the bridge, they begin their ascent through hostile 'black brooding roadside cattle' and watch a black hound running silently, 'swiftly up towards the mist, running as if with definite purpose'. Always they are in sight of water—runnels conjoining into a stream that grows into a torrent. To reach the cottage door they wade through plashy ground and ford 'in the half-dark a sort of seasonal stream'. When they knock on the door, no dogs bark. 'No calves or cocks made comforting farmhouse noises. The wind was raucous in the bare dripping hazels that overhung the wreck of a house from the slope behind. An evil wizard might live here.' A foreboding quality transforms the overgrown thatched roof for the narrator into 'a rubbish heap a maniacal mass-murderer might pick as a burial mound for his victims'. The black hound, we now might realise, was both an

omen of the decay they have now discovered and the threshold
guardian which Campbell discerns in many mythic journeys.[8]
The dog is spotted as soon as the trio crosses the bridge, representing entrance into another world. When they leave the cottage,
they refrain from talking until they re-cross the bridge, signifying
re-entrance into the common world.

The journey is an incursion into a paradise ruined and blighted
by some malignant agent. Unlike the Ireland of the Fireside
Songs and of the confused memory of the returning Americans,
this had been a tangible paradise. 'God help us,' exclaims the
narrator's mother before the trio sets out, 'I recall that house
as it was when Aunt Sally was alive. It was beautiful.' 'Good
God in heaven,' starts the father, when they come upon the
decaying wreck to which the house has been reduced. However
responsibility for the blight is distributed, 'Homes on the Mountain' brings to fulfilment the imagery and symbolism of water
that runs through rural Ulster fiction. Half-crowns are 'rained'
on the narrator and his friend Lanty; the Americans build on the
'wet' side of Dooish; during the building whiskey 'flowed like
water', rivalling the exaggerated torrents of the mountain runnels;
Thady could never as a youth let 'a salmon in the stream' alone;
the route to the cottage is across water, and throughout the story
rivulets weave and flow. Though the narrator's recitation of
Irish songs for his godmother results in a 'steady downpour of
half-crowns', this benign water-image contrasts ironically with
the symbolic use of water in the rest of the story. When not a
threshold symbol ('the seasonal stream' the trio crosses to reach
the O'Neill cottage), it is representative of decay and dissolution.
There is simply too much water : bogging down, drenching,
drowning. The fires of passion are quenched in it. Building is
rained out by it. Spirit is doused.

In his rain and overflowing rivulets, Kiely has found imagery
and symbolism for the spoliation of paradise—the 'paradise' of
a man's idyllic boyhood, the 'paradise' of a family's ancestral
home, the 'paradise' of a doomed and lonely mountain lifestyle.
And, remembering the irony of the story's songs, perhaps the
'paradise' of a pre-Plantation, pre-Famine or even pre-historic
Ireland, a nation of rebellious and passionate men who gave rise

8. Campbell, 77 ff.

to the songs and legends in the beginning. It is a multiple vision open to the same reservations that I entered against the stories of McLaverty and Friel. For Kiely, in rejecting the popular myth of Ireland, does not deride myth. Rather does he install a more remote, more poetic and, in the end, less vulnerable myth.

3

DOGS AMONG THE MOLES

THE writing I discussed in the two previous chapters indulges, one way or another, the ill-humour of the land. The rural naturalists accept its moral standards, record its tantrums, mourn its loss, while in the short stories of McLaverty, Friel and Kiely, authors and characters retreat into fantasy and wan, somewhat self-piteous humour. What is missing so far is a willingness to expose the darker side of life on the land—its pettiness, its obduracy, its violence and savagery. We receive only glimpses of this in rural naturalism, for example in the St Patrick's Day brawl in *Come Day—Go Day* and the ambush scene in *December Bride*. The precedent is there, of course, in Carleton whose sentimental attachment to the peasantry was offset by a readiness to expose evil and brutality on the land. Modern rural writers who share something of Carleton's readiness—Patrick MacGill, Benedict Kiely (in his two most recent novels), Patrick Boyle, Anthony C. West, Maurice Leitch, Jack Wilson, John Montague—also share his acquired urban consciousness and his critical attitude towards the land.

The fictional account to which a critical and unflattering attitude to the land is turned varies with each writer. Lynn Doyle produces muscular comedy with the appearance rather than the reality of satire. Patrick MacGill writes passionate but repetitious propaganda against the social evils of town and country. Altogether more faceted than either, Patrick Boyle and Benedict Kiely (of the later novels) combine comedy with satire and to Doyle's comic roughhouse and MacGill's black rural poverty add their vision of rural neurosis, repression and even diabolism.

The short stories of Lynn Doyle can be superficially dismissed as fictional stage Irishism, but they do reflect either directly (in

85

the occasional serious story such as 'The Rapparee') or obliquely (in the comic bulk of his canon) the irruptive, manic energy of the countryside. Doyle (real name, Leslie A. Montgomery) wrote dozens of quirky little stories, many of them set in the imaginary and folksy Co. Down town of Ballygullion, a kind of Ulster Everytown. His publishing career spanned the best part of a half-century, from *Ballygullion* (1908) to, aptly enough, *Back to Ballygullion* (1953).

The typical Doyle story is a fleet, humorous, perhaps over-coy romp among the foibles of errant humanity, and written through a participating narrator in thick Ulster dialect. Though in the end innocuous as a perception into the rural psyche and the wellsprings of sectarianism, the Doyle story does transform the violence of the countryside into knockabout comedy. The transformation functions to make light of rural violence and bigotry and in this sense is indulgent. But it is also meant to satirise the land by poking fun at its idiocies. It is difficult to know where indulgence ends and satire begins, or where satire ends and self-indulgence begins. Consider 'Sham Fight', one of Doyle's better stories.[1]

The plot of this story strikes a good many satiric sparks. A rich American whose father came from Ballygullion hires an English director to film a re-staging of the Battle of the Boyne 'that should give fair-play to both sides'. The folly of the Irish-American is matched by the greed of the Ballygullionites who sink their differences in order to fleece him. All goes well until the raging battle-scenes threaten to grind to a halt when the local historian unearths some unfamiliar facts about the Battle of the Boyne : that King William's side included not merely Ulstermen but 'the whole sweepings of Europe' and that the pope gave his blessing to William's campaign in Ireland. Nothing daunted, Protestants and Catholics unite in rejecting 'facts' which endanger their chance to make some quick money, and the film is completed.

The kernel of the story's satire is the insight that the sectarian reliance on mythology (the 'sham fight' of the title is not only the re-staged battle but also the Ulster concept of the historical battle) is exceeded by the avarice of the Ballygullionites. It is a comforting delusion, avarice being easier to contemplate than

---

1. 'Sham Fight' appears in *A Bowl of Broth*, London 1945.

hatred. Rather than contemplate hatred, Doyle effects its comic removal. After the film is completed, William McTallow, the Orangeman who played William, is convinced by the historian's facts about the Boyne, resigns from the Orange Order and becomes 'friendly and neighbourly with every class and creed'. When he dies even the Ancient Order of Hibernians wait to follow the hearse. Satire has become wish-fulfilment, reality turned once more into dream-fantasy. 'In the end we can always laugh at ourselves when there's nobody killed,' remarks the narrator, Patrick Murphy. Doyle's comedy is premised on this illusion. Doyle (was he Catholic or Protestant?) is not so much a neutral explorer of sectarian psychology as a sectarian hermaphrodite unwilling to offend either side. He is a funny and highly entertaining writer and, in a way of which he was unconscious, his prolific and obsessive comedy with its riotous anecdotage and music-hall rough-and-tumble captures a manic aspect of small-town rural life. On the brink of real satire, alas, Doyle falters and retreats.

Patrick MacGill, a contemporary of the early Doyle's, has a very different approach to life in rural Donegal, Derry and Tyrone. Doyle's Ballygullion, for all its sectarian violence, is a sheltered east-coast toytown compared with MacGill's windswept locations. MacGill saw not only sectarianism but a destitution of which we catch only a glimpse in McLaverty's Down and Antrim and Bullock's Fermanagh. Poverty in rural naturalism is depressive and the impoverished are passive and enduring, but whereas MacGill showed this side of peasant life, he also showed how poverty can erupt, without the sectarian catalyst, into violence. His stated theme approaches the pure naturalism of Zola—'life in all its primordial brutishness'—and if that is a characteristic overstatement, there was undoubtedly colossal penury on the wilder fringes of Donegal and Derry seventy years ago. His older characters remember the Famine and the disease, cannibalism and death it caused. Half a century later they still languish on bad land, suffering crop failure, unending poverty and hopelessness. On occasions MacGill comes close to Carleton's almost apocalyptic vision of the blighted land. *The Rat-Pit* (1915), for example, opens with a group of women crossing an estuary to the village of Greenanore to collect yarn for some underpaid home knitting. When Norah Ryan, the novel's heroine, joins the women they are sleeping in the snow awaiting the tide's retreat :

A face like that of a sheeted corpse peered up into the greyness, and Norah Ryan looked at it, her face full of a fright that was not unmixed with childish curiosity. There in the white snow, some asleep and some staring vacantly into the darkness, lay a score of women, some young, some old, and all curled up like sleeping dogs. Nothing could be seen but the faces, coloured ghastly silver in the dim light of the slow dawn, faces without bodies staring like dead things from the welter of snow. An old woman asleep, the bones of her face showing plainly through the sallow wrinkles of the skin, her only tooth protruding like a fang and her jaw lowered as if hung by a string, suddenly coughed. Her cough was wheezy, weak with age, and she awoke. In the midst of the heap of bodies she stood upright and disturbed the other sleepers. In an instant the hollow was alive, voluble, noisy. Some of the women knelt down and said their prayers, others shook the snow from their shawls, one was humming a love song and making the sign of the cross at the end of every verse. (p. 6)

The town of Greenanore is dominated by the police barracks, the Catholic chapel and the workhouse, images of bondage and oppression along with prison and the factory in MacGill's fiction. According to MacGill, the brutishness of life on the cruel periphery of north-western Ireland is due as much to exploitation as to the land's barren nakedness. Distribution of guilt is neatly summarised in a newspaper article on MacGill by Benedict Kiely: 'In the far Rosses, there were at the time three predominant wills: the will of God, the will of the priest and the will of the gombeen man.'[2] Farley McKeown, the gombeen man who owns the knitting industry and who made his money during the Famine, is a skinflint and tyrant. Little better is the gombeen priest, Father Devaney, milking the people of their money so that he can build a lavatory costing £250 in his new house.

Priest and merchant help to drive MacGill's characters to Scotland for seasonal work picking potatoes. The intertwined adventures in Donegal and Scotland of the two sweethearts Norah Ryan and Dermod Flynn (a largely autobiographical figure, according to the author) compose the loose narratives of

2. Benedict Kiely, 'Return to the Rat Pit', *The Irish Times*, 23 Feb. 1973.

Children of the Dead End (1914) and *The Rat-Pit* (1915). The
former is told from the viewpoint of Dermod, the latter from the
viewpoint of Norah, so these two books are really halves of the
same novel. The narratives are picaresque, bristling with ructions
and quarrels.. Like Doyle, MacGill is inclined towards burlesque,
but unlike Doyle he has a puritan didactic urge (too blunt to be
called a gift for satire) as befits his bedrock socialism. On occasions *Children of the Dead End* and *The Rat-Pit* resemble
Orwell's *The Road to Wigan Pier* in their episodic form, their
autobiographical cast and their concern for down-and-outs. Like
Orwell, MacGill was anti-capitalist and anti-employer, though
the Irishman's insight into economic exploitation was a good
deal cruder than Orwell's. To his Orwellian socialism MacGill
added a particularly Irish anti-clericalism and a sympathy for
that British industrial phenomenon, the Irish navvy.

MacGill's novels labour under many literary shortcomings. His
social criticism is ideologically simplistic, his poetry bad, his
characters too often caricatures, his endings sentimental. For all
this, his novels are mysteriously engaging. Their world, straddling
the famine-racked countryside of nineteenth-century Ireland and
the urban industrial squalor of twentieth-century Britain, is a
unique one. Unique, too, are characters like Moleskin Joe and
Gourock Ellen. And the stories rattle along at a fine pace. In the
context of rural Irish fiction, MacGill is Carleton's successor in
his refusal to be tyrannised by the land and its exploiters. He
flays not only the obvious villains but the peasants themselves for
their gullibility before the Church and employers, and for their
cruelty, for instance towards the hapless 'Beansho' who offends
them by having an illegitimate baby and by seeing through
Father Devaney. Even when strenuously striving for a saleable
manner (in which he was successful as 'the navvy poet'), MacGill
could not prevent himself from penning some powerful and
tenebrous scenes.

(2)

Most of the writers I have discussed have been concerned with
economic and political repression. By genre or default, there is
little or no psychology in rural naturalism, in short stories by
Kiely, Friel and McLaverty, in Doyle or in MacGill. Instead,
drama is created by the interaction of social forces. The solitary

or defiant character who might seem to cry out for analysis is simply regarded as the rural community regards him, i.e. as a 'character' in the colloquial sense, as a transgressor and as a potential victim. More recent writers of the Northern landscape such as Boyle, West, Leitch, Wilson, Montague, and Kiely of the later novels have tried to bring some psychology to bear, especially in the creation of solitary and defiant characters. Instead of economic and political repression they write, sometimes unconsciously, of sexual and cultural repression. Violence in their work can be seen in terms of this repression rather than MacGill's economic exploitation. McLaverty's distraught peasants are transmogrified into comic-horrifying idiots and demonic obsessives, just as his characters' passivity becomes sickness and disease, their almost 'healthy' poverty rankness and decay, the threat of violence its grotesque realisation. Blight for these more recent writers is no longer the crushing impersonal weight it is in the local naturalists, a weight that renders impotent (though sexual impotence is indeed a threat even in the most thrashing moments of sexuality in Leitch, Wilson and Boyle), but instead an active curse that drives men to violence and nightmare. To recognise the power of this curse is *ipso facto* to be alienated from the land and its people. All of these writers have a tinge of contempt for the rural Ireland from which they have sprung. This city-cultivated contempt makes itself felt in an aesthetic distance from the raw material despite the writers' intimate knowledge of rural ways. It is this aesthetic distance that makes me hesitate in calling any of these writers 'regionalist' in the way that the local naturalists are regionalists.

There are, nevertheless, strong inducements to the Irish writer to turn away from psychological realism. Two talented writers who have so far failed to resist the blandishments of their Irish literary heritage are Benedict Kiely and Patrick Boyle. If rural naturalism involves an isolationism in content and a moral abstentionism in approach, Boyle and Kiely are decidedly other than rural naturalists. Both are very funny and inventive and have a range and power beyond that of the local naturalists. Both are aware of a larger world outside rural Ireland, and it comes as no surprise to learn that they have access to the most prestigious and lucrative creative writing markets in the United States. A mutual defect, indeed, is a worldliness that is a little too brothy. Boyle and Kiely represent the senses rather than the intellect in rebellion against the atrophying constraints of Irish life. Their satire is fictional artifice rather than social threat or exorcism, a product, one feels, of exuberant personality and literary inventiveness more than of a burning sense of grievance. Their satiric victims are soft targets because they are all in a sense begrudgers, hypocrites, abstainers or philistines. These are the 'moles' of Irish life among whom Boyle and Kiely are randy and mischievous dogs. They are interested in means rather than ends and energetically turn the world of local naturalism on its head to produce mock-allegory, mock-romance and mock-heroics more sophisticated than anything in Doyle. In the end the jaundiced eye they cast on rural and small-town Ireland is not that of the satirist but of the literary alchemist who like Volpone loses sight of his satiric object amid his own brilliant machinations.

In Boyle and the later Kiely sentimentality can become black comedy, dream can become nightmare, and repressed sexuality can turn into the obstreperous and often perverted sexuality of inverted puritanism. Boyle and Kiely are the Burke and Hare of contemporary Irish literature. Clearly, though, we are dealing with either end of the same syndrome, and for all their rambunctious iconoclasm, Boyle and Kiely remain Catholic writers in a profound sense: the more they try to ignore and rebel against them, the more they confirm a Catholic upbringing and sensibility. Conscience and guilt are motivational lynch-pins in their fiction. Not surprisingly, then, their work does not only have its brash and noisy side but also its quiet and pathetic side. Both oscillate emotionally between the depression of the rural naturalists and a kind of manic joy-in-despair. Blight is not only for them a quiet dying or a matter for elegy but a kind of diabolism which Kiely has explored mock-romantically in his two most recent novels and Boyle mock-heroically in his single novel to date.

Like his short stories, most of Kiely's early novels are subdued, several of them, e.g. *Honey Seems Bitter* (1954) and *There Was an Ancient House* (1955), having as their central character a learned and poetic clerical student who loses his innocence and faith when initiated into sexuality. These novels do not impress me as much as many of the short stories, and as though he recognised where his strength lies, Kiely has begun to space his

novels out (six between 1947 and 1955 but only two between
1960 and the time of this writing) and to concentrate equally on
longer and more richly textured stories and novellas. In his two
most recent novels, *The Captain with the Whiskers* and *Dogs
Enjoy the Morning,* he has abandoned the relative quietness and
celibacy of the early novels and, no doubt taking advantage of
relaxing censorship in the Republic of Ireland where he is based
and of changing mores in the United Kingdom and United
States where his largest readership is, has turned to a muscular
and busy fiction, fired by a manic energy which foreign blurb-
writers are apt to call Celtic blarney and bawdry. As is to be
expected, the parodic element in these novels is an altogether
more theatrical affair than the mock-heroics of his stories that
conceal, as I have shown, a genuinely mythic quality.

The Captain with the Whiskers (1960) is at once realistic
Bildungsroman and mock-romance bristling with dubious heroes,
surrogate aristocrats and hardly chivalric love. It recounts the
young manhood of the narrator, Owen Rodgers, who in the
course of the novel leaves his Co. Tyrone village (is he named
after the Tyrone place-names Owenkillew and Owenreagh?)
to be a medical student in Dublin, returns disillusioned to become
a hotelier in Derry and closes the book in Dublin again, a somewhat cynical and world-weary widower. His maturation is inex-
tricably bound up with the eccentric and demonic Captain
Conway Chesney of Bingen House, a Boer War and Rhine
Valley veteran of the British Army. The captain is a ruthless,
violent, semi-cultured patriarch who runs his household on military lines and with a borrowed Teutonic efficiency. His wife,
unable to live down her servant background, remains faceless,
his daughters are cowed, and his three sons are made to drill in
Boer War uniforms and with heavy rifles.

Anyone hapless enough to become involved with the captain
suffers, even long after the captain is found drowned in the River
Gortin. One son becomes an incorrigible impregnator of young
girls, another a racing-driver who crashes and is left weak in the
head, the third a rigid priest; of the two daughters, one flees to
seek unsuccessfully the good life, while the other throws herself
from a high window of Bingen House. The curse upon the House
of Bingen and its devil of a captain (who keeps a stuffed serpent
upon the mantelpiece) stalks even Owen Rodgers who throws

over a local girl to woo one of the captain's daughters who in turn ditches him to join a gay social set. At the novel's end we learn that Owen re-met the local girl and married her but that she died prematurely, the curse of the captain apparently lingering still.

The Captain with the Whiskers is written in a rich, yeasty prose and seethes with anecdotes and allusions, many of them irrelevant and sensational. The over-ripeness of theme and language might recall for us the gothic novel, and the captain is a figure who would not be out of place in Poe or Mrs Radcliffe. Another tradition, too, might come to mind. Recollecting his youthful pal who had planned to write a book about Bingen and the captain, Owen at the end of the novel remarks : 'He had never written The Book : a deep south novel, suh, *the Book of Bingen* or *the Monster of Magheracolton* by Geoffrey Austin Macsorley.' (p. 276) *The Captain with the Whiskers* is that very novel in the sense that it shares with the fiction of the American South a gothic preoccupation with congenital evil and corruption and the notion of an imperial or aristocratic order gone bad. But Kiely's treatment of these themes is self-consciously different from that of, say, Faulkner or Tennessee Williams in so far as *The Captain with the Whiskers* is *mock*-romantic tragedy and is conducted in an iconoclastic singing or chanting voice that satirises its own pretensions. This verbal tightrope from which he seems reluctant to dismount means that Kiely's characters, in the manner of opera, talk *at* each other rather than *to* each other, and this can become irritatingly mannered in a novel which is also to an extent realistic *Bildungsroman*. This operatic quality of *The Captain with the Whiskers* (and of much of Kiely's fiction) blurs the distinction between dialogue and narration and the distinction between characters, and leaves the writer in omniscient control rather in the manner of a pub balladeer who will brook neither interruption nor respite. Here is Kiely in full and genial cry describing Owen's and his friends' search in Dublin for Alfred, the captain's son :

Separating by the dawn's early light the three searchers went by their various paths through the enchanted forest, asking questions of cottagers and wayfarers, roisterers in taverns, hermits in sylvan grots, or of bluff soldiery or halberd-bearing watchmen on the city walls.

Meeting again in the evening they conned the sum of the day's discoveries to find out, after a week, that even in a gossipy city like Dublin it was possible to mislay such a conspicuous object as an Austrian dog. Pubs and garden suburbs, presbyteries, cheap restaurants in backlanes where earnest working girls enticed sailors and where by night whiskey was secretively, illicitly consumed out of cracked teacups, football matches, dog-tracks, a day at the races, a night at the opera, careful scanning of all visible forms and faces produced never the face and form of the hunted satyr. (pp. 240–1)

The Captain with the Whiskers is mock-romance not only because of Kiely's laughing archaisms, inversions and metonymies, but also because it charts a young man's search for love through the adversities we associate with romance. Owen's initiation, however, is not so much into love as into evil, squalor and putrefaction, and a nose for these things is part of the legacy of the captain to those who came in contact with him. Kiely's gothic, like all gothic, is 'decayed' romance (as the Irish love-song of the novel's title is bewitched into a ballad of evil), his ugliness the ugliness of beautiful fruit left too long upon the branch. Although alive to the lovely landscape of West Tyrone, Kiely is even more alive in this novel to squalor, for instance of Derry, 'a rough, northern city where men's palates, calloused by sour heavy beer and burning spirits, were insensitive to the rich blood of the earth and the sun' (p. 147), or of Dublin : 'flat, dirty Dublin built by a stinking river on a lazar's marsh . . . Anna Livia Plurabelle, a dirty old woman, rotten weeds disfiguring her stone thighs' (pp. 116–17). In Dublin as a medical student Owen is initiated into sex by a drunken prostitute upon whom he takes pity : 'Beginning in charity, that night went on to curiosity, then to heat, disgust and a colony of persistent body lice.' (p. 118) Acidly, Owen–Kiely quotes the decent Dublin citizen roaring down the stairs of the old Abbey Theatre after Sean O'Casey : 'There are no prostitutes in this city.'

The Captain with the Whiskers is a novel in which Kiely comes closest to bitterness and personal exorcism. Anti-clerical sentiments are put into the mouth of the unsympathetic captain, but anti-hierarchical ideas are also voiced by the more sympathetic and persuasive priest, Dr Grierson, who maintains a running fight with his asinine clerical superior. It is difficult, though, to distinguish the author's bitterness from the novel's theme of blight, a blight that infects not only dirty Dublin and iron-grey Derry but even the lovely landscape of Gortin. What is the captain's curse? It is in part his despicable treatment of his wife and children. It is partly his dogmatic anti-clericalism and anti-nationalism. More damningly, the captain has tried to inject foreign names and ways into the native tissue of Gortin (e.g. by renaming the old Gaelic area of Magheracolton 'Bingen'), and by subjecting his household to foreign military discipline. The curse on the captain and his family and intimates, what we might call the bad blood of Bingen, can be read as the land's rejection—in a fashion familiar to readers of Bullock and McLaverty—of what is alien to it: the land remains. Yet in the final analysis the evil resides in the land itself and has resided there long before the captain came to activate it. It is a propensity for violence, superstition and dark magic that manifests itself in the shadowy figure of the wizard Doran who sliced off the official's finger and allowed his wife's body to moulder in her room while he drew her pension (a motif that aptly reminds us of Faulkner's 'A Rose for Emily' and which we will meet again in Patrick Boyle's 'Myko' and Anthony C. West's *The Ferret Fancier*).

As he has tried to wed *Bildungsroman* to gothic romance, so Kiely has tried to give the theme of evil a contemporary ring by weaving the captain's conundrum ('Is it better to be born and damned than not to be born at all?') through the novel, an aspect of the novel explored through the Graham Greenesque figure of Dr Grierson, 'twisted by celibacy and sustained by drink'. But the lingering impression of *The Captain with the Whiskers* is hardly likely to be of moral and theological quandary or of the psychology of adolescence or even of the realistic rendering of the surfaces of everyday life. Kiely is hypnotised by his own verbal facility and the folkloristic associations with his theme: moral evil vies with dark magic, narrative vies with ballad, realism vies with alchemy. The result is a novel that is a *tour de force* but one that suffers from generic confusion and tonal indecision.

The narrator of *The Captain with the Whiskers* refers to himself as Peeping Tom Rodgers because it was by accident he discovered from the stable-loft at Bingen the captain drilling his sons. In a larger sense Owen Rodgers, as narrator, is an eavesdropper on everything that happens in the novel. There is a more conventional Peeping Tom in *Dogs Enjoy the Morning* (1968), Gabriel Rock who haunts the hospital and frightens the nurses, but when Gabriel possesses hopping, daft Nora on the top of the ruined tower in full view of everyone, we are all, characters and readers, made Peeping Toms. No one is more of an eavesdropper and Peeping Tom than the author himself, of course, since he not only creates but constantly betrays his characters by retailing intimacies in the novel's continuing gossip. In this, Kiely, like all authors, is aspiring to the omniscience of God ('gossip', after all, derives from the root 'god'): fittingly, God in *Dogs Enjoy the Morning* is referred to as a Peeping Tom, the original Peeping Tom we might say.

Pursuing this trope to the end, Kiely has created in *Dogs Enjoy the Morning* a nutshell of a world, the village of Cosmona. Into this microcosm of just over 250 pages of junketing prose are crammed all the anecdotes Kiely has ever told, all the characters he has created, all the plots he has envisaged. A number of figures (including the shiftless ex-convict Christy Hanafin, three Dublin pressmen and a Liberian sailor) converge upon Cosmona—a village of the fevered imagination that could be almost anywhere in Ireland outside the straitlaced North-east —swelling a veritable grotesquerie of characters: King Kong Hoban, Peejay, Sister Thermometer, The Mouse, Shadow and Substance, Mickey Rooney. 'All human life is here,' remarks one of the reporters, echoing the advertising slogan of the *News of the World*. Cosmona is Kiely's Sunday-morning Cosmos.

Each character has his own reason for being in Cosmona or for going there, and the coincidence of all being there at the same time lends the novel an air of mischievous fantasy. At the end of the novel, after doing their bit to get the harvest carnival off the ground, the visitors disperse and the village reverts to its normal, still-zany self. Cosmona is a world both brutal and comic, a world of suicide and idiocy, of voyeurism, bestiality and sadism rendered with feisty prose and rampant laughter. If *The Captain with the Whiskers* is mock-romantic tragedy, *Dogs Enjoy the Morning* is pastoral comedy turned black.

The novel's climactic actions concern the satisfaction (licit and illicit) of that concupiscence of the flesh that is the novel's motivating force : all occur under the influence, it seems, of the standing stone and disused abbey tower in the shadows of which the villagers live. Monolith and steeple are repositories of local mythology but also phallic symbols : thus, the village picnic on the hill near the edifices (the novel's central communal event) is not only a re-enactment of a pagan harvest rite but also a metaphoric version of the major characters' surrender to fleshly desire. Some do not make the journey, figuratively speaking, to tower and standing stone, consequently the reader is faced with the conflict between sexuality and celibacy, a conflict reflected in the rather simple deployment of characters. Kiely has always been a Manichee of the spirit, seeing his characters either for or against the right to enjoy life to the full. In his novels fun-loving dogs carouse and copulate while pennypinching moles creep grudgingly from darkness to darkness.[3] It is the task of Peter Lane, hero of *Dogs Enjoy the Morning*—clerical student, hospital patient and 'postponed celibate'—to cross the invisible boundary between prodigals and pennypinchers and prove himself on the side of life. As with *The Captain with the Whiskers*, a *Bildungsroman* lurks within the voluminous fleshy folds of *Dogs Enjoy the Morning*.

The life-force which finally abducts Lane from priestly celibacy is given expression in the myths and legends that shroud Cosmona. There is the legend of Dark Dan (Domhnall Dubh) the horse-thief who allegedly abducted a farmer's daughter in 1835 and disappeared into a cave, never to return.[4] This legend is re-enacted in the novel by the black sailor's rape of Amantha, but it also reaches back into the subterranean mythology of Ireland. Charles Roe, the novel's local historian, sees behind the figure of Dark Dan a darker and more ancient force : 'I see the

3. My animal nomenclature is inspired by Kiely's novel and by his review of Hogan and O'Neill's edition of the unpublished journal of Joseph Holloway, 'Joe the Post: or A Portrait of the Irishman as Mole', *Northwest Review*, Eugene, Oregon, IX, No. 2 (Fall–Winter 1967–68).

4. This would appear to be a common motif in what Vivian Mercier in *The Irish Comic Tradition* calls Ireland's 'Otherworld literature'.

shape of someone greater, more terrible, the unconquered god of the shadows, Pluto, our Crom Dubh, our giant Balor of the Evil Eye, champion of our ancient faith in stock and stone, taking refuge in the earth and leaving Lugh, the young god of Christian light to be king of the castle.' (p. 53) Here Kiely, with tongue partly in cheek, has lent legendary and mythic dimension to the blight on the land, seeing it as a subterranean pagan force of violence that can erupt at any time and which erupts in *Dogs Enjoy the Morning* as comic perversion, sadism and bestiality.

In Cosmona Christian celibacy has little chance against pagan desire. The author hopes to plot Peter Lane's conversion to the flesh as a gentle curve in contrast to the brutal sensuality of the other characters, but Lane's sexual initiation with Nurse Walters is a clumsy and ugly affair on the floor of the hospital lavatory. In Kiely's Manichean world, it is usually the uncertain character, neither dog nor mole and in conflict with his conscience, who fails to come alive and to provide the novels with a serious centre. The serious side of Peter Lane's maturation, for example, simply jars with what is happening around him, and the upperworld of theology, rationality and psychological explanation subsides violently into the underworld of Kiely's black comedy. Kiely's thirst for scatological anecdote, grotesquerie and muscular comedy is unquenchable, as may be witnessed in a roll-call of the novel's chief events : 'A white cock that can shake hands. A darling girl that saw a ghost. A tinker woman who can dance on the seat of a chair while her husband holds the back-rung of the chair between his teeth. A dying man who was kicked by Japs into the River Kwai. A Peeping Tom performing in full view of all. Ned and Bob happy with the town whores. . . And a rape, Art said, a grade-A rape performed by a sailor, and a black one at that.' (p. 242) *Dogs Enjoy the Morning* is Irish anecdotage and pub gossip run rampant, at once a Peeping Tom's and a journalist's dream.

Like *The Captain with the Whiskers, Dogs Enjoy the Morning* has its serious commentary on Irish life buried beneath the grotesque surface where it can barely breathe. Kiely in this novel symbolises the whole of present-day Ireland by juxtaposing Dublin and rural town, worldly pressmen and bucolics. The mobile X-ray unit, like the influx of Dubliners into Cosmona, images the increasing impingement of city on countryside, while the plight of Mortell's ancient mill is a reminder of the changing face of workaday rural Ireland. The miller is the dignified nineteenth-century self-employed being ushered grumbling into the mid-twentieth century with its organised division of labour and impersonal techniques of production—all the paraphernalia of what Kiely has elsewhere called Ireland's Grocer's Republic.

Kiely is clearly unhappy with much of what he sees in Ireland today, an unhappiness he expressed through the character of Jeff in *The Captain with the Whiskers*: 'The sadness of the land we live in', said Jeff, 'is no longer the melancholy Celtic sadness of low skies, soft rain and birds crying on the bog. It's the exhausted sadness, the slough following in the wake of exasperation, of the little man who missed the train. We were too late for everything. We were too late even to be free.' (p. 283) These words give vent to the post-revolutionary tristesse of second-generation republicans. Unfortunately this theme is unexplored realistically and remains, in *The Captain with the Whiskers* and *Dogs Enjoy the Morning*, at the allegorical level as parody of romantic Ireland.

As we have seen in *The Captain with the Whiskers*, Kiely is equally unhappy with the Catholic aspect of Ireland's yesterday, and so in *Dogs Enjoy the Morning* he harks back to the day before yesterday, to Ireland's pagan past. In contrast to the new factories is the disused abbey tower standing on holy pagan ground: this is an image doing triple duty, for besides being a phallic symbol it testifies to the pagan roots of much of Christianity and also to the failure of Christianity to project its relevance into the twentieth century. Kiely's pagan Ireland is a brutal place but also a place of hedonism, sensuality and bacchic festivity. *Dogs Enjoy the Morning* is, as the title implies, something of an orgy in which both the Grocer's Republic and Holy Catholic Ireland are swept aside in the reenactment of ancestral rhythms and energies. But there are inherent dangers in a novel celebrating these things, and I find myself resisting both *Dogs Enjoy the Morning* and *The Captain with the Whiskers* for their 'overkill' in language and motifs: the inveterate pub balladeer springs again to mind. The world created in *Dogs Enjoy the Morning* is almost worthy of Hieronymous Bosch yet is off its axis, too jaundiced for its own satiric good. By so obviously *displaying* his large talent, Kiely fails to transcend his satire to say something serious about Ireland and the Irish psyche.

(3)

Whereas Kiely has been writing and publishing steadily since the late 1940s, Patrick Boyle ceased writing at one stage and did not, by his own account, take up the pen for seventeen years.[5] His precipitous success in the mid-1960s, aided immensely by the interest Grove Press in the United States has shown in his work, has been recognised as something of a literary phenomenon. On the strength (and I use the word advisedly) of one novel, *Like Any Other Man* (1966), and two volumes of stories, *At Night All Cats Are Grey* (1966) and *All Looks Yellow to the Jaundiced Eye* (1969), Boyle has been acknowledged as a brash and original talent by readers whose resolve has already been stiffened by such writers as J. P. Donleavy, Joseph Heller and Philip Roth. In his work the naturalistic theme of blight has been neatly wedded to a black comedy that has found a ready American audience.

Although Boyle's fiction has a familiar setting, it is illuminating to contrast a descriptive passage from a Boyle story with a superficially similar scene from, for example, a story by Michael McLaverty :

McLaverty

As the day advanced the sun rose higher, but there was little heat from it, and frosty vapours still lingered about the rockheads and about the sparse hills. But slowly over the little field horse and plough still moved, moved like timeless creatures of the earth, while alongside, their shadows followed on the clay. Overhead and behind swarmed the gulls, screeching and darting for the worms, their flitting shadows falling coolly on Paddy's neck and on the back of the mare.

'The White Mare'[6]

Boyle

A sting of heat was beginning to creep into the morning sun. Like a warm hand, it clamped down on the old man's scrawny

5. See Rosita Sweetman's interview with Patrick Boyle in her book *'On Our Knees'*, London 1972, 102–9.
6. 'The White Mare' appears in *The Game Cock and Other Stories*, London 1949, and also in an earlier collection to which it gives the title.

neck as if it meant to push him down into the mounds of cut turf he was so busily spreading. It wormed its way through the layers of cardigans and undershirts, it scorched his meagre shrunken buttocks, it soaked through his boots so that his scalded feet chafed against the damp wrinkled socks. Sweat trickled down his face, smarting his eyes and salting his mouth, but he worked on steadily, rolling the heaped-up sods back through his straddled legs like a terrier rooting frantically at a burrow.

'Go Away, Old Man, Go Away'[7]

Both scenes of small farmers at work, McLaverty's is characteristically pictorial, frieze-like, while Boyle's is fired by a menacing physical energy (heat 'worms' its way through the farmer's clothing) and an equally menacing emotional energy (the farmer works busily and in irritation not with but against the forces of nature). Boyle's farmer is diminished, rendered churlish and dog-like, but McLaverty's is raised almost to the power of myth.

Boyle's passage is something of a microcosm of his fiction. In it we see that nature and natural processes (e.g. of the body) are not to be eulogised or worshipped but instead feared and distrusted. Moreover, man himself is for Boyle a pathetic, ugly, animal-like creature who falls far short of our idealisations of the species. It is typical that Boyle should describe his farmer as terrier-like: almost always his characters are likened to unprepossessing animals—vulture, hedgehog, lizard, mouse, calf, balding eagle, goose, house-cat (and all these in the same story). Animals play a large role in rural Ulster fiction, but Boyle lends his own twist to this by a persistent and grotesque zoomorphic vision of man that is vaguely Swiftian.

Boyle is fascinated by the absurd foibles of the countrymen and country townsmen of Donegal, Derry and beyond, and these he transcribes with a perfect ear for colloquialisms and with a surface realism that both borders on caricature and tickles the reader with the shock of recognition. His portrayal of dodgers, malingerers and grafters is made even funnier because the narrator of the story is very often one of the boys himself whose perceptions have the ringing truthfulness of the insider. Boyle's world is a nest of hucksters and boozers into

7. From Boyle's collection, *At Night All Cats Are Grey* (1966); except where otherwise indicated, all the Boyle stories I discuss are from this volume.

H

which the outsider and the reader stray at their peril. Not content to chide his people gently, Boyle follows them into the urinal, under the bedclothes, on to the bar-stool the better, as he jokingly said, 'to savour the hum and reek of creation'.[8] Boyle has comically envisioned the writer as one suffering from 'prolapse of the croup—better known as Duck's Disease', built close to the ground that he might miss nothing untoward, indiscreet or debasing. It would give too much psychoanalytic weight to Boyle's fiction to say he shares what has been called Swift's excremental vision, but certainly Boyle's orificial imagery is as characteristic as his animal imagery. The author is fascinated with bodily orifices in their fundamental capacities and his stories are positively awash with drink, vomit, urine, blood and catarrh. Perhaps it would be more accurate to say that he is fascinated simply by the flesh, flesh in rigor mortis, as in 'Oh Death Where is Thy Sting-aling-aling', flesh in disfigurement, as in 'The Port Wine Stain', flesh in putrescence, as in 'Myko', flesh dismembered, as in 'The Metal Man', flesh bloodied and flayed, as in 'Go Away, Old Man, Go Away'.

Withal, the moral face worn by Boyle's fiction is more apparent than that worn by the work of the local naturalists or even of Kiely. McLaverty weaves the foibles of his people into the texture of his vision of rural Ulster in such a way that we cannot take offence at those foibles without threatening McLaverty's entire vision. Boyle, on the other hand, draws attention to those foibles—the scandal-mongering, the hypocrisy, the petty acquisitiveness—and not only exposes them but magnifies them into sin and crime. Sin followed by penance, crime followed by punishment : these are the commonest moral progressions in Boyle's fiction. There is, for example, the young narrator's betraying cruelty to the birthmarked cobbler in 'The Port Wine Stain', a betrayal exorcised in the boy's subsequent and even greater cruelty that is, in its simultaneous self-infliction, penitential. Then there is the skinflint publican-cum-undertaker Myko in the eponymous story who gets his comeuppance when a band of tinkers leave the mouldering body of their leader on his hands. The husband in 'At Night All Cats Are Grey' who enjoyably imagines he committed adultery while boozed the

8. Quoted from a little-known article by Boyle, in Jack Matthews, 'An Interview with Patrick Boyle', *Malahat Review*, Victoria, B.C., Oct. 1970.

night before suffers the pain of suddenly realising he did not, a pain of guilt rather than of illusion deflated. The progression is inverted in 'Square Dance' in which conscience and compassion in one character are mistaken for lust by another character. A greater crime in Boyle's moral universe than lust, miserliness, adulterous desire and cruelty, though all of these can be aspects of it, is betrayal. Two of his best stories, 'The Betrayers' and 'Meles Vulgaris', deal with betrayal. Both employ animal symbolism for obliquely sexual purposes in a way reminiscent of Friel's use of cockfighting in 'Ginger Hero', but even more powerfully than in Friel's story.

Stableman Willie Nesbitt in 'The Betrayers' lavishes love and compassionate patience on his unbroken skewbald mare but is seduced into paying attention to Cassie, the maid. Willie's tender and successful methods of breaking in his mare are plainly inapposite for use on Cassie and through his slow-bloodedness he loses the maid's attentions to a visiting policeman. When Cassie and her policeman come upon Willie training the mare they bait him until he loses his temper and concentration and begins to beat the mare who has, through the bloodshot eyes of Willie's failure, become Cassie herself. The mare bolts and Willie is knocked down. Conniving, cruel, fickle, Cassie (and her boyfriend) suggest worldliness laughing at the slow, backward countryside, yet Willie ends the story magnified in stature : 'Crippling along, one shoulder up to his ear, fisted hand held stiffly to his sides, blood-soaked long-johns hanging from the torn trouser-leg, he should have looked ridiculous. Instead there was something tough and resolute in his bearing that made you forget he was balding, chinless, splay-footed : that lent inches to his puny stature and dignity to his limping gait.' (p. 196)

Toughness, dignity and resolution are rare in Boyle's countryside where meanness and boorishness abound; they are what Boyle professes to admire and those who embody the solitude of dignity are like lonely mesas above the rubble and slack of connivance and avarice. Accordingly, to be true to oneself and one's own nature is in Boyle the ultimate virtue, to betray oneself the ultimate transgression. Kinsella remains true to himself in 'Square Dance' but gives the appearance of doing otherwise; Jim does not in 'At Night All Cats Are Grey' and suffers conscience because of it. Amid the temptations of life it is difficult to remain true to the self-image one has painstakingly tried to build up, in one's best moments, over the years, but it is all the more important to try because it is certain that all around one are dishonesty and hypocrisy. Boyle's is a slightly paranoid view of humanity, and he has one of his characters describe it as 'a world of meddlers, a vast conspiracy of busybodies intent on our destruction'.[9]

Self-betrayal is perhaps most painfully explored in 'Meles Vulgaris'. While Sheila endeavours to make herself seductive, her husband lies in bed with a book about the badger (Latin name, *Meles vulgaris*) and recalls a day in the Blue Stack Mountains in Donegal during their first holiday after their marriage when he attended a badger-baiting with men of the area. His memory of the badger's death (interrupted by Sheila's seductive advances and interpolated with scientific descriptions of the badger from the book) is acutely painful and expressed with numbing realism. He remembers the badger's tenacity in face of the torturing ring of dogs and men and how one of the men at length cracked into compassion and shame when the death becomes a scene of horrific bungling, admonishing: 'Let none of you ever boast of this day's work. It was pure butchery, that's what it was. A cowardly bit of blackguardism. There's more spunk in the brock than in the whole bloody issue of you.' (p. 140)

In his remembrance of that day, the husband sees the badger as having embodied tenacity, courage and ferocity, but above all tenacity: 'for surely, without tenacity, courage and ferocity were futile'. The badger's tenacity, like Willie Nesbitt's dignity, is what shines amid the countryside's dark cruelties. Tenacity is what is required if we are to remain true to ourselves, and the husband bitterly realises he has not shown this quality. The voice of the dying badger has been a reproach to him for his own failure and self-betrayal:

For all these years it had resounded in his memory with the urgency of a trumpet call—the wild defiant shout of an animal ringed about with enemies. He had thought to cast himself in this heroic mould. To be a maverick. Forever in the ranks of the embattled minority. Instead there had been a slow erosion of

9. From 'Interlude', a story in *All Looks Yellow to the Jaundiced Eye* (1969).

ideals, a cowardly retreat from one decent belief after another
until at last he found himself in the ranks of the majority. The ring
of craven curs that hemmed in and crushed the unruly, those few
who dared cry : '*Non serviam!*' . . .

Desolation—a grey waste of futility and failure—engulfed him.
His skin crawled. His limbs cringed in revulsion at the extent of
his betrayal. (pp. 140–1)

But in Boyle self-betrayal is almost always aided and abetted
by other betrayers (often women who are flirty when they are not
staid), and so Sheila is cast as one of the majority, tempting her
husband into a life of mediocrity and sameness. 'Grrr!' she
growls happily at the end of the story like a dog, as her husband
submits to her seduction as the badger never did to its tormentors.
Their intercourse at the end is depicted as a fierce fighting, a
baiting, just as earlier the husband recalled the dog and badger
locked together as though coupling.

Two things damage this fine story. One is overstatement.
Boyle is frequently overcharged, of course, with his novel and
many of his stories written in a prose that gallops urgently towards climactic revelation. But in a serious rather than comic
story, Boyle's urgency can overload his fictional structure;
'Meles Vulgaris' is charged with action and imagery like a small
circuitry fused by a giant voltage. In addition, something more
specific damages the story. It is difficult to know just what has
been betrayed by the husband. What ideals have been eroded?
What decent beliefs retreated from? What heroic mould broken?
The wish to cry '*Non serviam!*' recalls Joyce with its suggestion
of artistic loneliness and the loneliness of apostasy, but neither
of these is substantiated in the husband's case. Unfortunately his
self-betrayal remains very much a blank cheque for the reader.
There is a hint that the couple's suburban existence represents
collapse into mediocrity, and certainly in Boyle's fiction sub-
urbanism is one of two enemies to life and vitality, the other
being the begrudging smallmindedness and cowardly boorishness
to be found among Boyle's country townsmen and demonstrated
that day in the Blue Stack Mountains in the 'vulgar melee' of
the badger-baiting.

The quieter horrors of suburbia remain a secondary preoccupation with Boyle, celebrated in his first book of stories

with 'Suburban Idyll' and with several stories in *All Looks Yellow to the Jaundiced Eye,* an altogether more subdued volume some of whose stories are set not in the North-west but in Dublin. In 'Suburban Idyll' middle-class respectability is confronted by low-class and foreign vulgarity and with heraldic irony triumphs. The inaptly named Charles Killingley Hunter is oppressed by an ultra-respectable wife. 'Bent on swaddling him in safe middle-class respectability, she had patiently moulded him throughout the years, rooting out a dangerous originality here, damping down an awkward indignation there, ever on the alert for the monstrous heresy of vulgarity.' The husband with delicious irony is knocked down outside the home of an ill-reputed foreign woman who is the blot on the neighbourhood's escutcheon, and Mrs Hunter has to stomach not only the possibility of her husband's having cut loose on the sly but also the comic vulgarity of the drunks who bring the body home. The story is written in mock-heroic tones and ends with Mrs Hunter retrieving her pseudo-aristocratic bearing in time to face the person for whom in this world she has most contempt, the foreign temptress from down the street. Mrs Hunter is the standard-bearer of besieged respectability for whom no sacrifice, in the eternal campaign that appearance wages against reality, is too great.

It ought to be clear just how conventional a moralist Patrick Boyle is in his stories. But I think the ostensible moral issues are a pretext and that something more subversive and perhaps only half-conscious is going on in his fiction. To begin with, Boyle's originality lies in the way he intensifies foibles into crime and sin, and regret and guilt into penance. On occasions sin and crime even generate a kind of mock-apocalypse which can be very funny. 'Suburban Idyll', for example, in setting up Mr Hunter's death, has concealed references to the apocalyptic cargo-cults of dark Melanesia. Hunter teases his wife with baroque tales of people jettisoning their worldly goods in preparation for Doomsday, a recurring motif in cargo-cults.[10] Unbeknown to either, Mr Hunter is himself about to savour the fruits of Apocalypse. Even in such a trivial story as 'Home Again, Home Again, Jiggety-Jig', Boyle can make the sight of a drunk father

10. See Peter Worsley's account of cargo cults in *The Trumpet Shall Sound: A Study of 'Cargo' Cults in Melanesia,* London 1968, the title of which Boyle works into 'Suburban Idyll'.

enmeshed in the bedclothes conjure up an apocalyptic vision. In more serious stories, however, the mock-apocalyptic inclination has the more dubious result of blurring Boyle's moral intent. There is, in such a story as 'Meles Vulgaris', a mock-apocalyptic approach difficult to distinguish from parody, though nothing else in the story suggests that parody is intended.

Just as sin and crime are intensified into mock-apocalypse, so punishment and penance are intensified into mock-purgatory. Again, 'Meles Vulgaris' is a useful example, for the husband's tortured re-enactment of the apocalyptic badger-baiting is a kind of purgatory. The question arises here too as to what is being achieved by parodic hyperbole and supercharged realism when they accompany emotional imprecision. Boyle's serious stories, while often large achievements, tend unintentionally to mock and thereby devalue the heroism from which Boyle means his chief characters unwisely to depart. This is one sense in which we might call his fiction mock-heroic. In the darkly comic stories he intentionally mocks the mean and lowly who absurdly aspire to a warped and bar-room sense of heroism. This is the other more conscious and successful sense in which his work is mock-heroic. Heroics of the second kind lie in ample readiness for the satirist in Ireland's pub life and rampant anecdotage and have been tapped by fiction writers from Carleton through Lynn Doyle to Kiely and in fact, as Vivian Mercier has shown, by all kinds of Irish writers for as long as there has been Irish literature. Boyle's mock-heroes are writ physically large, boozers and lechers of gigantic appetite : a diverting task is to keep track of the myriad whiskeys and pints downed in an average Boyle pub scene.

Whereas other writers have turned to Ireland's Otherworld literature for their archetypes, Boyle has often turned to the Bible. Since betrayal is the characteristic crime in his fiction, it is not surprising that Judas is a recurring evil genius. It is unsurprising, too, that since infinite appetite (for drink, food and women) is his characteristic deadly sin, the figure of Samson should suggest itself. In Boyle's one novel to date, *Like Any Other Man* (1966), Jim Simpson, a bank manager somewhere on the western sea-board of Ireland, plays Samson, and Delia, a Cassie-like out-of-towner, his temptress. This novel strafes all of Boyle's favourite targets but does so with a promiscuity that leaves Boyle's own position ambiguous. To be more specific, it is hard to know in which of the two senses Boyle has meant his novel to be mock-heroic. What we are left with is an impression of vast and directionless energy on the part of the author and chief character and which in the case of the latter is even more pathological and self-destructive than the energy that drives the demonics of Kiely's recent novels.

The novel's parallels with the story of Samson and Delilah are deliberately protrusive. Simpson is a big man of unruly and exhibitionistic strength, an aggressive womaniser who is seduced by a visiting barmaid (Delia) in his small west-coast town. Simpson is a gargantuan drinker and during one binge Delia shears off his sparse hair, but he is going downhill physically by that stage anyway, suffering retinal haemorrhages from what he later learns is probably inherited syphilis. At the novel's end he apparently goes totally blind during a Samsonian orgy of destruction.

The writing in *Like Any Other Man,* for all the play with biblical allegory, is realistic in a muscular and coarse-grained way, like flesh under a magnifying glass. Simpson's haemorrhages give Boyle a chance to indulge the vivid anatomical imagery which supplants imagery from the natural landscape but which on occasions manages to make Simpson's haemorrhagic vision akin to that of a psychedelic landscape :

He saw it happen. Against the white paper it showed up as though on a cinema screen. For a moment he could not grasp the significance of the scarlet column rising like a volcanic eruption and, like an eruption, mushrooming at its peak. Only when he remembered that the retina inverts all reflected images did it dawn on him that he was witnessing the onset of another haemorrhage. Fearfully he watched the mushroom cloud swell and thicken as the small steady trickle of blood kept leaking out of the ruptured blood vessel.

He closed his eyes. . . His face was turned towards the window through which the morning sun had begun to blaze. Through his closed eyelids he could detect the different texture of darkness. To his horror he found that he could see against the mottled background a slender pillar of darkness surmounted by a cloud of deeper darkness. The cloud had settled lower. No doubt of that.

Soon, if the haemorrhage continued, the sinister cloud would sink down till all was engulfed. (pp. 118–19)

This detachment of Simpson's from the processes of his body (he 'witnesses' the haemorrhage) is characteristic of Boyle for whom the body is capable of betrayal as though it were another person.

The sheer obviousness of the Samson-Delilah parallels results in an innocuous parody of the biblical story. The novel's ending, which echoes the novel's opening passage (describing Simpson waking with a hangover), also gives an ironic nod to those novels in which we realise on the last page that the entire plot has been the hero's nightmare. More importantly, however, Boyle seems to be parodying, in Simpson's relation to the Church, those apostatic and confessional novels so beloved of Irish Catholic writers. In one scene Simpson refuses to make confession, in another he cannot remember the Act of Contrition, in a third is recalled his failure to take the sacraments. Simpson veers between lecherous desire and a peculiarly Catholic guilt, and the concluding nightmarish scene of the novel can be seen not only as a re-enactment of Samson's apocalyptic destruction of the house of the Philistines but also as Simpson's descent into purgatory. In typical Boyle fashion, then, the moral conflict is at once 'resolved' and satirised by reducing (or heightening) it into macabre and grotesque parody.

On the one hand, it is a merely literary resolution that does not decide the moral issue at all. Certainly Boyle's attitude towards the Catholic Church remains ambiguous. Equally ambiguous is Boyle's attitude towards his possessed hero. During his fall from strength and sanity Simpson castigates himself : 'With envy, he remembered this callous swaggering somebody, who barged his way through life, his very bulk insuring the respect of his fellows, contemptuous of the weak and ailing, harsh in his judgements, unrelenting in rancour. He had ridiculed love, scorned sobriety, despised respectability.' (p. 285) Yet whatever Simpson's faults, Boyle clearly prefers him to the moles around him who play the parts of the biblical Philistines and who, far from being respectable, sober, weak and loving, are swindling, drunk and hypocritical. Often Simpson seems one of the 'unruly' championed in 'Meles Vulgaris', a badger ringed with enemies. *Like Any Other Man* seems to set out to satirise

Simpson's perverted Irish sense of heroism and strength but hypnotises itself into a literary indulgence in it.

On the other hand, the use of macabre and grotesque parody can be regarded as a psychological resolution. The collision between Simpson's desire and guilt induces in him a manic-depression in which bouts of vitality and exhibitionism are succeeded by bouts of melancholy and self-castigation. Each swing of the emotional pendulum is exaggerated in Simpson's attempt to compensate for his lack of psychological stability which stems from the crude conflict between his Church-inspired conscience and guilt and his bodily-inspired desire. If Simpson is a schizophrenic, it is a condition he shares with a large number of Irishmen. Manic-depression, morbidity and schizophrenia have a high and almost crisis incidence in contemporary Ireland, and because the figures pertain to rural as well as urban Ireland, there is no reason to doubt that the high incidence has obtained for some time.[11] Boyle's novel is too highly charged for us to treat it as a realistic exploration of schizophrenia, but we can view it as an allegory of the sickness of the land and Simpson as a demonic and wounded giant harbouring within his bulk the venom that resides in the countryside, the evil currents that flow through the dark land. In Boyle's giant weakening through congenital syphilis we have the most vivid picture yet both of rural debility and of the land's mindless violence.

Like Any Other Man demonstrates the continuing ability of Irish writers to transform manic-depression into rich literary styles and subject-matter. If some writers (e.g. the local naturalists) tend to be merely depressive, others (e.g. Boyle, Kiely and others we have mentioned in this chapter) are rather more complicated. Boyle's heroics reflect not only his characters' manic-depression (their mania turned into apocalypse, their depression into purgatory), but also the conflict between his own wish for expression and the repressed, puritanical society in which he lives. As Mercier intimates, heroics and giantism in Irish literature represent the literary sublimations of real desire and longings. By holding heroics up to mockery, Boyle is de-

11. See Dr David Nowlan's analysis of the third annual report of the Medico-Social Research Board in the Republic of Ireland, during which he discusses the crisis incidence of schizophrenia and morbidity in Ireland and relates it to such factors as loneliness on the land and to the emigration of the healthier and more ambitious, *The Irish Times*, 23 Aug. 1972.

livering a liberating blow against repression. And so *Like Any Other Man,* published in America, was seized by the (Southern) Irish customs authorities and only released on appeal to the Censorship Board. It is a welcome extended in similar fashion to many of the novels discussed in this study. At the same time, the offending sensationalism and bawdiness into which Boyle turns the giantism and heroism of Irish legend and myth merely confirm the repression he is operating with and against. Sexual grotesquerie is a way of at once mocking and complying with the dictates of a society terrified of sexual expression. Unable to see this, some have been hostile to Boyle's work even though, like Kiely, he is not a satirist who threatens the foundations of social order but instead contents himself with highlighting social foibles. Perhaps, however, those hostile to his work, and to Kiely's, have sensed that it subverts the officially projected image of Ireland as a psychically healthy nation by being, in its macabreness and grotesqueness, *too* Irish rather than *un*-Irish. It seems to me that such has often been the real, if unspoken, complaint against allegedly obscene or indecent literature in the Republic of Ireland.

In the case of Patrick Boyle and other Irish Catholic writers, censorship and intolerance have paradoxically created a fictional tension that is enriching. Beneath Boyle's grotesque and macabre humour we can read a tremendous and subterranean struggle going on between the imagination and the intellect, the *id* and the *ego,* freedom and suppression. Unfortunately the moral and psychological price paid is immense, for the real issues are not resolved or even clarified by this literary response.

4

THE ARMED WATCH

(1)

THE alienation of its children is, in a good deal of the fiction I have discussed, a chief symptom of the land's debility and dearth. This can easily become allegorical. Youthful characters who grow into a sense of privation and a desire to leave for the town or city can symbolise that part of the rural population that responds to privation in the same way. Young Simon Lennox in Anne Crone's *My Heart and I* (1955), Hugh Griffin in *Lost Fields,* Ned Mason in *In This Thy Day* and Alec MacNeill in *Call My Brother Back* are in this sense allegorical figures. Growing up on the land becomes a metaphor for the 'maturation' of the land faced with the disturbing mysteries and seductions of city-born innovation and 'progress'. The simplest allegories I have read representing this progress are two threadbare little novels by Hubert Quinn, *The Land Remains* (1944) and *The Soil and the Stars* (1943). *My Heart and I* fleshes out the allegory with substantially more novelistic texture (including character-psychology) than one would expect from rural naturalism.

Not only have rural writers exploited the real and symbolic connection between youth and the countryside, maturation and the city, but their own writings and careers also tend to act out the connection. The desire to write and publish is almost synonymous with a young writer's move to a city—Belfast, Dublin or London—so that he re-enacts, albeit for different motives, the city-bound motion of many of his characters, or they his. Furthermore, the fiction of such writers tends to become 'urbanised' as they age, not only in terms of setting but also in terms of style and conception. A clear example is Benedict Kiely whose two most recent novels, *The Captain with the Whiskers* and *Dogs Enjoy the Morning,* could not in their worldly and urban conception have been written before, say, *Honey Seems Bitter.* To contrast *Dogs Enjoy the Morning* or Anthony C.

West's *The Ferret Fancier* with McLaverty's novels is to contrast worldliness with regionalism.

Despite the symbolic equation of youth with the land, maturity with the city, genuine novels of adolescence set on the land are uncommon, if by adolescence we mean that period in the middle and late teens characterised by psychological and biological ferment and a lust for knowledge and travel. In the fictional characterisation of the rural young, a desire for knowledge and travel is less important than the defects of a rural existence geared to old and settled people. The tensions built into the rural family, the incapacity of small farms to sustain more than one son, the lack of entertainment—these goad the departing youngsters more than the city lures. Adolescence in rural fiction is not so much psychological and biological as sociological, with the young man engaged in generational rivalry (usually with his father but often with a dominating mother) and in sibling rivalry with his brothers. The greatest ferment in the lives of the rural young is created by the conflict between their love for the land and their discontent with rural life. Such tensions and conflicts do not produce the dramatic turbulence or psychological realism we associate with urban novels of adolescence, for the social allegory of adolescence in rural naturalism takes precedence over the exploration of adolescence as a literal transition from boyhood to manhood.

Indeed, in rural fiction and to some extent in real life, adolescence as the city knows it is missing from the land, the boy assuming the labours of manhood early and being initiated just as early into the mysteries of animal, if not human, sexuality. If there is little real adolescence on the land, there is certainly 'little sign of adolescent rebellion', as Rosemary Harris reported for an Ulster rural community in her book, *Prejudice and Tolerance in Ulster*. The age of ferment in the rural young is not the teens but the middle or late twenties or even thirties at the time when the rivalries and tensions built into the inheritance system come to a head. As Arensberg points out, even middle-aged men (however long they have been engaged in the work of men) can remain 'boys' if they have not yet inherited their father's land on which they labour.[1] It is upon the inheritance of the land that

---

1. *The Irish Countryman*, 66.

the crucial transition in a countryman's social and ritual status
from 'boyhood' to 'manhood' is made, a transition equivalent to,
but very different from, the transition from adolescence to
manhood in urban society. Moreover, very often the crises of
love and marriage are deferred until the age of inheritance
because they are bound up with the transfer of the land from one
generation to the next. The young man coming into his parents'
land may legitimately seek a wife not as a lover but as a necessary
accompaniment to his new social and ritual status. In much of
the rural fiction, love and marriage present social rather than
sexual complications, e.g. disagreement over a wife's dowry,
rivalry between two parties for the hand of a socially desirable
third party. If there are no social complications, the sexuality of
the situation seems to present little problem. At the same time,
social and ritual demands frequently collide with sexual demands.
For example, a couple's social and sexual compatibility can
conflict with their childlessness, a socially unacceptable condition
in rural marriage. Or sexual incompatibility in terms of great
disparity in age between husband and wife can conflict with the
social and ritual convenience of the marriage. Whether or not
sexual demands on the one hand or social and ritual demands on
the other actually triumph, the point is that the two sets of
demands are on the land inseparable. Sometimes conflict does
not reach these advanced stages, for if a young man cannot gain
a wife without losing the land, he may choose to remain a
bachelor.

Rural fiction, then, does not depict the three great forms of
adolescent 'awakening' we find in *Bildungsromane* : the initiation
into sexuality, the questioning of religious faith, and the discovery
of literature and art. Anthony C. West's brilliant novel, *The
Ferret Fancier*, constitutes a notable exception. Of the three
Ulster writers whose adolescent fiction I discuss below—
Forrest Reid, St John Ervine and Brian Moore—two are Protestant and one is Catholic, a distinction of paramount importance. It is impossible to speak of the spiritual, sexual and
cultural crises faced by Brian Moore's adolescent hero Gavin
Burke without confronting the immense role played by the
Church in the lives of Irish Catholics. So ubiquitous is the social
influence of the Catholic Church that in adolescent fiction as,
presumably, in real life, crises of sex and culture are inseparable

J

from the spiritual condition of the adolescent. Sexual desire is trammelled by Church morality and dogma and spawns tremendous guilt and a morbid preoccupation with sinfulness on the part of the young protagonist. Intellectual and cultural curiosity must similarly confront the dictates and influence of the Church with the result that in the fiction art and literature create psychological stresses not unlike those created by sexuality. Indeed, the Church's attempted quarantining of the intellect is often due to its fear of sexually provocative or sublimative material falling into the hands of the adolescent.

The supreme ordeal in Catholic adolescent fiction, of course, is the loss of faith during which the most resonant guilt feelings are aroused, feelings which may not always be distinguishable from those guilt feelings aroused by sexual or cultural experimentation. The interdependence of these three matrices—faith, culture and sex—can perhaps best be envisaged as a network. From this network the Catholic adolescent seeks to extricate himself. Tactics of escape dominate Benedict Kiely's novels of adolescence (*Honey Seems Bitter*, 1954, *There Was an Ancient House*, 1955, *The Captain with the Whiskers*, 1960, and *Dogs Enjoy the Morning*, 1968), Brian Moore's *The Emperor of Ice-Cream* (1965) and another, unpretentious novel of Catholic adolescence, Joseph Tomelty's *The Apprentice* (1953). Tomelty's young protagonist spends the novel trying to flee his self-consciousness, his aunt, the neighbourhood busybodies, and sectarianism. Behind these images and states of bondage stands the Church, ever-ready to stifle and contain. The most vivid and famous imagery of bondage in Catholic fiction is to be found in the greatest Irish novel of adolescence, Joyce's *A Portrait of the Artist as a Young Man*. The nets which Stephen Dedalus strives to fly by refer to puritan constraints on sexuality, subservience before priests, parents and ancestors, and cultural and political nationalism. All of these also threaten Moore's Gavin Burke. Like Joyce, Moore bridled at the political implications of nationalism. Like Joyce, Moore found it necessary to leave Ireland in order to escape cultural and social restrictions, a process of repudiation recorded in their respective *Bildungsromane*. In one sense Moore in exile has not shown the same lofty detachment from Ireland which Joyce showed in Europe. In another sense Moore's exile has been the more complete : unlike Joyce, he has not limited his subjects and settings to Ireland; moreover, the young Irish heroes in Moore's American novels are more consciously preoccupied with the problems of incorporation into America than with the problems of separation from Ireland. For some time now, Moore has been claimed in some quarters as an American or Canadian writer.[2]

It would be difficult for the conspiratorial imagery of nets to function in quite the same way in the fiction of Protestant adolescence. For one thing, the Ulster Protestant usually feels himself to be British as well as Irish (again, Anthony C. West is an exception here) and so has an added and often confusing dimension to his nationality which helps avoid claustrophobia. For another, without the pervasive and binding influence of the Catholic Church, sex, faith and culture are more or less separate issues in the mind of the Protestant adolescent. Loss of faith is important in the novels of youth written by Forrest Reid and St John Ervine, but not nearly as important as in Joyce, Moore or Kiely. The young heroes in Reid and Ervine rebel against the darker, more puritanical and fundamentalist aspects of Ulster Protestantism, but it is not a searing or traumatic rebellion. Just as commonly, religion in Protestant fiction takes the form of the discovery of 'the other side', i.e. of Catholics. This discovery is empirical rather than spiritual, however, and presents no theological problems: there are few converts from or to either side in Northern Ireland.

Neither sex nor culture in the fiction of Protestant adolescence has the frightening mystique that it enjoys in Catholic novels of maturation because of the Protestant churches' unwillingness or inability to meddle in moral or intellectual affairs. The issue facing the young heroes of Reid and Ervine is what *kind* of sexual, cultural and spiritual life they will lead. Faced with various choices, the young heroes search for a psychological stability and balance that is right for them. (A similar search for stability dominates, as we saw, the adult Protestant fiction of Shan Bullock.) On the other hand, the issue in Catholic novels of adolescence is whether, when and how a sexual, cultural and spiritual life is possible at all. This problem is huge in its

2. Even his name has undergone metamorphosis: in Ireland he is called *brĭ'ən mōor* but in America *brē'ən mōr*.

fundamentality and makes at once for greater psychological imbalance and overstatement and for greater dramatic possibility than we find in Protestant fiction of maturation.

The issues that dominate fictional adolescence, as novels by Reid, Moore and Ervine demonstrate, encourage a high degree of realism. The very physicality of adolescence can in itself be a theme. Tomelty's *The Apprentice,* for example, is a self-effacing little novel whose hero, Frankie, the apprentice house-painter, tries to overcome self-consciousness about his lack of inches, his stuttering, his shyness and his fear of heights. This novel, at the end of which Frankie escapes from his problems into the arms of an older woman in a non-sectarian part of Belfast, is tenderly done. In fact, it suffers finally because Frankie, though a realistic adolescent, is too pitiable (and self-pitying) for the novel's good and so the book slides into sentimentality. Ervine, Reid and Moore have also a good deal of surface realism, but are realistic also in the sense that the hero tries, amid unlikely possibilities, to find a rational and lifelong solution to his problems.

The realism engendered by adolescence is offset by its romantic associations, and so realism and romance vie with each other in the novels of maturation we shall look at in this chapter. Octavio Paz sees the ambivalence throughout literary history and folklore:

Since adolescence is extreme self-consciousness it can only be transcended by self-forgetfulness, by self-surrender. Therefore adolescence is not only a time of solitude, but also of great romances, of heroism and sacrifice. The people have good reason to picture the hero and the lover as adolescents. The vision of the adolescent as a solitary figure, closed up within himself and consumed by desire or timidity, almost always resolves into a crowd of young people dancing, singing or marching as a group, or into a young couple strolling under the arched green branches in a park. The adolescent opens himself up to the world: to love, action, friendship, sports, heroic adventures. The literature of modern nations—except Spain, where they never appear except as rogues or orphans—is filled with adolescents, with solitariness in search of communion: of the ring, the sword, the Vision. Adolescence is an armed watch, at the end of which one enters the world of facts.[3]

3. Octavio Paz, *The Labyrinth of Solitude: Life and Thought in Mexico,* New York 1961, 203–4.

This romantic concept of adolescence, rooted in the ritual process of initiation into manhood, can be elevated into myth. Joseph Campbell's 'hero with a thousand faces' who participates in what Campbell calls the universal 'monomyth' of initiatory trial is usually an adolescent who is actually or figuratively isolated from his community, who undergoes trials, and who then returns actually or figuratively to the community, re-born, changed into manhood.[4] It is against this universal pattern that we can interpret the major events in the novels of youth written by Ervine, Reid and Moore. Two of the authors involve their hero or heroes in a literal or fantastic journey; all three authors have their hero or heroes undergo trials, usually in the city. It is difficult to think of a genuine 'adolescent' fiction without thinking of the city as a labyrinth that has to be penetrated by the initiate. Because rural naturalism does not involve adolescence, the city does not play a central role : even McLaverty's people in the ghettoes of Belfast yet live on the city perimeter without, as it were, penetrating its dark heart or distant reaches.

The city in the 'adolescent' fiction of Ervine, Reid and Moore is Belfast. It is a city that symbolises the ambiguity of nationality suffered by Ulster people. On the one hand it is intimate with the surrounding Irish countryside and has a large Catholic population. On the other hand it is an un-Irish city, cousin of those British Midland and Northern towns begotten by the Industrial Revolution. The image of Belfast depends upon the eyes through which it is viewed. Rural Catholics and Protestants tend to see it as dark, damp and menacing, which is how it appears in local naturalism and in stories by outsiders (e.g. Kiely's 'Ten Pretty Girls'). Belfast Catholics may love their city, but it is a love tempered by their comparative exclusion from the heavy industry that characterises it (witness the views of the Catholic stranger in Ervine's *Mrs Martin's Man*, 246–51) and by the Protestant domination of its customs and laws. The love which Belfast Protestants have for the city (a love which informs Ervine's novels) is mingled with pride in the industrial achievements of Belfast. Yet many Protestants live with a suffocating sense of the city's provincialism when compared with Dublin or London; Ervine's love for Belfast, for instance, has in it an element of

4. The word 'monomyth', Campbell tells us, is from James Joyce's *Finnegans Wake*.

contempt. All are agreed that bigotry and prejudice are a blight
on the city, preventing it from realising its economic and cultural
potential. Middle-class Protestant writers such as Forrest Reid,
Stephen Gilbert and Janet McNeill are less concerned with
sectarianism, perhaps because it has always affected the middle
class less than the working class. These writers frequently depict
the green and handsome suburbs of Belfast well away from
sectarianism and industry. Reid's *Peter Waring,* a novel discussed below, is, however, a notable exception. In *Peter Waring,*
as in *The Emperor of Ice-Cream* and Ervine's novels, the dark
heart of Belfast has to be penetrated as a condition of young
manhood.

(2)

Possibly because he had already covered the painful ground in a
first novel that brought him international acclaim (*Judith Hearne,*
1955), Brian Moore chose not to chronicle his young hero's lapse
from faith when he came to write what he has described as his
Bildungsroman, The Emperor of Ice-Cream (1965).[5] This is not
to say that seventeen-year-old Gavin Burke, fresh out of school
and into the Belfast ARP at the beginning of the Second World
War, does not suffer occasional pangs of apostatic conscience.
He does, especially in his bedroom, a profane grotto—like most
adolescent bedrooms—given over to private sin, sloth and worldly
daydreams, and in which the Divine Infant of Prague, 'only
eleven inches tall yet heavy enough to break someone's toes if he
fell off the dresser', vainly attempts to win Gavin back to childhood faith. But *The Emperor of Ice-Cream* is mercifully devoid
of spiritual wrestling-matches in the confessional and chapel pew
and of brimstone sermons by irate priests which feature in so
many Irish novels of Catholic adolescence. There are, of course,
potshots at the Catholic Church, but no real attempt to resurrect
the crisis of faith so intensely explored in *Judith Hearne.*

Gavin Burke's post-lapsarian condition has allowed Moore to
concentrate on re-fashioning Ervine's working-class and lower
middle-class Belfast, half a century later and from the Catholic
side. The dramatic heart of *The Emperor of Ice-Cream* is
Gavin's rift with his father, a rift that is ostensibly caused by

5. Quoted by Hallvard Dahlie in *Brian Moore,* Toronto 1969, 85.

Gavin's examination failures but is really caused by his father's pathological Anglophobia and passionate belief that, as the maxim goes, England's difficulty is Ireland's opportunity. Into this rift between father and son, brought to boiling-point during the Second World War, can be read Moore's contribution to a discussion of national identity, a dilemma that confronts the Northern Irish even more so today, thirty years after the setting of Moore's novel. It is fitting that the novel is set in Belfast, sectarian capital of Ireland and a city in which only private fantasy such as Forrest Reid's could permit anyone to forget to which sect he belongs. Gavin Burke refuses sectarian membership and becomes alienated not only from his father's Catholic United Irelandism, but also, less unnaturally, from Ulster Protestantism which Gavin encounters in its raw and brutal form while on ARP duty during the German blitz of Belfast.

This is the more assured part of *The Emperor of Ice-Cream*, but the novel has other less expected and successful themes and settings. Rather unhappily in terms of results, though certainly not in terms of motive, Moore has tried to crash what is usually psychic off-limits to a writer of his background, the Protestant middle class, and his scant portrait of bohemian Protestant homosexuals might appropriately reflect Gavin Burke's sequestered Catholic adolescent mind, but does not, being close to caricature, really enrich the novel. Marginally more successful is the author's attempt to re-live for us the bohemian leftism of the thirties, but using Belfast as a setting in which to do this is probably more courageous than wise; as we shall see, the intellectual bohemianism of the thirties is more successfully captured in the London scenes of George Buchanan's *Rose Forbes*. Lastly, if we add that Moore has also tried to recapture in imagery what Belfast was like during the blitz, it is clear how crowded a short novel is *The Emperor of Ice-Cream*. The novel has an un-orchestrated, catch-all quality about it, as though Moore, with two American-based novels behind him (*The Luck of Ginger Coffey* and *An Answer from Limbo*), were retracing his steps to pick up anything important he may have overlooked on his post-haste trek out of Northern Ireland en route to New York City.

When the novel opens, religious faith has already been displaced in Gavin's mind by half-baked thoughts on sex and culture. Religion has been reduced to the puppet-like Divine

Infant against which he conducts a running propaganda war. Morality, too, has been reduced to the Black and White Angels who squabble for his soul in Gavin's overwrought imagination. *The Emperor of Ice-Cream,* then, is not vitally concerned with the relative validity of opposing moralities and beliefs but more prosaically with the struggle within Gavin between the will to succeed and the will to fail. Gavin's biggest problem is what to do with his life, and to this problem philosophical and moral considerations are subordinated. Compared with Reid's Peter Waring, Gavin Burke is intellectually backward, and his devotion to poetry is little more than a fascination with the sound rather than the sense of the lines. There is, for example, the Wallace Stevens line Moore borrows for the novel's title : 'He liked that line,' Moore has young Burke muse. 'He was not quite sure what it meant, but it seemed to sum things up.' (p. 8) What the line does is satisfy Gavin's adolescent self-consciousness by permitting him to translate his own indecisiveness about a career into a near-apocalyptic pessimism about the future of the world. This is one of the novel's charms, the author's memory of how the adolescent romantically mistakes the practical and immediate for the cosmic and objective.

Uncertain what to do for a career, Gavin has left school and on the outbreak of war joined the Belfast ARP. Goaded, however, by his father's wounded pride in academic distinction, he continues to study desultorily and longs ineffectually to follow his elder brother to university, not so much for its intellectual as for its sexual and financial possibilities. His belief that he is 'doomed to fail' is made up of equal parts self-pity and lack of will, for since his father is a solicitor and his brother Owen is already at university, there is no question of class or sectarian discrimination in the novel. His sexual adventures reveal a similar adolescent concoction of self-pity and lack of drive which, rather than moral or religious scruples, are the obstacles that stand between Gavin and the fulfilments of manhood. He would appear, for instance, to have no moral qualms when the offensive Bobby Luddin offers him his wife and with a clear road ahead to sexual initiation ruins his chance by getting drunkenly sick. There is more excuse for Gavin in his off-on relationship with his girlfriend Sally, a good Catholic girl of formidably intact purity, one of that legion of girls Gavin deems 'nuns in mufti'. Here again, though, the failure (to break with Sally) is Gavin's, for unlike Sally he would appear to have no moral compunction about premarital sex. What *The Emperor of Ice-Cream* chronicles is the galvanising of Gavin through circumstances into decisiveness, action and will.

I do not want to underestimate the power of Gavin's vestigial Catholicism, but I do think that this operates in the novel psychologically rather than morally. The fact that it remains to inhibit does of course testify to the power of the Catholic Church, even over the apostate. Had Gavin the will to sin, he would do so; the notion of sin in the absence of real faith has thus become for him, as it becomes for Moore's earlier heroes, Judith Hearne and Diarmuid Devine, a way of camouflaging psychological failure. To this extent, premarital sex and the lapse from Catholic faith are dramatic *factors* but not really *issues* in *The Emperor of Ice-Cream*. It might be said that the only substantive issue in the novel, one that Moore debates and resolves dramatically in such a way that it has relevance to the reader's own world, is that of Irish nationalism. Even this issue is clouded, dramatically and intellectually, by a couple of pseudo-issues which are there more for ballast than for any sense of their urgency. Curious and somehow out of place in Moore's Belfast is the Protestant homosexual bohemian coterie Gavin is introduced into by Freddy Hargreaves, a fellow-recruit to the ARP. The coterie is headed by an improbable clergyman, the Rev. Kenneth McMurtry, and because neither McMurtry nor the coterie is explored, they remain Catholic stereotypes of Protestant free-thinking artiness, similar to the stereotype of the fast Protestant girl : 'To think that people who wrote poetry, burned joss sticks, and built puppet theatres were living here in Belfast, not a mile away from his own home,' Gavin wonders. 'They were Protestants, naturally. Why was it that no Catholic could grow up in an interesting atmosphere?' (pp. 94–5)

Somewhat fuller is Moore's portrait of thirties socialism, embodied in the figure of Freddy Hargreaves, a character who recalls Brendan Tierney's Protestant mentor, Ted Ormsby, in *An Answer from Limbo*. Again, the spirit of the Spanish Civil War, middle-class leftism and the radical poetry of Auden & Co. seems somehow misplaced in Moore's Belfast and never properly developed. Like Protestant bohemianism, it remains little more than caricature. Moore might be considered successful in showing how important movements and causes are distorted and reduced in the fevered adolescent imagination, but I would be more inclined to this view if at the same time Moore transcended the caricature to reveal something of the adult reality of middle-class, intellectual life in the Belfast of the 1930s.

Moore is on much surer ground in his portrait of a city suffering from an inferiority complex, so painfully conscious of its provincialism that it can even discern flattery in Hitler's attempts to bomb Belfast and insult in his mistaken bombing of rival, neutral Dublin a hundred miles to the south. The way the war stalks Belfast, Gavin and his ARP unit across two seas is the admirable dynamic of *The Emperor of Ice-Cream,* and much of the rest—the bohemianism, thirties radicalism, sex, apostasy—is so much packing and buttressing. No one believes Hitler would bother with Belfast, but at last the war becomes a reality and before Gavin discovers the meaning of the previous, apparently futile months in training, he experiences an exaltation that at the same time lends meaning to his years of indecision and frustration. It is a moment trapped beautifully :

Two more explosions boomed on the far side of the city. The guns were silent. Then, beautiful, exploding with a faint pop in the sky above them, a magnesium flare floated up in the stillness, lighting the rooftops in a ghostly silver. Freddy was revealed, a few paces away from Gavin, his face uptilted, his glasses silvery opaque as they searched the sky. And in that moment, with Gavin there started an extraordinary elation, a tumult of joy. He felt like dancing a Cherokee war dance on the edge of the parapet. The world and the war had come to him at last. Tonight, in the Reichschancellery of Berlin, generals stood over illuminated maps, plotting Belfast's destruction. Hitler himself smiled in glee, watching the graphs of the planes' progress. Tonight, history had conferred the drama of war on this dull, dead town in which he had been born. (p. 199)

All along, we might realise at this point, Gavin has symbolised Belfast (in the way, as we shall see, Ginger Coffey symbolises Canada)—callow, provincial, unrefined, waiting for the bestowal of maturity through suffering. The blitz paradoxically allows Belfast to reveal its bravery and resilience (as well as occasional cowardice) and to transcend its bitter sectarianism. In short, a chance to redeem itself from death ('this dead town') into life. The war even extends a similar, though lesser opportunity to Dublin, a neutral city that nevertheless sends its fire-engines to the aid of stricken fellow-islanders across the sectarian and geographical divide, one of the few gestures of non-sectarian solidarity in the history of modern Ireland.

Belfast is redeemed from the metaphoric deadness of its spirit by the visitation of real and mass death upon its streets. So, too, Gavin is redeemed from the metaphoric deadness of the attitudes around him (bohemianism, faddish socialism, Catholic and Protestant bigotry) and of his own limbo-like existence by his sudden intimacy with real and ugly death. When Gavin is put to work undressing and arranging corpses in a morgue—a job for which with Hargreaves he bravely volunteers—his initiation, begun so dramatically when the German bombers droned up Belfast Lough, becomes a kind of purgatory, a motif we shall encounter in Ervine's *The Wayward Man* and which arises quite naturally out of the symbolic nature of adolescent initiation in myth and in primitive societies as a kind of rebirth into the adult community. What Gavin's grisly task teaches him is the ugliness of death and also its anonymity, for death recognises no sexual, class or sectarian distinctions :

Gavin had seen his first corpse when he was eleven years old. Corpses were elderly relatives, dressed sometimes in brown shrouds, more often in their Sunday best. They lay in the downstairs bedroom on white linen sheets, their hands crossed over their breasts, fingers entwined in rosary beads or crucifixes, black-edged Mass cards strewn around them in tribute. . . But now, in the stink of human excrement, in the acrid smell of disinfectant, these dead were heaped, body on body, flung arm, twisted feet, open mouth, staring eyes, old men on top of young women, a child lying on a policeman's back, a soldier's hand resting on a woman's thigh, a carter, still wearing his coal sacks, on top of a pile of arms and legs, his own arm outstretched, finger pointing, as though he warned of some unseen horror. (p. 231)

From his terrible experience Gavin emerges purged : his triumphant completion of this final trial suggests he has thereby developed the will to achieve what still elude him at the novel's end—sexual relationships, a career, moral stability.

The blitz and his experience in the morgue not only precipitate Gavin into manhood, but also justify him to the reader and to himself in spite of the mistaken and biased attitudes of the other characters. During Moore's descriptions of the war's devastations, we might recall an earlier passage in the novel when Gavin's White Angel takes him to task for his uselessness and tells him : 'This war is a phony war and one day it will be over, with the only Irish casualties you and your buddies who will then be out of work. Take a look at yourself. You're what you feared. A flop.' (p. 76) The White Angel is wrong, for the war turns out to be horribly genuine. Its reality comes as a blow to Hargreaves who is forced to realise the fatuity of seeing it as an ideological irrelevance, a private squabble among capitalists. More significantly, it is a blow to Gavin's father, inveterate hater of the British and early champion of the Fuehrer. Hitler, he and like-minded anti-Britishers discover, is no respecter of sectarian allegiance or of Eire's neutrality. When the war comes to Belfast, people like Gallagher, the ARP man who clandestinely shines his torch skyward in the hope of attracting German bombers to the city, are hoist by their own petard.

Gavin's relationship with his father forms the dramatic central theme of the novel. Not only do Gavin's examination failures incense his father, but also the fact that Gavin, product of a good Catholic family, should join the ARP to help John Bull fight the Nazis. Burke Senior, a less sympathetic character than even Brendan's dead father in *An Answer from Limbo,* exhibits a mentality Gavin and his creator despise. That mentality is summarised for us in a scene in which Burke Senior opens the (Catholic) *Irish News* :

He shook the paper out and began to read, his full lips pouting at the news. Gavin, watching him, decided that his father read the newspaper as other men play cards, shuffling through a page of stories until he found one which could confirm him in his prejudice. A Jewish name discovered in an account of a financial transaction, a Franco victory over the godless Reds, a hint of British perfidy in international affairs, an Irish triumph on the sports field, an evidence of Protestant bigotry, a discovery of Ulster governmental corruption : these were his reading goals. (p. 32)

The Emperor of Ice-Cream is Moore's dismissal of the absurder reaches of Irish nationalism and the religious bigotry that often attends it. Ireland being Ireland, however, it is necessary to add that Moore makes no implicit or explicit defence of Northern Protestant supremacy or of the orange equivalent of green nationalism. Gavin is surely destined to become as impartial as his author who remarked to Hallvard Dahlie : 'I felt, and I feel that both Protestantism and Catholicism in Northern Ireland are the most desperate tragedies that can happen to people. . . I feel there should be a pox on both their houses.'[6] Moore's impartially led him to see nothing wrong with enlisting for Great Britain during the Second World War, though perhaps he was enlisting less for Britain than against Nazism. Britain and her armed forces offered Moore (as they did, and do, many Irishmen) a way out of a poisoned provincial pond into the anonymity of larger seas beyond. In taking the way out, Moore rejected not only Irish Catholic bigotry but its equally unpalatable Protestant counterpart.

Despite the neatness of the novel's ending, Moore does not resolve convincingly, in all its aspects, the conflict between Gavin and his father. Gavin's father wants him to come south to neutral Eire with the rest of the family, but Gavin stubbornly elects to remain with his ARP unit. After a bombing raid, Gavin visits their old house, now deserted and, significantly, 'condemned'. While he is there he hears someone come in with 'the step of the dead'. It is his father who has come back to look for him and who speaks to him with the gestures of surrender :

In the candlelight, he saw that his father was crying. He had never seen his father cry before. Did his father know that the house was condemned, did his father know that everything had changed, that things would never be the same again? A new voice, a cold grown-up voice within him said : 'No.' His father was the child now; his father's world was dead. . . 'Oh, Gavin,' his father said. 'I've been a fool. Such a fool.'

The new voice counselled silence. He took his father's hand. (p. 250)

6. Dahlie, 3; Moore's alienation from the politics of the North was confirmed when he made a visit to Belfast during the current troubles recounted in 'Now and Then', first published as 'Bloody Ulster' in *Atlantic Monthly* (Sep. 1970) and re-published in *Threshold*, Belfast, 23 (Sep. 1970).

In this last passage of the novel, Gavin's novel-long thirst for change and for escape from the dead is slaked. Yet in spite of of the tidy way Moore has ribboned up the book with an almost oedipal completeness most befitting a novel of adolescence, the conclusion raises an important question. For if 'his father's world' is intended to mean not merely Mr Burke's personal world, but also that of like-minded members of his generation, then the ending is disingenuous. Many people in Ireland did, as Moore has claimed,[7] perform a *volte-face* similar to Mr Burke's during the Second World War, but the essential features of the world of Gavin's father—the prejudice, bigotry and hatred—were in no way affected. In *The Emperor of Ice-Cream* Moore has won a victory against narrowness and intolerance, but one akin to that of a man who picks up the ball and proclaims the game over when he is winning. Sadly enough, Moore could not possibly have written the same ending three years after the novel's publication without its seeming unacceptably sentimental. I am not charging him with lack of prophetic insight. In his ending Moore confuses Gavin's entrance into manhood with a spurious corollary—the defeat of psychological and social attitudes around him. It is an unwarranted corollary to make. Moreover, it is the kind of confusion that throughout the novel is characteristic of Gavin's adolescent egocentricity. It is very fortunate that the conclusion to *The Emperor of Ice-Cream* does not seriously endanger its earlier, finer parts.

(3)

St John Ervine, in a long and illustrious career in drama and fiction, produced several fine novels set either in the Ballymacarrett area of East Belfast (where he was born) or on the Newtownards-Donaghadee shoulder of the Ards peninsula. His is a world of small shopkeepers, often vain and ambitious, among whom a few black sheep come down with wandering fever and sail the seven seas in clippers and schooners during the time of Ervine's own boyhood in the 1890s. In his three Ulster novels, *Mrs Martin's Man* (1914), *The Foolish Lovers* (1920) and *The Wayward Man* (1927), wanderlust not only

7. Dahlie, 97–8.

propels the narrative but is a lifestyle that threatens the stay-at-
home shopkeepers. These shopkeepers are Protestant and Scots-
Irish and their names have a resilient Ulster cast that suggests
an ancient family residence in the area—Clegg, Mawhinney,
McDermott, Greer, Mahaffy, Magrath, Dunwoody. This sense
of place is especially important in Ervine's fiction because of
the wanderlust it opposes, and is both a good (suggesting security
and ancestral pride) and an evil (suggesting staid provincialism
and unadventurousness).

Like the rural writers who came after him, Ervine makes use
of the motif of bad blood, particularly in *Mrs Martin's Man* in
which family quarrels play a big part and metaphorise the sectarian feuds in Belfast at the beginning of the anti-Home Rule
agitation in the 1880s and 1890s. Like these writers, too, and in
a manner occasionally recalling Carleton, Ervine captures with
realism the mores of the country town and working-class Belfast.
However, Ervine's naturalistic elements belong to a different
literary school from that of the writers we have so far discussed,
and his sweeping narratives, as John Boyd has said,[8] are of the
same Edwardian tradition in which Galsworthy, Wells, Bennett
and the early Maugham participated. Ervine's interest is not in
social forces which preclude moral choice (as in local naturalism)
but in moral choice within rather practical contexts. Adolescence
in Ervine is a pre-Joycean concept in which the young hero seeks
an appropriate lifestyle instead of truth or vision. The basic
choice facing his young men as they approach manhood is
between travel and sedentariness, independence and commercial
ties. Because wanderlust is one of the choices, Ervine's novels are
romantic in a vulgar sense, for they recount adventures that take
the young heroes to Belfast, London and America. There is a
second, equally vulgar sense in which his work is romantic.
Frequently the choices facing the hero are embodied in women
among whom he has to choose not merely a wife but a lifestyle.
Frustrations in love are major stumbling-blocks for Ervine's protagonists as they flounder indecisively among prostitutes, demure
hearth-lovers and hard-bitten business-women. This is how sex,
like other relationships, is presented in Ervine's novels, as symbolic
of a lifestyle or a value-system rather than in terms of pleasure or

8. In *The Arts in Ulster,* 118.

beauty. Ervine is not really a romantic writer despite the romantic trappings. His strength as a novelist lies in the fluency of his storytelling and in the realism of occasional and powerfully atmospheric episodes. His weakness lies in the basic moral simplicity of his fictional universe and the running to type of his characters.

Part One of *The Wayward Man* recounts how young Robert Dunwoody, whose sailor father was drowned, turns his back on his mother's plans for him to take over her shop in Ballymacarrett, and stows away on a boat to Scotland before signing as a seaman on a ship bound for Australia. In Part Two he is initiated into Paz's world of facts, meeting all kinds of trouble and people in storm-tossed ships and seaport brawls. It is in this part of the novel he has his first woman, a San Francisco whore with whom he falls momentarily in love. In Part Three, seven years having elapsed, he returns to Ballymacarrett and is inveigled by his mother into marrying a childhood acquaintance, Brenda, and taking over a branch of his mother's shop that Alec, his conscientious bachelor brother, has built up. Finally, he has a brief affair with a girl he makes pregnant, tells his wife and leaves them all to go back to sea, certain now that his real home and friends are there.

The first part of *The Wayward Man* is fictionally the richest. Ervine recaptures the atmosphere of East Belfast around the turn of the century, a homely neighbourhood of small streets and busy corner shops. One shop in particular haunts young Robert's imagination : Mr Peden's 'Italian warehouse', a shop redolent not only of Protestant commercial zeal but also of exoticism.

Robert could not understand why it was called an Italian warehouse, for there seemed to be no difference between it and any other grocery, but he did not greatly trouble himself with explanations. That it was called Italian was sufficient for him, and he would open his atlas and gaze at the boot-shaped map of Italy, with its heel in the Adriatic and its toe almost touching the rump of Sicily, and tell himself that it was next-door. There was a volcano in Italy, and Robert would not in the least have been astonished if it had suddenly erupted in the middle of Mr Peden's shop. . . Sam Peden would let him thrust the white scoop into the flour or bury his hands deep in the corn-bins or lift tea in a copper-coloured scoop from the stencilled wooden boxes in which it had been brought from India and China and Ceylon. There were pictures of tea-plantations on some of the boxes. Indian girls with big, dark eyes daintily gathered the tea-leaves or paced along sunlit roads with jars of water poised on their dusky heads![9]

But there is another kind of exoticism on Robert's own doorstep. To Ervine's East Belfast Protestants, Catholics and the Catholic religion are foreign, myth-enshrouded and to be feared. When young Robert wanders into a Catholic chapel, he steps into a strange world of imagined hostility.

Sometimes he peered through the windows of repositories at the crucifixes and scapulars and rosaries and statues of saints and Holy Families and, most of all, the pictures of the Sacred Heart. These last oddly repelled him, though he could not have said why. There was Jesus, in a blue and red robe, pointing to a hole in His side, where a large and very regular heart was visible. Flames rose from it, and a wreath of thorns encircled its head. Great gouts of blood dropped from it, and a cross stood up from the flames! . . . There were similar pictures of the Virgin, whose Heart, sometimes, was pierced with swords. Robert, horribly fascinated by them, gazed at the pictures and felt sick. They made him remember the one-armed man who sat in the gutter of the Queen's Bridge and exposed his mutilation to the gaze of the charitable. Always, when he had approached this man, Robert had resolved to shut his eyes, but they could not close, and when he came abreast of the beggar, he felt himself, half-horrified, half-fascinated, gazing on the stump! The Holy pictures filled him with disgust, yet he was compelled to look at them. Trembling and awe-stricken, he would creep to the chapel-door and peep in at the symbols of idolatry. He was astonished to find himself enthralled by the clusters of candles at the Virgin's feet and the flickering red light burning before the altar. Once, when he saw the High Altar itself richly lit up, he went into the chapel and, lest he should be discovered to be a Protestant prowling about in a Catholic church, he dipped his fingers in the holy water stoup, and made the sign of the Cross and genuflected to the Host, as he had seen a woman do. He slipped into a seat, and became frightened when he found that he was kneeling near a confessional in which a priest was sitting. Supposing the priest

9. *The Wayward Man* in *The St John Ervine Omnibus*, London 1933, 7–8; subsequent quotations from this novel and from *The Foolish Lovers* are from the editions in this Omnibus.

K

were to force him to confess his sins ! . . . He hurried out of the chapel again, not daring to look behind him, but even in the street, surrounded by good Protestants, he could not forget the fascination of the lit candles at the Virgin's feet or the lovely light they made in the dusky chapel. (pp. 14–15)

The fascinating mixture of sensuous repellence and mysterious attraction of Catholic churches is a motif in Protestant fiction and its experience almost a mild initiatory trial in Protestant adolescence. There appears to be no counterpart in Catholic fiction.

Robert's sortie into the more familiar world of the Salvation Army begins and ends even more abruptly. He lies on the roof of the 'barracks' eavesdropping on the service until one night the roof gives way and he crashes on to the startled 'soldiers' beneath. Although Mrs Dunwoody has hopes that Robert will become a Presbyterian minister, it transpires that he does not have the faith. Restless and venturesome, he stows away on a lighter on the River Lagan and explores the other side of Belfast. So begins a series of adventures that make Part One a microcosm of the entire novel, for during these adventures Robert becomes a man in many ways. When thrown off the lighter he wanders to the Giant's Ring where he meets a countryman who tells him the legend surrounding it. If he has here encountered other-worldliness, he encounters sectarian violence as he makes his way home through the Catholic Short Strand area where he is set upon and beaten up. He returns home, rows with his brother Alec, strikes his brother and runs away again, this time stowing away on a boat to Scotland. On board he meets madness, personified in the shape of Boak, a fellow stowaway. His greatest trial, however, is reserved for that same night when he wanders around Glasgow in search of a bed. He sleeps in a brick-kiln with tramps and when driven out by a policeman stumbles on to slag-heaps in a scene that in its desolation at once recalls the opening of Patrick MacGill's *The Rat-Pit* and prefigures the dramatic world of Samuel Beckett :

There seemed to be no one but the tramp and himself alive in this dank world of clay and ashes, and for a melancholy moment he imagined that mankind had perished, that the earth had been consumed, that presently he and the tramp would turn to a heap of white dust and cinders and drift down to the pool and be buried in green slime! . . . His thoughts were suddenly dispelled when his foot caught in something soft that was half-covered with the warm white dust and he fell forward on his hands and face, scraping them on cinders. A horrible fear filled him as he fell, for he had felt the soft thing yield as he trod on it, and he wanted to get up and run away even if he fell into the pool in his flight. But his fear left him when he heard himself cursed and reviled and he turned and saw that a tousled head was emerging from a heap of rags with which its owner had covered himself after he had dug into the warm ash. Presently other heads were lifted, and Robert saw that he was surrounded by men who had nearly buried themselves in the slag. As they sat up in the white ash and let the rain dribble in dirty streaks down their dusty cheeks, it seemed to Robert that the grave was giving up its dreadful dead. On some horrible battlefield corrupting men must lie in heaps as these men lay on that hill of slag. The rain and sleet still fell and the bitter winds still blew, but he no longer felt them, for the air was warm and seemed to be getting warmer! . . . Perhaps he had died in his sleep in the brick-kiln and his damned soul was now meandering along the first slopes of hell. Those red and orange flames that splashed across the black sky and turned the green pool to a copper colour came from infernal fires. He was dead and damned! (pp. 130–1)

In the morning, having witnessed the death of one of the tramps caught in one of the rolling 'pugs' of molten slag, Robert stumbles out of hell and 'seemed suddenly to himself to be a grown man'. Ahead of him lie the adventures of the sea and the return to Ballymacarrett.

For all the promise of Part One, with its moments of almost epiphanic horror, and the brash American adventures of Part Two, the nub of *The Wayward Man* is a rather pedestrian one. Ervine's young men do not seek sexual, spiritual and cultural experiences as ends in themselves, but stumble upon them accidentally as they 'shop' among various possible lifestyles. In this sense, the experiences are used by Ervine to create local colour and atmosphere (whether in Belfast or San Francisco) rather than dramatic penetrations. Ervine's portrait of Robert's flirtation with evangelism in Ballymacarrett is an example. Robert is not a spiritual character, neither is he, really, a sexual or artistic character. Ervine's young men grow up into the pedestrian life of small shopkeepers in Co. Down and either they reject or accept that life. In acceptance or rejection there is little character development. When Robert returns to Belfast he is temporarily forced to accept his mother's shopkeeping life but shares neither her business-sense nor her snobbish pride in her side of the family. His resistance is steeled when he finds that his wife Brenda becomes something of a mini-tycoon, ruthless and competitive. Rejecting family snobbery and commercialism (as we knew he would), he seeks love not in his wife but in an impoverished girl and a home on the high seas. Taken at face-value, *The Wayward Man* would seem to be the quasi-romantic novel of a man who repudiates the two chief characteristics of his Protestant Ulster heritage—its philistine mercantilism and its provincial Scots-Irish arrogance.

Just as easily, however, Ervine provides the battle between family pride and the commercial instinct on the one hand and rootless solitariness on the other with a different outcome in *The Foolish Lovers*. He has his young hero embrace at the novel's end what his counterpart spurns in *The Wayward Man*. The family business is, in *The Foolish Lovers,* a laudable way of life, partly because it rests on that very family and ancestral pride that Robert Dunwoody found so obnoxious and partly because rootlessness and solitariness, as embodied here in the decadent poet Palfrey, are cast as sheer humbug and wishful thinking. Before making his choice, John MacDermott undergoes trials similar in their tribulation to those of Robert Dunwoody, but in London's sleazy literary world rather than on the high seas. These tribulations are meant to represent the deflation of John's romantic notions of travel and literature when all the time romance awaits him in his own backyard. 'By the Hokey O . . . there's a romance at the end of it all,' cries John at the end of the novel after he has returned to carry on the family shop in the face of competition. But *The Foolish Lovers* is only on the surface romantic; in fact it is basically anti-romantic and anti-heroic for it is a defence of bourgeois existence and of practical compromise, neither of which have a part, save as foils, in genuinely romantic fiction. If it is a lesser novel than *The Wayward Man,* it may be in part because it pours its bourgeois content into a romantic mould.

Headstrong John MacDermott, discontented with the prospect

of inheriting his Uncle William's village grocery shop, seeks excitement in the city, first in Belfast where he discovers for himself the literary and theatrical culture peddled in anecdote by his eccentric Uncle Matthew, and then in London where he goes to seek his fortune as a writer. In London he is buffeted by adversity and though he publishes a novel (at his own expense) and has a tragedy produced, he has to fall back on Fleet Street hack-work and in the end returns home to the Ards peninsula. While in London—a part of the novel busy with characters such as Cream and Gidney who could almost have stepped out of Dickens—John is confronted with two very different approaches to literature, neither of which he finds to his liking : Palfrey's lofty decadence and Hinde's Grub Street journalism. Repelled by these lifestyles and disenchanted with London, he finds himself less impatient with the qualities of staunchness and practicality he left in abundance at home in Protestant Ulster. This, of course, is for him a compromise, as is his love-life, but then compromise in this novel is presented as being synonymous with good sense and maturity. Having been betrayed early on in Belfast by Maggie Carmichael, a girl he adored and who threw him over for a policeman, he woos and marries Eleanor in London. His pursuit of Eleanor is romantic, but when she returns with him to Ireland, she becomes enamoured—like a pale prefiguration of Brenda Dunwoody—of the MacDermotts' commercial exploits. At first he resists the pressures on him to abandon his life in London, but weighed down by the growing responsibility of his wife and child he bows to the pressures and decides that his destiny lies in carrying on the family business rather than in the loneliness of the ambitious writer.

What is possible in *The Wayward Man*—solitariness and independence—is mere fantasy in *The Foolish Lovers*. What is to be avoided in *The Wayward Man*—commercialism and immobility—is virtuous in *The Foolish Lovers*. The poetry of one is the doggerel of the other. And so we have John MacDermott wandering through industrial London, like a mirror-opposite of Robert Dunwoody, singing a hymn to Commerce that is at the same time a hymn to his native Ulster :

That poet fellow . . . what was his name? . . . whom he had met at Hampstead . . . Palfrey, that was the man's name . . . had

sneered at Commerce! John had not been able to make head or
tail of his arguments against Commerce, and he had found himself
defending it against the Poet . . . 'the very word is beautiful!' he
had asserted several times . . . mainly on his recollection of his
Uncle William. Palfrey had had the best of the argument, because
Palfrey could use his tongue more effectively, but John had felt
certain that the truth was not in Palfrey, and here tonight, in this
place where Commerce was most compactly to be seen, he knew
that there was Beauty in the labours of men, that bargaining and
competition and striving energies and rivalry in skill were elements
of loveliness. (p. 310)

In total contrast to *The Wayward Man, The Foolish Lovers*
reads like a novel by a man who wants to justify his lower middle-
class Protestant origins and his inherited business gifts. Explicitly
in its action and dialogue and implicitly in its three-act structure
that imitates the archetypal triadic pattern of adolescent romance
(separation, initiation and return), *The Foolish Lovers* parodies
romance.[10] *The Wayward Man* which ends with the hero's departure and which champions heroic solitude seems, conversely,
to be romantic. I do not think there is cause to doubt Ervine's
sincerity because of this disparity. These two novels can be seen
in tandem as the initiation of the hero into different aspects of
the planter psyche: on the one hand, the Protestant ethic,
mercantilism and business acumen without which the Plantation
would have foundered and which Ervine himself, as adminis-
trator and theatre manager, had in fair measure; on the other
hand, the emigrant psychology born of Nonconformist persecution in the eighteenth century, along with a penchant for travel
born of a unionist loyalty to Britain's far-flung empire. These
two strands in the Ulster planter psyche are frequently interwoven in Ervine, for instance in the loving description of the
Ballymacarrett shops in *The Wayward Man* that not only hum
with petty bourgeois industriousness but also with the aroma of
colonialism.

Considered together, then, these two novels are as close as an
Ulster Protestant writing about the lower middle class could

10. According to Northrop Frye, parody of the romance and its ideals is
an important theme in the more bourgeois novel ('The Four Forms of
Fiction', a selection from *Anatomy of Criticism*, Princeton 1957, reproduced
in *The Theory of the Novel*, ed. Philip Stevick, New York 1967, 34).

possibly come to romance. But even in *The Wayward Man* it is only within hailing distance. The garrulously hard-headed characters in this novel militate against the thrust of the narrative towards romance, with the result that the novel ultimately approaches parody of romance after the fashion of *The Foolish Lovers*. Ervine's characters are more sexually alive than those of the rural writers who came after, but love in his fiction is a matter of lifestyle, not of joy. Furthermore, culture in his novels is really a kind of higher philistinism—exciting London-born opera, ballet and drama : the kind of culture, in fine, to which the young provincial Protestant aspires. Ervine, said John Boyd, borrowing Ervine's own opinion of Arnold Bennett, 'fights the battles of the romantic with the weapons of the realist'.[11] I am more inclined to think the reverse is true.

(4)

The lower middle-class mercantile spirit that informs Ervine's novels is something which fills the young heroes of Forrest Reid's novels with dismay and occasionally disgust. For Reid, mercantilism, as one of the least deniable manifestations of the real and practical world, was to be avoided at all costs, especially when it took the forms of squalid money-grubbing and sordid philistinism. It would be truer to say, however, that what really offended Reid was the notion of social *descent* from respectability into squalor. Product of a Presbyterian merchant family that had come down in the world, Reid was early imbued with both disdain and apprehension at the sight of seediness and frayed decency. This was transferred to his boy-heroes, for whom the prospect of degradation, material and moral, has an exquisitely painful fascination.

This ambivalence is reflected throughout Reid's body of fiction. There is a very English, elitist side to it, an affected fragility as though its presiding muse were some Pre-Raphaelite ghost or Georgian elf. Its feyness is surely what attracted the attention, and to its creator the friendship, of such delicate sensibilities as Edwin Muir, Walter de la Mare and E. M. Forster.[12] It has also ensured Reid's eclipse as a relevant force in contemporary

11. In *The Arts in Ulster*, 118.
12. Brief essays on Reid can be found in E. M. Forster's collections, *Abinger Harvest*, London 1936 and *Two Cheers for Democracy*, London 1951.

Irish fiction (apart from influencing the early novels of Stephen Gilbert), a situation which was not helped by Russell Burlingham's full-length *Forrest Reid : A Portrait and a Study* (1953) which, though useful to the student of Reid, aspires to cultic fellowship rather than insight and tries to spirit Reid's work away from the rude gaze of common men. But anchoring Reid's fiction is his sense of that which invokes his elitist fear and disdain and which he feels moved, at least in the early novels, to re-create—the dark industrial heart of Belfast and the grubbier aspects of Protestant materialism. Moreover, the author of the most formidable and consistent canon of any Ulster novelist this century was not above a joke at his own expense, and in the acknowledgement of his own limitations and fragilities lay a resilience that I like to think sprang from the fact that he was an Ulsterman who spent almost his entire life in his native Belfast when many inferior and less secure writers have shown the city a clean pair of heels at the first opportunity. 'I alone knew, how much, as an author I resembled Mr Dick,' he noted in his second autobiography, *Private Road* (1940). 'I could get on swimmingly until I reached my King Charles's head—the point where a boy becomes a man. Then something seemed to happen, my inspiration was cut off, my interest flagged, so that all became a labour, and not a labour of love. I supposed it must be some mysterious form of arrested development'. (p. 12) Almost totally confined to childhood and early adolescence as it is, Reid's work can appear marginal, an impression the author himself fostered, even going so far in *Private Road* (published when he was sixty-five) as to withhold all but diplomatic recognition to his own adulthood.

Reid's remark about arrested development is, of course, a characteristic piece of coyness; one suspects Reid of praising himself with faint damnation, a device used constantly by his boy-heroes who have an insatiable appetite for smothering affection. True, as a man he apparently loved childhood games and pastimes and as a novelist explored at his peril adult and female characters; nevertheless, Reid always writes out of a sense of strength not weakness, even though like his young protagonists he occasionally affected in his autobiographies an arch naïvety reminiscent of Dickens's Mr Skimpole. An incident from his first autobiography is illuminating in this regard. Whereas Reid was pretty hopeless at representing heterosexuality in his novels, there is a scene in *Apostate* (1926) in which, on a holiday in Ballinderry, the young Reid encounters a neighbouring woman of blemished repute and visits her in her cottage. Aroused and longing for her caresses, the boy coyly works his way round the room and into her arms, feeling 'strange little electric thrills' passing through his body and 'queer little noises' rising in his throat. The scene is sexually alive in a way Reid rarely achieved in his novels, and is so because of the almost perverse tension set up between the boy's knowing insinuation of himself as a reluctant lover and his sense of helplessness as an overgrown child. An analogous and larger tension in style and point of view between passive self-absorption and droll self-reliance—a species of irony—enlivens Reid's fiction and often saves it from flabbiness. We might even speak of an analogous tension between Reid's realism and his elitist fantasy. AE and Edmund Gosse considered him a realist,[13] but one could with more justification call him a dreamer of dreams; the point is that realism and fantasy vie with each other in his work. Psychologically, what this little scene demonstrates is the conflict between nascent sexual desire (the boy's wish to impose himself on events) and a natural passivity (the boy's desire for the anonymity of childhood or of the womb). This conflict is within almost every central boy-character of Reid's and most vividly in those characters who come closest to manhood. *Denis Bracknel* (1947), a rewrite of an earlier novel, *The Bracknels* (1911), heavily weights one side of the conflict, for the fifteen-year-old titular hero indulges in morbid fantasy before strangling himself, the passive desire for both the world's pity and the anonymity of the earth-womb thereby consummated. It is the kind of tale, melodramatic and psychologically transparent, that too often attracted Reid and as a novel is inferior to the beautifully controlled *Peter Waring* (1937), itself a rewrite of *Following Darkness* (1912) and both dedicated to E. M. Forster. *Peter Waring* is a success in terms of its tone and shape, qualities that Reid sought more than ideas, hence the obsessive rewriting during his later years.

Less decadent than *Denis Bracknel*, *Peter Waring*, without sacrificing any of the essential elements of Reid's fiction, presents the psychological ferment of adolescence with the right balance

13. Cited by Reid in *Private Road* while discussing critical reactions to his novels.

between fantasy and realism, active desire and passive longing. It is nostalgically set in the 1880s or 1890s, an appropriate *fin de siècle* context for the hero's confusion about his sexuality and the function of art, but Reid also exploits the Ulster setting, and the differing attitudes towards morality, religion and class facing Peter Waring relate very directly to the North of Ireland. The novel is probably the closest Reid came to writing a psychological rather than magical work in which the final form of the young hero's personality remains in doubt until the end of the book, and to this extent *Peter Waring* is a genuine *Bildungsroman* in a way Ervine's novels are not meant to be.

Almost sixteen when the novel opens, Peter Waring lives with his father, a grass widower and schoolteacher in Newcastle, Co. Down. His home life, due to this cantankerous and puritanical father, is unhappy and he spends much of his time with Mrs Carroll, a widow who lives in Derryaghy House. The spacious world within, and the luxuriant landscape outside the house compose a dreamlike existence for the boy as he communes with the ancestral spirits of the house and the pagan spirits of the green Mourne country. His greatest influence is Mrs Carroll, warm and sympathetic yet conveniently unrelated so that she is free from suggestions of parental authority and can function as a focus for the boy's sexual stirrings. With his own mother and Mrs Carroll's husband out of the way, it is an ideal and Freudian situation, and one out of which, in Reid's terms, only a fool would want to grow—which indeed is what the novel on one level sets out to prove.

When Mrs Carroll's nephew and niece come to visit her from England, Peter falls in love with Katherine. At first she returns his attentions and he is deliriously happy despite the uncomfortable relationship with Gerald, Katherine's languid and musical brother. The idyll is shattered when Gerald and Katherine Dale leave and Peter travels to Belfast to attend school. He is unhappy living with pious relations of his father's and on the eve of the school holidays rows with them and returns to Newcastle with a friend, Owen Gill. When Katherine and Gerald come to Derryaghy again, he discovers that she no longer loves him. He tries half-heartedly to kill himself by courting pneumonia and ends the novel in the comforting arms of Mrs Carroll where, we might suspect, he has longed to be all along.

Even more dramatically than in Ervine, the city in *Peter
Waring* is the location of adolescent tribulation. Reid's own twist
to this is to make working-class and lower middle-class Belfast
a specific kind of purgatory. If the southern suburbs of turn-of-
the-century Belfast are shown as beautiful in most Reid novels,
it is the least attractive and most industrial parts of the city that
frighten and fascinate Peter Waring. The McAllisters, his father's
relations, live above their shop in exactly the same street in
which Alec has his shop in *The Wayward Man,* but Reid sees
the life of the small shopkeeper in rather a different light from
Ervine. 'It depressed me,' recalls the elderly Peter who narrates
the book. 'I hated all that it implied—ugliness, discomfort, sordid
economies, and a ceaseless struggle to keep up appearances.'
(p. 163) This seediness afflicts his own father, too, whose grubbi-
ness as well as puritanism makes him repulsive to Peter. We
might even suspect that it was a disparity in class and breeding
that caused Peter's parents to separate (a disparity Reid detected
in his own parents) and that the same disparity helps to destroy
the father-son relationship.

As with many of Reid's young heroes, it is hard to know to
what extent Reid has unconsciously created a snobbish character.
For all his contempt for his father, Peter is not truly at home at
Derryaghy House, especially in the company of Gerald, a youth
of aristocratic bearing. Peter's taste in literature and his sensitive
nature lift him above his father's lower middle-class shabbiness,
but he is yet unschooled in decorum (not knowing what RSVP
means, for instance) and feels socially misplaced. 'I was ashamed
to let him see the kind of people I had sprung from,' the narrator
writes when recalling his desire to take Owen home to Newcastle;
on another occasion he is 'purposely uncommunicative, being
ashamed of the class to which [he] belonged'. Such social shame
is fairly normal among adolescents in the presence of those they
imagine to be social superiors, but its recurrence in Reid suggests
that it had in his case a real and lifelong basis. Neither Ervine
nor his young heroes seems to have been stricken with such class
confusion, perhaps because their families went up, not down, in
the world.

In total contrast to Derryaghy House with its upper middle-
class murals is the tatty room in East Belfast in which the
McAllisters treat Peter to a welcoming meal :

The furniture was worn, the carpet was worn. The curtains, the vases and ornaments, were cheap and gaudy. I even preferred our parlour at home, where, if things were not less hideous, there were at any rate fewer of them. Here, as well as the inevitable texts, several pictures adorned the walls, and a large engraving hanging directly in front of me was the first example of its kind I had seen. It represented a young man in armour, for the possession of whom two classically draped females were struggling : one flaxen-haired and virtuous, I supposed; the other dark and wanton, for she held a champagne-glass in her hand, which she waved aloft like a torch.

'A fine picture! A fine picture!' Uncle George commented, pleased by my fascinated gaze. 'It's a Royal Academy picture that. "The Choice", they call it. You can see the lesson, Peter, the artist had in mind.'

Yes, I saw the lesson. (p. 154)

Ironically, the relation between art and morality is a problem Peter wrestles with throughout the novel. He has endless discussions with Owen Gill who worships Tolstoy and who practically eviscerates *Anna Karenina* to reach all its moral implications. Art is nothing if not moral for the humourless Owen, and in his righteous zeal he writes to Tolstoy and receives from the Master a directive to underline everything he understands in the Gospels with a red pencil ('a red pencil?' asks Peter with a sarcasm that escapes Owen) and live his life accordingly. Owen the moralist is ribbed mercilessly at Derryaghy by Gerald Dale who, living his musical life in London in the margins of *The Yellow Book,* takes an altogether more Wildean view, seeing Tolstoy's *What Is Art?* as 'a sort of Child's Guide to Morality'. From these discussions Peter garners only bewilderment.

The tension between Peter and Gerald is, psychologically, the novel's most interesting feature, though because of Reid's reticence and the climate of opinion in which he wrote the tension is never resolved. All along, one feels, the unfulfilled love is not between Katherine and Peter but Peter and Gerald, and that the Peter-Katherine affair is a metaphor for the relationship Reid really wanted to explore. Dramatically the novel is none the worse for this unresolved tension. Moreover, homosexual attraction (or what Reid, perhaps less than ingenuously, calls 'the friendship theme'[14]) is not given the status of a quasi-philosophy in *Peter Waring* as it is, as we shall see, in the Tom Barber trilogy, and can be seen simply, if we choose, merely as part of the sexual ambivalence of adolescence.

Whether we are thinking of Peter's love for Katherine or of the attraction between Peter and Gerald, the problem of the nature of love remains for Peter the same. His love for Katherine has about it a detached kind of purity (though Reid does not flinch from the physical symptoms), a kind of idealism that is to human relationships what the doctrine of *l'art pour l'art* is to works of art. We can take the analogy further, for just as Peter is faced with not one but two alternatives to Gerald's aestheticism in art (the McAllisters' philistinism and Owen's moralism), so he is faced with two alternatives to the shattered idealism of his love for Katherine. There is George McAllister's prurience, harmless enough when we consider that it consists of hoarding pornographic pictures and remorselessly dating girls, but symptomatic nevertheless of a kind of philistinism in human relationships. Then there is Mr Waring's brooding and obsessive puritanism and anal-retentive dread of pleasure and especially sexual pleasure. Little wonder that Owen gets on so well with Peter's father— his attitude to art is like Mr Waring's attitude to life, humourless and heavily moralistic.

Mr Waring's puritanism is not only a matter of temperament but of religious conviction, for he is a North of Ireland fundamentalist who reads the Bible every day and prays at the drop of a hat, even stealing into Peter's bedroom at night to kneel by his bedside. The guilt which racks Peter over his unwilling connivance at George's prurience and over the Katherine affair springs from his religious upbringing and almost compares with the guilt that afflicts the young heroes of Irish Catholic *Bildungsromane*. Nor are the organised churches any more appealing to Peter than his father's private one. He seeks help from the Rev. Henry Applin but is sorely disappointed. In desperation he seeks succour in a Catholic church but is offended by its iconolatry, a kind of spiritual and aesthetic philistinism no more acceptable than his father's pious moralism. Peter's experience in the chapel recalls that of Robert Dunwoody in Ervine's *The Wayward Man:*

The curiosity that had drawn me into the church was rapidly

14. *Private Road*, 88.

ebbing. Everything—the smell of stale incense, the lighted candles,
the cheap gaudy decorations—now struck me as vulgar and repel-
lent. It all somehow seemed wrong—gross rather than spiritual—
and my idea of confessing to a priest seemed wrong too. I rose
and went out, the last thing I noticed being a thick sediment of dirt
at the bottom of the stoup of holy water. (p. 257)

Peter is not, in conventional terms, a religious person at all and
is merely seeking a way of resolving his guilt and quandaries that
are at base sexual. His mind when free of sexual preoccupations
is inclined towards the metaphysical and not the theological, a
kind of intellectual idealism grappling with what Reid calls
Herbert Spencer's 'unknowables', problems of infinity and
identity. 'These insoluble problems were, nevertheless, just what
fascinated me. The practical ethics of religion—that I should be
good and encourage in myself a variety of Christian virtues—
that kind of thing did not interest me at all.' (pp. 27–8)

There is, then, a pattern underlying Peter's adolescent tumult.
In each of the realms of art, sexuality and religion, he is confronted with three different attitudes which we might roughly
designate moralism, philistinism and idealism. Delirious with
guilt and confusion in the midst of these, and wounded by
Katherine's imminent departure for Italy, Peter tries half-
heartedly to commit suicide by lying down in a rainstorm, and
ends the novel being nursed by Mrs Carroll. Sickness is a periodic
condition of Reid's young heroes and seems to represent their
temporary return to the womb or to childhood with all their
physical and emotional needs taken care of by an older
woman summonable by a bellpull. Like dream and fantasy, sickness is courted by the youngsters during a crisis and because they
detest the prospect of manhood and its responsibilities. In Reid's
fiction the final barrier between adolescence and manhood is
never really breached and there is a turning back at the last
moment, the final initiatory trials funked.

Dream, fantasy, sickness: all are part of the same psychological syndrome and represent a solution to Peter's adolescent per-
plexities. But they are not altogether an evasion of the problems,
not a total reversion to childhood which is, anyway, impossible.
Not only are they capable of being given philosophical justification (as in the Tom Barber trilogy) but they can also be projected

into the real and adult world. For example, it is characteristic of Reid that Peter should try to commit suicide by lying on the ground at the edge of the sea, for the return to the womb of the mother is also return to the womb of the earth (the sea being a natural symbol of the womb throughout Reid's fiction). The real religion that is given expression in *Peter Waring* is a pantheism that springs from certain psychological needs and sublimations. The high moments of the novel are those in which Peter experiences temporary epiphanies of joy or sorrow. I use the word 'epiphanies' advisedly, for in a few rare instances in *Peter Waring* we are reminded of Stephen Dedalus' epiphanies in *A Portrait of the Artist as a Young Man,* a work published four years after *Following Darkness.* Burlingham has rightly drawn attention to the coincidental similarities: both Joyce and Reid, for example, use a post-nineties sensuous prose (from which Reid never wholly graduated) to describe the swooning of the hero's soul and its momentary consubstantiation with the matter of the universe, a kind of half-willed suicide of the spirit. The following passage from *Peter Waring* might recall for us comparable passages from *A Portrait* or even the conclusion of 'The Dead':

A deep silence overhung the earth. Behind me were the white frozen mountains; on either side was an endless stretch of snow; and before me was the dark and sullen sea. The day was closing in, and already more light rose from the ground than fell from the sky overhead. Snow had begun again to fall—a few flakes, drifting and fluttering down out of the grey clouds. But I knew this was only the beginning, and that there would be more soon. I walked to the edge of the sea, and watched the cold desolate waves rolling in to break at my feet. At that moment I felt infinitely alone.

Alone spiritually, and alone as one might be in a dead or dying world. The whirling flakes of snow fell ever faster out of the winter sky; the barren, frost-bound land was wrapped in stillness; the only sound I heard came from the breaking waves. And it seemed to me that the darkness gradually approaching was like the final extinction of life, and I could imagine that there would be no further awakening—that the end had at last been reached. (pp. 238-9)

I would not want to push the occasional similarities too far.

Besides, there is one essential difference between the two books: whereas Stephen Dedalus 'wakens' from his epiphanies and goes forth, sunward, to forge and create (just as Joyce 'wakens' from the self-indulgence and occasional decadence of *A Portrait* and goes on to write *Ulysses*), Peter Waring stands on the threshold of adulthood and reality and turns back to a life of dream and night-sojourns (just as Reid chooses to write and rewrite his dream-fiction during a forty-year career).

If Peter's pantheism is inseparable from dream-fantasy, so too are his attitudes towards art and sexuality that are incipiently formed at the end of the novel and given fullest expression in certain other Reid novels. Peter is clearly not going to seek or achieve happiness in normal heterosexual relationships; he is attracted by physical beauty and a sympathetic nature but in a way that bestrides or transcends the sexes, a passive way that permits consummation or sublimation in dreams and private fantasies. And as for art, if Reid does not pursue Peter's latter thoughts on this subject, we might justifiably let *Peter Waring* itself symbolise his thinking for us. The realistic scenes of the novel, set in lower middle-class Belfast, are enveloped within a Georgian dream of luxuriant countryside. It is essentially a city-dreamer's landscape, idealised in the manner of eclogue or pastoral. Purportedly set in the striking Mourne country, *Peter Waring* gives us a landscape where nothing is particularised or recognisable, a dreamland of dells and glens and silver rivers to describe which Reid need not have moved out of his suburban Belfast study.

Nonetheless, *Peter Waring* is a very fine novel—rich, fluent and assured, spiced by Reid's inimitably droll humour, full of feminine emphases and coy observations. Moreover, we ought not allow the novel's *fin-de-siècle* nostalgia and fantasy-romance to overwhelm its realistic kernel, its deft re-creation of a sensitive Protestant adolescence in the North of Ireland in the 1890s. Unlike Ervine's young heroes, Peter Waring does not at the end of his ordeals enter the world of facts, but his is an armed watch nevertheless.

5

PASSAGE THROUGH LIMBO

(1)

B RIAN M OORE is the North's best-known novelist since Forrest
Reid and has achieved an international reputation, chiefly in
America and Great Britain, that Reid never enjoyed. *The Lonely
Passion of Judith Hearne* (1955) is perhaps the best novel to
come out of Northern Ireland. Of all Northern fiction writers,
Moore has been the most uncompromisingly urban—there is
almost no landscape or sense of nature in his work. And yet the
broad social movement charted in Moore's succession of novels
is one which clearly begins—offstage, as it were—on the land.
Belfast, in which Moore's early novels are set, may be the
North's largest city but it is a city still fairly close to the land in
spirit and space. *Judith Hearne,* apparently a novel of urban consciousness, is in fact peppered with those whom Belfast residents
would call country people : Mary, the maid James Madden
rapes; Moira O'Neill, in whose house Judith seeks warmth and
normality; and Judith herself, born in Ballymena and educated
in Armagh. Judith's Belfast is a mere enlargement of the villages
and towns we met in the rural fiction, an inquisitive, scandal-
hunting, puritanical, passionless place characterised by the burger
mentality of its Presbyterian rulers and the apathy of a vestigial
Catholic peasantry. It is a world dominated by ceremony and
rite : *Judith Hearne* reflects this not only in its use of Catholic
liturgy but also in the stilted human relationships it painfully
dissects. The static, ritual quality of Irish life is imaged, too, in
Moore's use of the Lupercalia in *The Feast of Lupercal* (1957),
in the pseudo-military ambience of *The Emperor of Ice-Cream*
(1965), and less metaphorically in the examination of ritual that
is at the heart of the recent *Catholics* (1972).

In Moore's ritualised Irish society, roles are sharply defined
and those who are foolish or desperate enough to step outside

social and community limits risk the worst that can befall the individual: notoriety and indignity. A great deal of the drama of *Judith Hearne* arises because Judith's social position balances on a knife-edge between respectability and disrepute. The novel's climax brings, among other things, the feared collapse into social disgrace. In Moore's Belfast the chameleonic skill of failures and dodgers in feigning social respectability matches the almost canine skill of friends, neighbours and even strangers in scenting out abnormality.

All of this is familiar to readers of Ulster rural fiction. However, whereas transgression in the rural community usually means the creation of bad blood or wilful solitariness and pride, Moore's Belfast communities are more incensed by failure. *Judith Hearne* and *The Feast of Lupercal* demonstrate how the failure and un-willing solitary becomes in the eyes of an urban but still ritualised society a transgressor and potential victim: 'The failure' I want to define as the hapless individual incapable of beginning or completing within his own community the necessary transitions towards appropriate social status and self-fulfilment. These transitions have come to be known, after Arnold van Gennep's classic 1909 work of the same name, as 'rites of passage'.[1] The term refers to those rites surrounding such temporal transitions as birth, adolescence, loss of virginity, marriage, childbirth, status promotion and death, and such spatial transitions as departure, welcome and incorporation.

Between transitions, the individual is in a dangerous limbo, and his inability to make a fresh transition at the appropriate time is the sign of failure. The more primitive the society, the more pro-nounced are the rites of passage; failure and isolation are there-fore easier to spot but also, by ritual means, to remedy. Ritual failure and isolation we would therefore expect to be *more evident* in peasant society but at the same time *less common* than in modern urban society. Normally the individual is well integrated in a heavily ritualised, rural and primitive society. If he is not, or if he is in conflict with the community (like the chief characters in local naturalism), there are ritual methods of exclusion with which he is familiar; exclusion in such a society does not usually

1. Arnold van Gennep, *The Rites of Passage*, trans. Monika B. Vizedom and Gabrielle L. Caffee, Chicago 1961.

produce anomie. The situation is very different in modern urban society which is de-ritualised and dehumanised. In such a society the ritual *methods* of aiding the individual in his transitions have diminished but his ritual *needs* have not. The predicament of the individual who moves from a ritualised to a de-ritualised society can be described as 'displacement' rather than failure. Moore's early novels are about failure, his later ones about displacement. His canon therefore spans that entire scenario that takes us from the ritualised land to the provincial town and then to the de-personalised cities of the New World. With his latest work, *Catholics,* he even returns us to the ritual and rural beginnings of modern Ireland to make the scenario, in time and space, circular.

Moore's Belfast is somewhere between the two extremes of primitive rural society and dehumanised cosmopolis. The city is still heavily ritualised but its ritual and ceremony are impersonal and the weaker individuals have to fall back on their own ritual resources. Moore's fictional approach in his Belfast novels reflects this ambivalence of setting. If the mental stress caused by loneliness is a feature of life in the big city, then the extent to which Moore in his early novels explores mental decline (Judith Hearne, for example, ends her novel in premature senility) re-creates a Belfast on the way to becoming a cosmopolis. But while Miss Hearne and Diarmuid Devine could remain unnoticed in a really large city, they cannot escape detection in Moore's Belfast. Detection means victimisation. Moore's ritual portrayal of their victimisation balances his psychological portrayal of their mental distress. In the Belfast novels, then, Moore's style is midway between psychologism and ritual naturalism. In *Judith Hearne* this ambivalence of style is very obvious. In the sixth chapter Moore suddenly depicts events from the successive viewpoints of several characters, using a rudimentary stream-of-consciousness technique. This chapter is a kind of psychological intermezzo framed by conventional, third-person, naturalistic narrative.

The failure can be described as a primitive outsider. Moore's later novels, set in North America, might on first impression be seen as novels about existential outsiders, but it is important to understand how the consciousness which informs these novels has developed out of an originally rural and particularly Irish situation. Beginning with Ginger Coffey, the later heroes flee their stifling Irish communities only to exchange one kind of limbo for another. If Judith Hearne and Diarmuid Devine are failures who become victims, the later heroes are Irish immigrants who suffer anomie and rootlessness in their adopted country. The failures suffer at the hands of a closely knit community; the displaced suffer by neglect at the hands of a depersonalised cosmopolis. But it is not the nature of cosmopolitan life which is the primary cause of unhappiness in the later novels, though this complicates the incorporation of the outsider into his new community. Unhappiness is caused firstly by the fact of displacement and secondly by the clash between life in America and that peculiar Irish experience which the displaced have fled. For these reasons I am inclined also to call the displaced 'primitive outsiders'.

It is not hard to share the novelist's enthusiasm for the dramatic and social possibilities of the primitive outsider, whether failure or displaced. Van Gennep, talking of the individual trapped in isolation between rites of passage, remarks :

This isolation has two aspects, which may be found separately or in combination : such a person is weak, because he is outside a given group or society, but he is also strong, since he is in the sacred realm with respect to the group's members, for whom their society constitutes the secular world. In consequence, some peoples kill, strip and mistreat a stranger without ceremony, while others fear him, take great care of him, treat him as a powerful being, or take magico-religious protective measures against him.[2]

The notion of the sacred will assume relevance when we discuss the scapegoat in Moore's fiction. At this point I am interested in the essentially ambivalent status of the outsider. Ronald Frankenberg puts van Gennep's concept of this ambivalence into contemporary jargon when he writes that

In nearly every group activity, it is possible to recognise someone who has only that activity in common with the other members of the group or is a deviant in some respect from the distinguishing criteria of the group mainly concerned. Such a person . . . is to some extent removed from the conflicts and social pressures of full

2. Van Gennep, 26.

members of the group. This makes him or her of central importance in the precipitation and resolution of such conflicts.[3]

In Moore, indeed in much Ulster fiction that has its roots in
land-consciousness, the significant character is someone removed
from the group ('weak' is van Gennep's term) yet in whom social
and dramatic conflict is precipitated and resolved ('strong' is van
Gennep's term).

It is through the 'strength' and 'weakness' of his outsider that
the novelist can give his narrative the dimension of social criticism. When Moore sets his novels in Belfast, in Dublin, in
Canada, in the cities of the United States, he is engaged in social
criticism. Society is held responsible for allowing individuals to
become isolated and for victimising them. In the act of victimisation, society is captured by Moore in the process of resolving the
conflicts within itself. To this extent, Moore's dramas are symbolic, not to say typical. Yet it would misplace the emphasis to
call the victims themselves symbolic or typical. Instead they are
freaks and originals. This is obviously true of Judith Hearne and
Diarmuid Devine and in part of Ginger Coffey. It is less obviously
but equally true of the Irish-American heroes whose displacement
is unusual in itself but is made even more unusual when we consider the nature of the society they have fled. Because of the
continuity in the scenario I have been talking about throughout
this book, a continuity reflected in Moore's canon, almost all of
Moore's outsiders have at some stage to be discussed in terms of
their indigenous or transplanted Irishness. Only when Irishness
is dimly rather than vividly presented may we begin to claim
that Moore's primitive outsider has become the existential outsider, that modern fictional hero whose alienation, springing from
no readily accessible or comprehensible social reality, carries the
burden of symbolising our own alienation.

(2)

Critics have persisted in forging similarities between Moore and
his compatriot-in-exile, James Joyce. Jack Ludwig, for instance,
saw Moore in 1962 as Joyce's heir in the genealogy of Irish

3. Ronald Frankenberg, 'British Community Studies: Problems of Synthesis' in *The Social Anthropology of Complex Societies*, ed. Michael Banton,
London 1968, 126.

fiction.[4] Hallvard Dahlie, in a fairly perceptive account of Moore's work, sees Joyce's progress from *Dubliners* to *Ulysses* reflected in Moore's own development from *Judith Hearne* (1955) to *I Am Mary Dunne* (1968).[5] He perceives in both authors not only a shift from naturalistic techniques to experimentalism but also a movement from despair to affirmation. An associated claim is that Moore's work, including his early work, is like Joyce's a fictionalisation of the central dilemma facing man today. That dilemma has been capsulised for us by two Moore critics. John Stedmond, in his introduction to the Canadian edition of *Judith Hearne,* asserts that this book 'probes what David Daiches has called the central question in modern fiction: "How is love possible in a world of individuals imprisoned by their own private consciousness?" '[6] According to Ludwig, Moore's characters 'ask themselves *the* question facing twentieth-century man: knowing what he does about all things political and social how does man still get out of bed in the morning?'[7] As a corollary to this, Ludwig sees Moore's Belfast as an appropriate symbol of the West's decline.

These approaches to Moore, as my previous section implies, are misguided. Moore's fiction, especially his early work, is interesting and refreshing as major writing because it does not focus upon an essentially twentieth-century predicament but rather upon ritual isolation. In consequence, Moore's Belfast is anything but a symbol of the decadent West's decline : instead it has the appearance of a primitive society almost unsullied by twentieth-century cultural and social conflicts. Unlike most of the Ulster writers we have so far met, who dramatise their society either sympathetically or with satiric tongue-in-cheek, Moore treats Ulster society with a savagery subdued only by the exigencies of novelistic form. The early novels are ruthless indictments of a compassionless Church and a compassionless community. Only his subsequent experiences in the godless, impersonal capitals of North America have led Moore to see that perhaps after all there is something of profit to the human soul, if not in

4. Jack Ludwig, 'Brian Moore: Ireland's Loss, Canada's Novelist', *Critique* V, Minneapolis (Spring–Summer 1962), 5–13.
5. Dahlie, 118–19.
6. *Judith Hearne,* Toronto 1964, v.
7. Ludwig, 11.

the terrorised, sectarian Belfast he revisited recently,[8] then in the *idea* of a community held together in co-operation and without bigotry and fear at its centre, a notion so idealistic that it has to be turned into fable in his most recent work, *Catholics*.

In a manner Ludwig does not recognise, decline *is* important in Moore's first two novels, *Judith Hearne* and *The Feast of Lupercal*. Seated before her mirror early in the book Judith Hearne sees a woman still to celebrate her sex and for whom in her early forties time is running out. At the novel's opening she is capable of fancifully transforming her image into that of a nubile woman :

Her angular face smiled softly at its glassy image. Her gaze, deceiving, transforming her to her imaginings, changed the contour of her sallow-skinned face, skilfully re-fashioning her long pointed nose on which a small chilly tear had gathered. Her dark eyes, eyes which skitted constantly in imagined fright, became wide, soft, luminous. Her frame, plain as a cheap clothes-rack, filled now with soft curves, developing a delicate line to the bosom. (p. 18)

Such self-delusion is destined at the end of the novel to give way, after a narrative of great poignancy, to terrible resignation : 'She sat at the bare white dressing-table and saw her face in the mirror. Old, she thought, if I met myself now, I would say : that is an old woman.' (p. 184) Miss Hearne's descent from hope and comparative youthfulness into loneliness and feeblemindedness is also a descent from respectability into social disgrace, and this in turn images a social decline independent of her own fate. Miss Hearne has staggered from flat to flat, spiralling downwards as her hopes of an ordinary family life fade, until the reader discovers her as she moves into Mrs Rice's boarding-house. Mrs Rice lives in Camden Street, a shabby-genteel area around Queen's University which 'used to be', as Judith remarks, 'one of the best parts of the city . . . a very good neighbourhood in the old days'. The social backdrop to the novel, then, is the decline of Victorian middle-class Belfast, a seedy scenery appropriate behind Judith's straitened material and spiritual circumstances. By no stretch of the imagination, however, can we call this backdrop the decline of Western civilisation. The Victorian

8. 'Now and Then', *Threshold*, Belfast, 23 (Sep. 1970).

Belfast of *Judith Hearne* has not degenerated into whatever decadence or proletarian anonymity Ludwig envisages as following upon Western decline, but rather into an Irish lower middle-class tattiness. Mrs Rice and her boarders symbolise this lower middle class whose members have not been 'reduced' from the Victorian middle class, as Judith Hearne has, but promoted from the working class and who have retained their stifling puritanism and bigotry.

The implication of Ludwig and other critics that Judith Hearne is the ultimate product of a declining society, that she is a terminal deposit of that society, holds water only if by 'society' we mean Victorian middle-class Ulster. Miss Hearne is set apart from the other characters by her anachronistic and self-conscious gentility, her use of words like *soupçon* when addressing an ignoramus such as Mrs Rice. On the other hand, she is set apart just as much by her timidity, her lack of personality and drive, her plainness and will to failure, and these have little to do with social decline. Miss Hearne cannot really be said to symbolise or embody the decline even of Victorian middle-class Ulster, though in a way her fate images it for us; like all of Moore's major figures, she is removed from her community, something of a freak, and only in an oblique way can be regarded as a product of it.

Furthermore, whereas the decline of Victorian Ulster has been a gradual process of decay, what happens to Miss Hearne, even though she has been slowly approaching this stage of her life, is really rather swift and terrible. The notion that runs through all of Moore's novels—and which is not satisfactorily meshed with that of social decline—is that of crisis. For the purpose of discussing Judith Hearne, Diarmuid Devine and Ginger Coffey in psychological rather than ritual terms, crisis can be defined as that point in their lives at which the horrifying perception strikes them that their failure and isolation might have become permanent. For the later American characters the nature of their crisis, as we shall see, is something different.

Like Judith Hearne, Diarmuid Devine in *The Feast of Lupercal* (a novel, incidentally, in which social decline is of minimal importance) is brought up short at a critical stage of his life, and in the act of being brought up short suffers agonies of isolation. He, too, at the outset of the novel believes there is still time. 'Since when was thirty-seven considered old?' he asks himself indignantly, but would not dare to repeat the question two hundred pages on. Devine's very outward bearing suggests imminent crisis :

He was a tall man, yet did not seem so : not youthful, yet somehow young; a man whose appearance suggested some painful uncertainty. He wore the jacket and waistcoat of a business suit, but his trousers were sag-kneed flannels. His black brogues clashed with loud Argyle socks. The military bravura of his large mustache was denied by weak eyes, circled by ill-fitting spectacles. Similarly, his hair, worn long and untidy behind the ears, thinning to a sandy shoal on his freckled brow, offset the Victorian respectability of waistcoat, gold watch chain and signet ring. (p. 12)

The state of neglect in which Devine and Judith Hearne languish is the neglect suffered by the spouseless and childless middle-aged. But their isolation runs deeper than this. Both stand at the threshold of middle age without having faced and ridden the crises of youth : of loss of virginity, of marriage, of parenthood. Both are made aware of the incongruity between their outward image as responsible adults and that inner trembling and desire that drives one towards a girl seventeen years his junior, and the other towards an elderly doorman. If with van Gennep we see regeneration as a law of life, guaranteed by the very rites of passage which spell failure to the unsuccessful, we can understand why the stories of Devine and Judith Hearne must end in resignation or madness. Diarmuid Devine might trade his rags for an Aberdowndie with Tattersall waistcoat, but he remains the same Diarmuid Devine : rebirth does not come at sixteen guineas.

Devine's faintheartedness and Miss Hearne's timidity and plainness suggest that they would be losers wherever they lived. But if there is a terrible inevitability about their fates, the specific counts on which the community indicts them are wholly unreasonable and are themselves indictments of an unchanging, static society. Thou shalt not consort with Protestant girls (fast or otherwise) it tells Devine, nor consume alcohol alone (especially if a middle-aged woman) it tells Miss Hearne, nor throw thyself at those whose social background has not been thoroughly investigated. If I have chosen to parody biblical commandments here, it is because the unchanging Church is as oppressive an agency in these two novels as the community itself.

(3)

Judith Hearne and *The Feast of Lupercal* explore the inextricable link between the spiritual and moral demands of the Church and the sexual habits and moral conscience of the individual. Religious dictates and constraints concerning the expression of sexual passion, the attendant psychological inhibitions, the way sexual and religious fantasies can commingle to the detriment of the individual's sexual and spiritual fulfilment : these lie fairly close to the heart of both novels. The Church in both is a rather primitive, over-ritualised institution, hardly less culpable than the community in its neglect and exclusion of the central characters. In *The Feast of Lupercal* both the Church and the community persist in confusing the sexual and the spiritual, spitefully translating Devine's alleged sexual shenanigans into religious terms. One can almost imagine Devine shaking himself free from the confusion, overriding his conscience, escaping the psychological inhibitions a hyper-developed conscience can cause, and taking the plunge into what for him would be liberating sex. Almost, but not quite. On the other hand, Judith Hearne seems far less salvageable, far less corrigible. It is Judith herself who cannot divorce the body from the soul, the sacred from the profane. She suffers for her sexual deprivation precisely in proportion to her piety, which is the novel's central irony. The religious doubt she experiences is provoked not by her yielding to the fleshly temptations of which she daydreams, but by sexual loneliness and anguish. When she tries to give vent to her doubt, she confronts in the confessional an unfamiliar priest who is bored by her chatter, and, mortified, she halts in mid-confession.

She had seen his face. A weary face, his cheek resting in the palm of his hand, his eyes shut. He's not listening, her mind cried. Not listening !

He began to speak : 'Now, my child, we all have burdens put upon us in this life, crosses we have to bear, trials and tribulations we should offer up to Our Lord. And prayer is a great thing, my child, a great thing. We should never be lonely because we always have God to talk to. And our guardian angel to watch over us. And we have a mother, our Heavenly Mother, to help us and intercede for us. Yes, we have a Holy Family, each and every one of us. All we need to do is pray. Pray, my child, ask God's aid in fighting these temptations.'

'Yes, Father.' (Oh, he doesn't understand, he doesn't.)

'Now, I want you to say five Our Fathers and five Hail Marys as penance for your sins.'

And then his voice, mumbling the Latin, giving the sacred words of absolution, the words in which, acting as God's medium, he washed the soul white as purest snow. His fingers raised in the sign of forgiveness. The confession was over. (pp. 144–5)

Later, when she goes to Father Quigley's house, he takes her to task for being drunk and sends her packing. The pathos of Miss Hearne's subsequent flight from piety is that despite her honest, though boring, confessions of wounded faith, she is rejected at a critical moment by someone whose spiritual obligation it is to dispense charity and understanding, not platitudes or school-masterly admonitions.

Despair breeds doubt in a beneficent God. Doubt demands demonstration. When Father Quigley rebuffs her drunken pil-grimage to his house, Judith Hearne demands, in her desperation for assurance, what Othello calls 'ocular proof'. In that terrible scene she attacks in what is a sexual assault the locked and resistant tabernacle to reach and embrace an elusive Christ. 'But the door rejected her,' Moore writes. 'It would not open. Blood ran from her nails.' In a mirage of self-pity and genuine thirst for certainty, she transforms priest and housewife bending over her into the grieving members of a pietà. Her bloodstained hands are the hands, her suffering the lonely passion, of the crucified Christ. Judith Hearne's attempted union with Christ is, like her passion, both spiritual and sexual. Her ecstasy is the ecstasy of spiritual onanism in which she becomes both female supplicant and the male redeemer she so imperiously seeks.

The 'revelation' in this scene is induced by Miss Hearne's anguish and, like the rough, dark-haired males of her life, is imaginary. Nevertheless, it is the high point of her 'lonely passion'. If we see a confusion on her part throughout the novel between sexuality and spirituality, then we can attribute what happens after this scene to post-ecstatic apathy. For if she can still at the end of the novel go through the motions of the Mass, Judith Hearne no longer understands the true meaning of the rites. Moreover, she now believes herself damned :

O Lord, I do not believe, help my unbelief. O You—are You—?
The Mass was over. The priest went to the foot of the altar and knelt.
'De profundis clamavi ad te, Dominum!' he cried.
The nuns joined in, reciting the prayer. Other prayers. And I have cried out. I am alone. Without prayer.
'. . . thrust into hell, Satan and with him all the other wicked spirits who wander through the world seeking the ruin of souls. Amen.' (pp. 185–6)

'Drifting in a sheepish calm', like Lowell's Lepke, Miss Hearne at the end of the novel is beyond the Church, as she is beyond the community. Judith—woman of Judah, praised by the Lord— returns to her Sacred Heart, private symbol now, and dwells in the companionship of its merely physical presence.

Intimidated and transfixed by the mere thoughts of sinfulness and faithlessness, Judith exaggerates and intensifies her spiritual dereliction. This is connected to what I have called the novel's central irony, for what Judith Hearne, like Diarmuid Devine, must 'expiate' are not so much sins as the very piety and inno- cence which stand in the way of fulfilment. Unable to commit those sins of the flesh she dearly wishes to commit, Miss Hearne turns to drink, a sin not of pride or wantonness but of despair and deprivation. Moore has captured perfectly the vicious spiral of Judith Hearne's descent. The longer she is deprived sexually, the more sinful she wishes to become. The more she flagellates herself for her sinful thoughts, the more vicarious sexual 'satisfaction' she derives.

Apart from Moore's biting perception of the distorted role of sexuality in Irish Catholicism, there is a real theological problem embedded in *The Lonely Passion of Judith Hearne,* which is: how do the rites of redemption accommodate one whose spiritual condition is neither really sinful nor lapsarian, but one of tortured piety, imagined sin and quiet desperation? Yet I do not think Moore is himself vitally interested in this problem. He is far more interested in the psychology and ritual of isolation. The character of Judith Hearne is shaped as much by isolation from the community as by isolation from the Church, and most of what I have said about her spiritual condition could be translated into social and psychological terms. One might even claim that she turns to the Church in total desperation (and, taking a stern view, with some hypocrisy) only when she has been rejected by the men and women around her and when her fantasies about marrying James Madden have come to grief. Church and community are really, in effect, one and the same in this novel, each a facet of the other, each judging and dismissing lonely individuals callously and cursorily. After the series of *faux pas* in the boarding-house, Moira O'Neill's, Earnscliffe Home and Father Quigley's, she is even more desperate for human intimacy. It is for this rather than for spiritual intimacy that she turns to the Church. When the Church fails her, she is forced to fall back upon her own meagre ritual resources, her own imaginary company : the picture of Aunt D'Arcy, the Sacred Heart and those winking shoe-eyes.

Solon T. Kimball, in his Introduction to a translation of van Gennep's *The Rites of Passage,* and thinking not of Ireland but of contemporary America, observes :

The critical problems of becoming male and female, of relations within the family, and of passing into old age are directly related to the devices which the society offers the individual to help him achieve the new adjustment. Somehow we seem to have forgotten this—or perhaps the ritual has become so completely individualistic that it is now found for many only in the privacy of the psycho-analyst's couch. The evidence, however, does not bear out the suggestion. It seems much more likely that one dimension of mental illness may arise because an increasing number of individuals are forced to accomplish their transitions alone and with private symbols.[9]

The psychological and ritual condition Kimball diagnoses is Judith Hearne's, and to a lesser extent Diarmuid Devine's, but the high social incidence he claims and the social cause he adduces, though pertinent to Moore's American novels, are not applicable to the Belfast novels. Moore's Belfast of the early 1950s is not contemporary urban America; Mrs Rice's boarding-house, rather, is a microcosm of the Ulster community as Moore sees it, and, on

9. Van Gennep, xvii–xviii.

another level, of Irish Catholic society. The community takes the time and trouble to visit recrimination on Judith Hearne once she has forced herself in her desperation upon it. We may contrast this with the fate of Mrs Tierney in *An Answer from Limbo* who can die in New York City without anyone paying the slightest attention. Judith Hearne is reduced to private symbolism not because the society has become de-ritualised but because it is *too* ritualised to accommodate anyone who cannot meet the strict demands of Church and community. Although it might most accurately be described as 'provincial', Moore's Belfast is a fairly primitive place. In consequence, Judith Hearne's painful and premature journey through crisis and social disgrace to a convent home has for most of us a grotesque, absurd, even surreal aspect which heightens the novel's drama and ensures that it is a much more powerful achievement than Moore's second and in a way anticlimactic work, *The Feast of Lupercal.*

(4)

Judith Hearne's reversion to private iconolatry, brought about by rejection and isolation, is explicable in the larger terms of Moore's sensibility which is ritualistic rather than theological or even ethical. Unlike Joyce in *A Portrait,* Moore is not primarily concerned with the truth-value of Catholicism but with its social and institutional extravagances. This is evident from *The Feast of Lupercal* : though the action takes place in a Catholic grammar school in Belfast (St Michan's in some editions, Ardath College in others), Moore's main structural reference is to a pagan festival rather than to Christian rites of spiritual passage. The novel further exploits the ironic disparity between individual desires and the ritual pound of penitential flesh the community and Church demand. Devine, like Judith Hearne, is prepared to sin in order to effect entrance to life's feast, but is unable to do so. And like Miss Hearne he is punished as much for his imaginary sins as for the actual peccadilloes he commits. He cannot make love to Una Clarke yet must still be pilloried in modern fashion—condemned by graffiti on school lavatory walls. An actual transgression, the betrayal of Una, is, like Miss Hearne's drinking, a transgression of weakness rather than of wanton strength. When he refuses to face up to his responsibilities as man, adult and friend by not telling Tim Heron in time that Una spent the night in his den, he brings down upon himself the wrath of a community which despises weakness as much as wrongdoing.

The scene in which Tim Heron canes Devine is the climax of the novel. It works on several levels. There is, first of all, minor irony in a schoolmaster being caned. More importantly, this scene concludes the ritual progression from Devine's betrayal through confession to the penance of bodily pain, a progression that is the structural spine, as it were, of both *Judith Hearne* and *The Feast of Lupercal*. But in the second novel, Moore has turned from Christian ritual to the ritual flagellation in the Lupercalia. Hallvard Dahlie focuses the irony of the scene upon the barren, sexless Devine being flogged in a re-enactment of the Roman fertility rite.[10] A stronger irony, and one that parallels the irony in *Judith Hearne*, emerges if, instead of seeing the original rite as a means of inducing fertility, we see it with Frazer as a means of purification. We can then view Devine's caning, with heavy irony, as a purging of sexual contamination. Wilhelm Mannhardt's theory that in the Lupercalia evil spirits are sent away by whipping also endows Moore's climax with appropriate irony. When the failure is punished by ostracism or violence for real or imagined transgression in such a way that the will and spirit of the community is reasserted, the victim has become a scapegoat. Heron's caning of Devine, in its obsessive severity, seems to transform the schoolmaster into such a figure, just as Judith Hearne seems to become a scapegoat in the fracas in Earnscliffe Home. At the moment of greatest persecution the scapegoat is at his most sacred and, dramatically, his most viable. The community endeavours to exorcise through punishment of the victim imagined threats to, and evil elements within, itself. In choosing the scapegoat as his central figure, the novelist in turn exposes and exorcises the rather different ills of the community; the moment of victimisation is also the moment of most intense social criticism. Finally, the caning must also be seen as a rite in which Devine can 'expiate' his real 'sin'. It is neither carnality nor betrayal. 'Why did I even fail to sin?' Devine asks himself. 'To fail to sin, perhaps that is my sin.' The final irony

10. Dahlie, 42.

M

is in the failure he shares with Judith Hearne, the failure to 'expiate' the worthless purity of frightened innocence.

Although Moore's picture of life in a Catholic grammar school is penetrating and his portrait of Devine's terrified failure is poignant, *The Feast of Lupercal* lacks the rich texture of the first novel, and substitutes fabrication for the inevitability with which *Judith Hearne* surges towards its conclusion. Devine is probably too slavishly a male version of Miss Hearne. Both characters change only in their recognition of their failure and, paradoxically, of their immutability. *Judith Hearne* begins and ends, aptly, with Miss Hearne's private objects of comfort and worship. Devine, making an appointment to see Una Clarke off to Dublin, knows he will never see her again. 'She was right, he couldn't change,' he tells himself. 'For the rest of his life he'd go on telling people what they wanted to hear.'

'Life itself', wrote van Gennep, 'means to separate and to be reunited, to change form and condition, to die and to be reborn. It is to act and to cease, to wait and rest, and then to begin acting again, but in a different way. And there are always new thresholds to cross.'[11] But not, we fear, for Devine and Judith Hearne, who languish in the limbo between becoming and having been. Like greening pebbles, they lie at the verge of a slow-moving stream.

(5)

Much of Moore's subsequent canon is concerned with the fate of those who, like Moore himself, have escaped from the kind of provincial, even primitive, communities that victimise Judith Hearne and Diarmuid Devine. The common denominator remains 'crisis': the central figure is forced to assess himself at a profoundly critical, even fatally critical, stage of life. But there are differences between those who languish at home in Ireland and those who try to make it in America. First of all, the Irish-American characters have come farther and are more preoccupied than Devine and Miss Hearne with the past and how it has moulded them. Whereas we learn a great deal about the early lives of Ginger Coffey, Mrs Tierney, Brendan Tierney, Mary Dunne and Fergus, we know relatively little about those of Miss

11. Van Gennep, 189.

Hearne and Devine, who seem to hover in a limbo that has no ascertainable beginning. Secondly, the later characters who have fled Ireland have had the will, strength and vitality to do so. This has lessened the ready-made pathos of his fiction, and forced Moore to reach more deeply into the minds of his main characters for his effects: the psychology of *Judith Hearne* is fairly rudimentary in comparison with that of *Fergus* or *I Am Mary Dunne,* though this does not make the latter two better novels. Thirdly, the later heroes are middle-class characters who leave Ireland because of cultural and commercial claustrophobia. They have a far greater potential for success than Moore's first two heroes, and in fact the implication of the fictional crisis shifts from the price of failure to the price of success. Whereas Judith Hearne and Devine are faced with intense isolation, the later characters are faced with the recognition that their success, their socialising and their friendships are all to an extent phoney and carry a heavy price-tag. These characters try in the course of the novels to find their real, and inevitably past, selves beneath the shiny surfaces of American life.

Regardless of their enhanced vigour and, occasionally, social status, Moore's central figures continue to be outsiders. The theme of 'ritual failure' extends with variation into the North American novels, but gives way to the cognate theme of 'ritual displacement'. Displacement occurs when the individual is unwilling or unable to perform the rites of incorporation into a new community and thereby find happiness and fulfilment. Both displacement and failure are conditions of isolation for, as van Gennep points out, the transitions we have to make within our own community parallel those we have to make if we move from one community to another. In the light of heavy Irish emigration over the decades, displacement might be regarded as a particularly Irish predicament. The psychic and spiritual passage through limbo of Moore's characters might, then, be seen as symbolising the passage of Irishmen and Irishwomen, across the centuries, from poverty, persecution and unfulfilled ambition to the New World.

If the nature of isolation has changed in Moore's North American novels, so too has the nature of society from which his heroes are excluded or apart. The social reasons Kimball adduces for the retreat of individuals into private symbolism now hold for Moore's American fiction, which becomes increasingly less Irish and more cosmopolitan. It is almost as if Moore's succession of novels traces the growing fortunes in a new continent of one hypothetical immigrant who has travelled from Judith Hearne's Ballymena through Devine's Belfast or Ginger Coffey's Dublin to Canada and from there to the United States. All along, though, the crippling image of Ireland stays alive, even in Moore's sixth novel, *I Am Mary Dunne*, whose only Irish connection is the titular character's Irish extraction. In his seventh novel, *Fergus*, the memory of Ireland is once more bright in the mind of the central figure, and *Catholics* is actually set in Ireland, though an Ireland of about twenty years from now.

The Luck of Ginger Coffey (1960), Moore's third novel, balances the two themes of ritual failure and displacement and is thus a pivotal work in the canon. Coffey does not fail sexually, as do Judith Hearne and Diarmuid Devine, but rather in his inability to carve out for himself a successful career in a world which deems professional success—something which is to preoccupy Moore after this novel—a desirable form of social advancement. As a result, he almost loses his wife and daughter to a more successful man.

Coffey attempts to conceal the failure of his life in Dublin by presenting a fraudulent *vita* to the Montreal employment agent, reminding us that he is, unlike the straitlaced Miss Hearne and Mr Devine, a bluffer and petty con-man. What, he asks himself, were the true facts of his life?

Facts : James Francis Coffey, failed B.A.; former glorified secretary to the managing director of a distillery; former joeboy in the advertising department after he was kicked downstairs; former glorified secretary to the manager of a knitwear factory; failed sales representative of three concerns in this new and promised land. Facts : husband of a woman who wanted out before it was too late; father of a fourteen-year-old girl who ignored him. (p. 81)

For Ginger Coffey failure in Ireland breeds failure in Canada, creating in him a besieged state of mind in which paranoia takes root. The 'CRIPPLE MATE CASE' he follows on newsstand headlines is a soap-opera fantasy of self-pity in which Coffey is the victim of a conspiracy, guilty only of an incapacity he cannot help. Self-pity gives way to infantile regression during which he envies his child neighbour for living in a world of toys where no demands are made and no responsibilities are exacted. Moore presents a cruel symbol of this regression when he has Coffey find a job at Tiny Ones Inc., a Montreal nappy service. The reversion to fantasy in the face of failure and bewilderment was a favourite resort also of Judith Hearne and Devine. In all three novels the social repercussions of failure are the same—exclusion from the community and the retraction of roles for the failure to play. Because he is not willing to take a job unequal to his ambitions, Ginger Coffey finds his roles as husband and lover, father and breadwinner, challenged and for a time seriously threatened. As in the two previous novels, the failure is relatively minor but the repercussions immense.

The Luck of Ginger Coffey, then, like its predecessors, is a novel about the price society exacts for failure. In each of the three novels there is a key scene in which the confrontation between victim and society is brutally apparent. In *Judith Hearne* it is the scene in which Judith is forcibly ejected from the convent home for having a bottle of gin; in *The Feast of Lupercal,* the scene in which Devine is caned. In *Ginger Coffey* it is the scene in which Coffey is charged with indecent exposure after urinating in a doorway, and the subsequent courtroom scene. In these two scenes, as in those from the other novels, there is injustice at work as society misinterprets and overreacts to—comically in *Ginger Coffey*—a minor transgression. But in one important respect, Coffey's humiliation is different from that endured by Devine and Miss Hearne. Ginger Coffey has been a failure in Ireland and has decided to try his luck in Canada, with the result that to the limitations of his own small talents is added the task of weathering the formidable if informal initiation rites facing him as a New Canadian. He brings with him small credentials: the slap-happy heartiness, transparent manner and sheepskin-jacket mentality of a bluffer who imagines himself a Dublin squire. He finds, alas, that these are flimsy credentials in a country preoccupied with hard talk, hard work and equally hard cash. Only by lying can he survive and even then it is a precarious survival. In one sense the novel is Ginger Coffey's education into the social and economic ways of Canada: it is no coincidence that the man to whom he almost loses his wife is a nattily dressed, smooth-talking, get-ahead native Canadian against whom New Canadians have to compete. The novel is strewn with New Canadians who found this competition too stiff and who went under—old Billy the Irishman, for instance, in whom Coffey sees a terrifying pre-figuration of himself. And yet, in another sense, Coffey is Canada herself, uncertain, callow, occupying that limbo between Dominion and sovereign Republic, between the old country and the United States, between the promise and the fulfilment of nationhood. Among the pub-frequenting proof-readers whose ranks Coffey joins, this is a favourite if obscurely understood topic. 'Poor old Canada,' laments one, 'not even a flag to call its own' (an indignity removed since the novel's publication). 'They sneeze in the States and we get pneumonia here,' observes another. 'Greatest mistake this country ever made was not joining the United States.' The same men defend Canada vigorously when Coffey denigrates it, thus exhibiting the ambivalence associated in the novel with Canada herself. Perhaps these two interpretations—Coffey both as hapless immigrant and as Canada —are not as far apart as they seem : the education of Coffey into the ways of a new and brutal world might be seen as the education of Canada into such a world. I imagine that such a view might strengthen the claim that in *Ginger Coffey* Moore has produced Canada's best novel to date.[12] This claim, however, ought not unjustly inflate this modest novel's reputation.

Part of Coffey's difficulty in adjusting to Canadian life is due to the fact that he has not separated himself fully or decisively from his past in Ireland. And so the mores of Irish provincialism continue to haunt him. They are even embodied in the figure of Eileen Kerrigan, the Irish immigrant who recognises Coffey from the old country as he stands, mortified, in his Tiny Ones uniform. And the patronising admonitions of his former parish priest ('If you burn your boats, you'll sink. You'll sink in this world and you'll sink in the next.') stay with him, illustrating graphically the vicious parochialism of a people who both despise and envy those who attempt to shake off the spiritual and moral shackles that bind.

But if Coffey cannot blot out the past, he can at least ensure

12. A claim made by Ludwig, p. 13.

a future. By the novel's end, he has successfully performed the rites of incorporation—hardship, humiliation, temporary loss of social and personal identity—into Canadian society. The indecent exposure charge and the comic-nightmarish courtroom scene can be viewed as the last 'initiation rite' Coffey must endure before becoming a genuine Canadian. The novel is therefore more optimistic than the two previous novels because it ends, though Coffey may not recognise it, on a note of modest success. But of course acceptance into Canadian society is only the beginning. In order to start afresh (and having won back his wife and his freedom, he receives emotional and legal warrant for this), he must drastically lower his standards. To this extent the ending spells resignation, though a healthier resignation than Judith Hearne's or Diarmuid Devine's. Whereas their resignation is the abandonment of all hope, he refuses to countenance total defeat. 'Life was the victory, wasn't it?' he asks himself with characteristic melodrama. 'Going on was the victory. For better or for worse, for richer or for poorer, in sickness and in health until—.' Like Judith Hearne and Devine he has come to know his limitations. But his are fewer and less crippling. He has his wife and his daughter and the genuine hope of a job befitting his meagre talents. He has stopped, acknowledged, and is ready to begin again in a new way.

(6)

If in *Ginger Coffey* Moore turned the pathos of his first two novels to modestly successful comic advantage, in *An Answer from Limbo* (1962) he opened up markedly new terrain and in so doing wrote what was then his best novel since *Judith Hearne*. *An Answer from Limbo* was Moore's first novel to appeal directly to Americans, set as it is in New York City (where Moore himself lived for some years after leaving Canada), with mostly American characters, dialogue in American-English and, a new departure, dashes of successful lovemaking amid the predictable failures.

The novel has three plot-lines, only one of which can be regarded strictly as an extension of the themes and motifs we have noted in the author's early work. The question whose answer echoes from the titular limbo is that confronting Brendan Tierney, the struggling writer who has emigrated from Belfast:

is he prepared to sacrifice anybody or anything for the sake of his work? He is, and the resulting emotional abandonment of his wife, children and mother constitutes one of the main crises of the novel. Behind the question of emotional sacrifice is another : should he sacrifice integrity and quality in order to gain instant success on the popular market? Brendan Tierney would be diminished as a character were we to see his plight merely in the ritual terms we have applied to Moore's central characters up to now, for among other things *An Answer from Limbo* is Moore's *Kunstlerroman*. As such, it is a successful evocation of the pressures and problems that face any struggling writer whose art is capable of lucrative prostitution, Moore's twist to this theme being a quick-blooded protrait of the New York publishing scene, a portrait sketched with something between the cynicism of the ambitious writer and the saucer-eyed wonder of the provincialite.

I am not especially concerned here with this aspect of the novel, nor with the book's second plot-line : Jane Tierney's lapse into infidelity during her search for a dark ravisher. This is the weakest part of the novel, for her dark ravisher, Vito Italiano, never in name or deed rises above the level of crude caricature. This might ironically reflect upon the kind of woman this writer's frustrated wife becomes, but no amount of intended irony could compensate for oversimplified character-isation, especially when genuine characters are being created alongside Italiano. The figure of Jane Tierney is better done and she seems in some respects a warm-up for a later, even better creation, Mary Dunne.

It is the novel's third plot-line that links *An Answer from Limbo* solidly with Moore's prior works : Mrs Tierney's passage from Ireland and her subsequent destruction at the hands of an alien culture. Brendan's mother, who shares equal billing in the novel with her son, differs from Moore's previous inhabitants of limbo in having been successful in worldly terms. She was pretty when younger, reflects Brendan at the close of the novel, she was married to a successful man, was well-off and widely loved. 'Yet,' he reminds himself, 'she died alone in the limbo of a strange apartment and lay dead until, by accident, a stranger found her.' (p. 316) Mrs Tierney's material success is not the only difference between herself and Moore's previous heroes. While the latter attempt to escape the bondage of their past, Mrs Tierney tries to preserve hers so that she may not be absorbed by an alien society. Aptly, her life ends with the ritual affirmation of her past in prayer and supplication and an implicit denial of the new world she found so hostile.

Mrs Tierney is a more admirable character than Ginger Coffey, if only because she makes an attempt to re-establish in New York the important values of her life in Belfast. This cannot be explained away simply in terms of her age and inflexibility as against Coffey's comparative youth and adaptability. Coffey never did and never will have values that promote any kind of spiritual well-being. He is, as he says, 'neither fish nor fowl, great sinner nor saint'. This typically hand-me-down Coffey metaphor is as far as he is prepared to pursue the matter. On the other hand, Mrs Tierney is a devout Catholic who suddenly finds herself in her son's godless home in a godless society when Brendan brings her across to America to look after the children while his wife works and he writes. Intolerant and atavistic, Mrs Tierney is the perfect foil to Brendan and to Jane, whose fashionable and facile tolerance renders her less unattractive to the reader than she would have appeared in any of Moore's previous novels. Alarmed at the spiritual condition of her part-Jewish grandchildren, she surreptitiously baptises them. The discovery of her act results in the final estrangement between mother and son. Neither her God nor her piety is welcome in the chic New York apartment and she goes off to die alone with her empty pleas for help and her invocations to an ancestral God. Her lonely death—a familiar Moore victimisation scene—three thousand miles from home, crippled by a fall in a strange apartment, is a cruel irony for a woman who sets great store by the primitive delights of community and faith. It is an irony compounded by the fact that she dies at the foot of a blaring television set, as though it were some Christian or pagan divinity instead of a mass-producible apostle of amorality.

Mrs Tierney occupies a limbo that ends only in death. It is an emotional limbo, caught as she is in the emotional crossfire between her son and his wife. It is a cultural limbo, a limbo of the unreal in which the amorphous content of life is reduced by American technology to the cold efficiency of manmade forms. Her dream of such a limbo is also a dream of that spiritual limbo occupied, according to the Church, by 'those souls who did not merit hell and its eternal punishments but could not enter heaven before the Redemption (the father's Limbo)'.[13]

> They brought Pilate. He was Sir Cedric Hardwicke. He called for water and washed his hands. He smiled. He screamed. Two angels cast him down to hell. 'Look over there,' the judge said. 'That is Limbo.' She looked and it was a quiet place like an airport lounge with green plants that were not real and food on a buffet that was not real food. There were many old men there, old men in white robes with long white beards. They were the just men who had died before the coming of Christ. They sat hopeless and silent, for they knew they must stay forever in oblivion. (pp. 210–11)

'The father's Limbo' becomes in her dream 'the children's Limbo' that awaited little Lisa and Liam before she baptised them. The dream is clearly set in New York airport, an appropriate dream-metaphor for the godless unreality of that city.

In *An Answer from Limbo* Moore has abandoned the theme of failure and concentrated upon that of displacement. Like Ginger Coffey, Mrs Tierney suffers the isolation of the newcomer, but unlike him she is unable to free-fall and to regain control of her life. For her, Octavio Paz's remark is only too true : 'Permanent exile, then, is the same as a death sentence.'[14] As always, Moore is critical of the community and society that victimise his character. Mrs Tierney is destroyed because she refuses to abandon the past and its values in order to gain entrance to the world of Brendan and Jane. That is not to say that Moore assents to her values; quite clearly he would reject many of them as he did in *Judith Hearne* and *The Feast of Lupercal.* It is rather a matter of comparative evil, as if during his Greenwich Village stint Moore found something even worse than Irish smallmindedness : the wilful jettisoning of integrity, dignity and belief. And so for the first time in Moore's work, primitivism and provincialism become virtues, bulwarks against the erosive hypocrisies of modern, cosmopolitan life. He has since fabulised these virtues and vices in *Catholics.*

13. *New Catholic Encyclopaedia*, VIII, New York 1967, 762.
14. Paz, *The Labyrinth of Solitude*, 206.

(7)

The theme of ritual displacement is extended even further in Moore's sixth novel, *I Am Mary Dunne* (1968), a *tour de force* and perhaps Moore's most crafted and accomplished work after *Judith Hearne*. Moore establishes in *Mary Dunne* an analogical series of movements which represent, literally and metaphorically, the stages leading to the crisis of limbo. Mary's husbands and suitors—Jimmy Phelan, Ernie Truelove, Hatfield Bell, Terence Lavery—constitute the series of roles Mary has had to fill, and at the same time roughly parallel her wanderings from Nova Scotia to Toronto, to Montreal and to New York City. These phases of her life she recalls during and after a day's activities that provide the chronology of her recollections in bed that same evening. *Mary Dunne,* reminiscent of but more structured than Joyce's Molly Bloom soliloquy, is a cleverly wrought novel and, less spacious than *An Answer from Limbo,* a return to the claustrophobic confines of a woman's fevered mind where it all began for Moore.

But the differences between Mary Dunne and Judith Hearne are several and large. For one thing, whereas Judith Hearne is imprisoned in her past and her unchanging identity, Mary Dunne struggles throughout the novel to find one identity among many in which she can heave to and seek refuge. This highlights one crucial difference between failure and displacement in Moore's novels. The failures, Judith Hearne and Diarmuid Devine, find themselves unable to change and to move forward. Theirs is the limbo of stasis. The displaced, Mrs Tierney and Mary Dunne, find their continuum of identity splitting and strive to mend the breach, Mary Dunne through a neurotic recapitulation of the past, Mrs Tierney through a sense of the past bolstered by her religious belief. Theirs is the limbo of instability. Ginger Coffey is the transitional figure in all this : the failure who forces himself to change by putting his identity up for grabs in a new country.

The threat to Mary Dunne's identity is much greater than that to Mrs Tierney's, though it does not have fatal results. She is now Mary Lavery but she was Mary Bell and before that Mary Phelan. Each marriage required of her a different role to satisfy each husband : 'I play an ingenue role, with special shadings demanded by each suitor. For Jimmy I had to be a tomboy; for Hat I must look like a model : he admired elegance. Terence wants to see me as Irish : sulky, laughing, wild. And me, how do I see me, who is that me I create in mirrors, the dressing-table me, the self I cannot put a name to in the Golden Door Beauty Salon?' (p. 41) Similarly, she accuses herself of obscuring her real identity behind a mask in each of her careers : 'Weren't they just roles I acted out? Even acting itself.' She has been student, writer, actress, provincialite, wealthy cosmopolite moving in sophisticated New York theatrical circles. She has cast off and put on so often that she seems to live between roles as frequently as she does within them.

Her upward social mobility is paralleled by a kind of upward sexual mobility. Two things haunt her : the memory of her father's death during an act of adultery, causing her to fear her own strong sexuality; secondly, her guilt-inducing treatment of her second husband, Hatfield Bell. Among the men in Mary's recollections it is Bell who dominates, eclipsing Mary's current husband as a character and force in her life, though it is with Lavery that she claims to have found sexual and emotional happiness. Mary outsexed Bell as she did Phelan before him. The inadequacies of her men she long believed were due to her own unattractiveness, and the feeling persists in nightmare. Her movements from place to place and from man to man can therefore be viewed as a quest after sexual and emotional stability and contentment.

But if Mary has achieved material and sexual success as Mary Lavery, why does she affirm her identity at the end of the novel, and after intercourse with Terence, as Mary Dunne? Has she, like Mrs Tierney in fantasy and death, returned safely to her origins and thus resolved the identity crisis of the novel?

A proper reading of the novel's ending is crucial for an understanding of what Moore is trying to do. Mary's crisis apparently lasts but one day, but we are to assume, I think, that this identity crisis, though precipitated by premenstrual tension, is an accumulation of the smaller identity crises of her past. How we interpret the ending will therefore determine how successfully we think Mary, postmenstrually, will pull out of this biggest crisis of her life. Here is the last part of the last ringing sentence of the novel :

I know who I am, my mother said tonight that I am her daughter and while she lives I will be that, I will not change, I am the daughter of Daniel Malone Dunne and Eileen Martha Ring, I am Mary Patricia Dunne, I was christened that and there is nothing wrong with my heart or with my mind : in a few hours I will begin to bleed, and until then I will hold on, I will remember what Mama told me, I am her daughter, I have not changed, I remember who I am and say it over and over and over, I am Mary Dunne, I am Mary Dunne, I am Mary Dunne. (p. 251)

Dahlie sees this as an act of desperate affirmation, believing that 'in the act of remembering her past, she attains the identity spelled out by the book's title : the identities she has temporarily assumed as Mary Phelan, as Mary Bell, as Maria, and now as Mary Lavery, cannot obscure the only unchangeable fact about her, that she is, and always will be, Mary Dunne . . . no legal or social vicissitudes can alter what she was born—Mary Dunne.' Elsewhere he calls Mary Dunne's affirmation an 'attainment of calm'.[15]

Dahlie misses the central irony of the novel. What looks like an affirmation is an *attempt* to affirm, not at all the same thing. Mary's repetition of her identity, in the anxiety of imminent menstruation, is like a captured soldier's repetition of his name, rank and serial number—affirmation of a formalised, legal identity that satisfies neither himself nor his captors. Moreover, Mary's dependence upon what her mother has said in a brief telephone conversation testifies to her utter insecurity, not to any degree of certainty whatever. This 'affirmation' caps the irony of the novel : in her current relationship with Lavery, Mary has found emotional and sexual satisfaction as well as material success, yet in a crisis she hearkens back to a past that she cannot bother to recollect in detail. For it is not Mary Dunne we come to know but rather Mary Phelan and, supremely, Mary Bell. We know Mary Dunne only as the schoolgirl who suggested to her teacher that the Cartesian maxim, *cogito ergo sum,* might better be rendered *memento ergo sum.* This is a curious emendation on the part of a child; we might even on the strength of it view Mary's subsequent life as a self-fulfilling prophecy, as if she had received philosophical licence during childhood to

15. Dahlie, 106, 115; the second Dahlie quotation is from 'Moore's New Perspective', *Canadian Literature* (Autumn 1968), 83.

wander whither and with whomever she pleased in the comforting knowledge that her identity remained safe at home in Butchersville, Nova Scotia. But even though she holds under duress of premenstrual tension to her Cartesian modification, her life and her recollections of that life disprove it. She is Mary Dunne, but is also each of her subsequent identities, not at once but successively. She is, in fact, the changeling she fears herself to be.

(8)

It is tempting to view Moore's North American fiction, with Hallvard Dahlie, as more optimistic than his Belfast fiction. The shift from parochial to cosmopolitan settings and from the burdensome piety of the chief Belfast characters to Mary Dunne's practical morality would seem to represent a movement from bondage to emancipation. Yet we should not simplify the direction Moore's work has taken. For instance, there are significant interruptions in the optimistic flow of the canon. *Ginger Coffey* is clearly more optimistic than *Mary Dunne,* and Mrs Tierney, a later and more sympathetic creation than Coffey, never in spirit leaves the restrictive world Coffey flees. Even more important than these interruptions is the discovery by Moore's latest characters that the absence of community identity and dogma is an even more terrifying predicament than their smothering presence. The world that Mrs Tierney rejects—a faithless, impersonal world—is the world Mary Dunne inhabits. Mary's response to her 'emancipation' is to deny it by mistakenly asserting that her identity resides in her beginnings. Yet it is clear that her problem, in so far as it is not merely premenstrual, can only be solved if she stays with Terence, establishes roots, forgets her past and constructs a future.

This is a difficult task in a society such as Mary's in which the ritual means to aid the individual in his transitions towards fulfilment have all but withered away, in a society where the individual is forced to impose past rituals and private symbols upon a hostile and impersonal present. Yet there is little in Moore's fiction to suggest that happiness and identity lie outside ordinary human relationships or group values, neither does he suggest that such things are no longer possible, even though his chief characters have difficulty in achieving them. For this reason

I hesitate to call even Mary Dunne an existential outsider. The crises weathered by Moore's later characters may be *aggravated* by life in a dehumanising cosmopolitan society but they are *caused* by the radical difference between that society and the provincial, even rather primitive communities from which the characters hail. It is this difference, the sense of limbo, that throws up all the fantasies and ghosts and upsetting memories. We might even regard Moore's most recent novels autobiographically as his own imposition of past rituals and private symbols upon the fluid impersonalisations of his life in the United States. In evidence we might recall that one of the characters tells the titular hero of *Fergus* (1971) that literature is for Fergus a substitute for religious belief. *Fergus* in one sense takes social displacement a step further than *Mary Dunne,* for it is set in Southern California to where Moore himself moved after New York City. Los Angeles, as one character observes, is postpossessions, post-capitalist, a place in which total artificiality, total efficiency and total depersonalisation seem to be the objectives of life. Against the backdrop of this society is set Fergus's memories of childhood and adolescence in Belfast. The novel also extends the aesthetic and ethical conflicts which Brendan Tierney faced in *An Answer from Limbo.* Fergus is Tierney with two novels behind him, a writer who has safely avoided the tantalising bait of popularity but who now faces an even greater temptation—that of prostituting his art for big money in the Hollywood dream-factory, of being a glorified joeboy in a film studio, to borrow one of Ginger Coffey's wisecracks.

On the other hand, *Fergus* is a kind of return : having swung as far away from Ireland as he could in Mary Dunne while maintaining tenuous links with the old country, Moore in *Fergus* begins a sharp curve back towards his native island. *Fergus* in fact is more of a re-hash than an advance. The hero is a familiar Moore figure in two respects : firstly, in being at a critical age (which in Moore's novels tends to be in the late thirties or early forties); secondly, in being, like most of the later creations, a man of talent and integrity who yet falls short of Moore's own personal standards. This last gives Moore's treatment of his chief characters a slightly patronising, there-but-for-the-grace-of-God tone.

Fergus's particular crisis is this : he awaits the reaction of the studio to a rewritten script; when the order comes down for him to change the ending, he neglects to call the studio as arranged and so by losing the assignment prevents himself from selling-out. It is a personal victory by default and one dwarfed by a much larger struggle in which his victory is a good deal more debatable. He fails to call the studio because he spends the day embroiled in confronting his past in Belfast—being judged by it, coming to terms with it, receiving from it what emotional and moral warrant it will bestow upon him. The past takes the embodied forms of his parents, his relatives, former school-teachers, priests and schoolfriends, some of them as they are now, some of them as they were, some of them resurrected from the dead. This exteriorising of guilt, hope, regret, anger and frustrated ambition would seem to have developed as a device out of Judith Hearne's winking shoe-eyes, Sacred Heart and Aunt D'Arcy, Gavin Burke's Divine Infant and two Angels and Mary Dunne's Mad Twin—the whole fictional apparatus by which Moore has expressed and disguised a seared Catholic conscience.

The figures from the past are perhaps over-familiar to Moore readers. There is Dr Keogh from *The Feast of Lupercal* (less benevolent now, and Fergus canes him in fantasy, thereby ex-acting sweet revenge for poor Devine); Paddy Donlon playing a similar role to Ted Ormsby in *An Answer from Limbo* and Freddy Hargreaves in *The Emperor of Ice-Cream;* Moore him-self as a young man out of *The Emperor of Ice-Cream;* and Fergus's parents who closely resemble Brendan Tierney's parents. The most interesting apparition is Fergus's father who gives Moore the opportunity of exploring the father-son relationship that lightly haunts several of the novels and is dramatised here so painfully that one suspects the private exorcism of guilt or regret, emotions naturally sharpened in a son who achieved fame and relative fortune only after his father's death and so was robbed of the chance to impress the one person above all whom he wanted to impress.

The self-indulgence of the novel is partially offset by Fergus's charming naïvety while living in cynical America, a naïvety which Moore himself seems not to have lost—he remains fascinated by his adopted country, he is still in love with the idea of making it as a writer in the United States, still invoking the names of great writers, Joyce and Faulkner, and wondering like some undergraduate how they would have handled certain situations. But though the interlocking dialogue between the ghosts and Fergus and between Fergus and the 'real' characters is interesting, there is no technical development in *Fergus;* the dialogue and descriptions are adequate but no more, and the book finally fails to escape its basic narcissism. The advance in theme and setting is so slight that a new departure was obviously called for after the novel's composition. Beyond southern California there is no frontier of Western decadence to be crossed, no society more dehumanised in which a Moore character can endure anomie. Nor can the dead and the remembered in Ireland be made any more alive—as accusers, prosecutors and judges—than the embodied apparitions in *Fergus* who walk, talk and leave physical proof of their existence. The problem was to find a new perspective in which Moore's abiding concern —the quality and shape of an emigrant Irishman's relationship to the past in Ireland and to the present in the most 'advanced' Western society—could be dramatically rekindled. At one point Fergus says acidly of the Irish : 'A nation of masturbators under priestly instruction.' 'All right, that will do,' checks one of the apparitions. 'You have a case of myopia. Unable to take the long view.' *Catholics* (1972) tries to give us a long view of the most important institution in Ireland, the Catholic Church, and at the same time a long and singular view of Western society.

(9)

The literary pilgrimage of Brian Moore which we have charted —and the metaphor is ironically apt in the light of his latest novel—crosses, at this point in time, the current attraction of the young and disaffected to romantic revolution (explored by Moore in his 'non-fiction novel' about the kidnapping and murder of Canadian cabinet minister Pierre Laporte, *The Revolution Script,* 1972) and their simultaneous nostalgia for pre-bourgeois, pre-technological certainties of faith and ritual. Because the setting of *Catholics* is futuristic, an island monastery off the Kerry coast at the close of the twentieth century, it could be thought that Moore is simply using the book as a platform on which to debate with himself current social and theological topics. It is true that, like many futuristic novels, *Catholics* is a

N

conflict of theses rather than of character and so loses power and conviction to this extent. But if in its spare hundred pages it bags none of the hares it starts, we at least have the brief spectacle of the quarry in full flight across an unexpected landscape. We must also view the novel on one level as Moore's attempt to dig up the roots of the kind of Catholicism under which he and his early characters suffered. It is almost as if Moore is asking himself whether the Catholic Church he and his characters know was always the over-organised, impersonal, superficially ritualised institution it appears in his novels. It is thus in the nature of a return journey but one that begins not from the present but from some point in the last quarter of this century, which enables Moore to project his view of Western society beyond the decadence anatomised in *Mary Dunne* and *Fergus* on through to the technocratic future. With a ring of vengeance, Moore's view of Ireland and the West, from penal days to the threshold of the twenty-first century, is a long view indeed.

Catholics envisages a world of rampant ecumenism in which the liturgical *fait accompli* of vernacularisation has been followed by the abandonment of private confession and the demotion of the sacraments to purely symbolic status. At a time when Christianity stands on the brink of 'interpenetration' with Buddhism, the central ecumenical powers cannot tolerate the spectacle of this island monastery, newly discovered by a television crew, conducting Mass in the pre-1966, sometimes even eighteenth-century manner (at a Mass rock) like some liturgical coelacanth. Orders go out in the pocket of a denim-fatigued American plenipotentiary, Kinsella, and the opposition he meets from the Abbot and other monks constitutes the novel's slight drama.

In Moore's future, ecumenism—a kind of Common Market of Christianity—is seen as a dilution, even betrayal, of a revolutionary ideal embodied in the offstage figure of Hartmann whose memory Kinsella worships. Hartmann (future avatar of today's radical American priests?) worked in South America and was a priest for whom faith meant revolutionary altruism and dedication but neither miracles nor mystery. Hartmann, in fine, is indistinguishable from Che Guevara.

If Hartmann, struggling for the good of mankind, has been betrayed by mere bureaucratic reform (of which Kinsella is a well-meaning but degenerate example), so too is the bloated supermarketry of today's Church seen by Moore as a betrayal of an older, different ideal. An encounter with such super-marketry while on a pilgrimage to Lourdes years ago (i.e. around our own time) has cost the Abbot his faith just as, we might add, its more primitive Irish version (all wind and brimstone) helped alienate Judith Hearne and Diarmuid Devine. The betrayed ideal is located in the monastic crudity of the rocky West and is represented in the image Moore invokes of the priest of penal days struggling for men's souls amidst social strife. To use a metaphor not in *Catholics,* the penal priest daily per-forming miracles is like the still, mysteried eye of a hurricane while Hartmann, two centuries later, opts to work instead amid the turbulent spirals of that hurricane. Moore offers us our choice in the definition and expression of faith.

It is a choice not just for Catholics but for all of us, for while *Catholics* is about the changing ideals and realities of one church, it is also a parable of what is happening to Western society in its political aspect. The Church's transition from being an inflexible, self-referable power structure (in which there were, and in Irish Catholicism still are, crevices for eccentrics and rebels to hide) to being a bargaining, reformist, dehumanised organisation mirrors the wider transition from colonialism to centralisation, EEC-style. Is there gain? As communications shrink our world (fittingly it is a TV crew who discover the monastery) we grow apart as people : whatever else it is, McLuhan's global village is no village. To accommodate ourselves to others may be to diminish ourselves : whatever else it does, ecumenism involves a dilution in faith and ritual.

This is what Moore is saying but what he is not adequately dramatising. Neither the plot nor the characters fulfils the pro-mise of their exposition. Even if the novel calls for him to be rather faceless, Kinsella is not a credible character and his Irish extraction, unpursued, seems gratuitous. Moore's prose is too loose, his similes and metaphors too inexpensive (one character looks 'like Dylan Thomas', Kerry is a 'Beckett landscape'), and his structure too tight and shortwinded : the technique of having brief scenes like camera angles, pioneered in *The Revolution Script,* is insufficient for proper character development. *Catholics* has the plot of a novel, the scene structure and dialogue of a short story, and the relation of action to theme of a parable or fable. Given this, it is not surprising that it cannot solve its own problems and that the attempt to combine the theme of apostasy from Moore's first novel, *Judith Hearne,* with that of revolution from the later *The Revolution Script* seems makeshift in these hundred pages.

Withal, Moore has stumbled on what I take to be a literary mother lode in tomorrow's bureaucratic desert, the nostalgia for religious faith and ritual already felt by the young. Moore has only begun to work a fictionally minor vein, and when the theme and fictional attitude develop, there will be, especially in Ireland, wry irony in the sight of yesterday's apostates becoming today's nostalgics. Yet there has been only limited and tactical recantation on Moore's part. The nostalgia that informs *Catholics* is not for the kind of Catholic society that is the antagonist in his early novels—hypocritical, repressive, self-advertising and puritanical—and which Moore sees as destined to pass away once the most remote and backward reaches, notably in Ireland, are discovered by the prying tentacles of bureaucracy and technology. His nostalgia is for something that only flickers vulnerably today—that still, mysteried eye shorn of pomp that was once the genuine spiritual centre of social and religious ritual. From this we will all, and therefore none of us, be outsiders tomorrow.

In the figure of the Abbot, sadly underdeveloped, are these notions adumbrated. For the Abbot the blandness of ecumenical ritual promises to be the perfect camouflage for his apostasy. We can see how the figure of the Abbot might have grown in the mind of the author out of Fergus and Brendan Tierney. The fear of falling short of his early ideals of faith and integrity haunts him as it does them, but unlike them he has been spared the purgatory of continuously selling-out because society (in the guise of Church liturgy) has diluted its ideals to the consistency of his own practical standards, thereby permitting him to conceal himself amid the surrounding mediocrity. Tomorrow, Moore seems to be saying, we shall lose even the right to be outsiders, with all the uniqueness and individuality as well as loneliness that that condition implies. Tomorrow there will be no outsiders because the notion of ritual and social failure will be eradicated. So too will the idea of being rooted, of belonging and expressing primary loyalty to a community, a place, a tradition. *Catholics,* were it expanded and developed, might be subtitled *The Death of the Outsider,* and with it Moore has come full circle in his treatment of a certain character-type. The novel is a requiem not only for societies such as today's Ireland where there are outsiders like Judith Hearne and Diarmuid Devine, but also for societies such as yesterday's Ireland where if there were no outsiders it was because the genuineness of ritual and mystery enveloped everyone. The New York of *Mary Dunne* and the Los Angeles of *Fergus* have advanced and spread, linking up with the bureaucratic, ecumenical capitals of Europe in pursuit of the perfect, dehumanised society. In *Catholics* the hoary description of Ireland as 'the last outpost' has been endowed with new and ironic meaning.

But of course there will continue to be outsiders, even if Moore's vision transpires, individuals already immortalised in Kafka, Camus and others, characters for whom the salve of fantasy, the refuge of memory and the delights of community are no longer available as they are, in practice or theory, to Moore's heroes. In conception if not in actual characterisation, Moore's Abbot is the closest the author has come to creating an existential outsider, but only at the price of ignoring the real Ireland of today, a price reflected in the novel's spare, parabolic form. Moore's best characters are cast adrift, but the success of the novels in which they figure depends not on the modest quality of Moore's thought but on the rich rendering of the community or society from which the outsiders have become unanchored. That rich rendering is to be found in *An Answer from Limbo, I Am Mary Dunne* and, above all, in *The Lonely Passion of Judith Hearne.*

6

STRANGE EXILE

By 1800 planted Ulster was the wealthiest part of Ireland, and the most significant effect of its prosperity was, according to one historian, 'the emergence of a strong middle class, at a time when such a class scarcely existed in any other part of Ireland'.[1] While the landowning class was closely identified with the Established Church, the rising mercantile middle class in the North was for the most part Presbyterian.[2] From this division of the spoils Northern Catholics were socially and economically debarred. Of the nineteenth century, one historian writes : 'There was in Ulster no Catholic aristocrat, no Catholic landowner, of any consequence, and very few Catholic professional men.'[3] This is reflected even in twentieth-century fiction, where well-off Catholic middle-class families are uncommonly represented, and even then they seem precarious and freakish—Friel's Hogan family in 'Foundry House' or Kiely's Chesney family in *The Captain with the Whiskers*.

The numerical strength of the planters and their waspish sense of independence were factors in there being no Northern Protestant Ascendancy comparable to that in the South. As a result, the Big House in Ulster fiction is not the potent symbol or richly textured backdrop it is in Southern fiction, though as we shall see large houses play their own important role in Northern Protestant fiction. In some Catholic writers, e.g. McLaverty, we often see the Big House from a distance, usually as a ruined hulk. In Bullock we glimpse it operating efficiently

1. J. C. Beckett, 'Ulster Society before 1800', in *Ulster since 1800,* ed. T. W. Moody and J. C. Beckett, London 1957, 20.
2. J. C. Beckett in *ibid.,* 22–3.
3. David Kennedy, 'The Catholic Church', in *ibid.,* 174.

but still see it through the eyes of an outsider. For a portrait of the Northern Ascendancy (albeit in decline) from the viewpoint of an insider, we need to turn to Joyce Cary's two Irish novels, *Castle Corner* and *A House of Children*. Such was Cary's sense of family history that he was able to flavour these novels with nostalgia not only for the Victorian past but also for the more distant graciousness of the eighteenth-century from which he saw the Victorian order as a falling-off. The decline continued in his own immediate family, and because his father was the first Cary for generations to follow a profession,[4] Joyce Cary provides a link between the true Ascendancy and the Protestant middle class that has dominated the North since 1800.

It is to writers of this latter class that we are likely to be referring when we speak of an Anglo-Irish strain in Ulster fiction, i.e. educated Protestants (whether Anglicans or Dissenters) whose social standards and values were established in England and who were as likely as not educated there. One thinks of such sons of professional, clerical or merchant fathers as C. S. Lewis, Louis MacNeice, Forrest Reid, Stephen Gilbert and George Buchanan, all educated in English or English-orientated public schools. This century it has become irrelevant, socially and literarily, whether the Protestant middle class is Church of Ireland or Nonconformist : a typically ambivalent figure is Forrest Reid whose father was a Presbyterian merchant and whose mother was Church of Ireland, a member of the distinguished English Parr family. Two rather different and more interesting facts connect these writers. First of all, they were all reared in or close to Belfast, a prosperous city which has a large commercial middle class. Joyce Cary on the other hand sets his two novels of Ascendancy life out in the land where the Big House held sway, in Donegal and in Derry where he was born in 1888. Secondly, all felt moved to recall their childhood in Ulster as though in nostalgic recognition that the social class into which they were born was no longer dominant. Memories of a Protestant middle-class boyhood are recorded by C. S. Lewis in *Surprised by Joy,* by Louis MacNeice in *The Strings Are False,* by Forrest Reid in *Apostate* and by George Buchanan in *Green Seacoast*. In the hands of these writers, the autobiographical mode is a shorthand

4. Andrew Wright, *Joyce Cary: A Preface to his Novels,* London 1958, 17.

way of plotting social decline. All of the autobiographies recall a leisured Victorian or post-Victorian boyhood of maidservants, spacious gardens, summer 'hols' and old books in dusty attics. The recollections are always nostalgic even when, as in MacNeice's case, nostalgia is disavowed.[5] They are also artistically shaped : the finely crafted autobiography is in the North primarily a Protestant middle-class form.

When we set Cary's *A House of Children,* a largely autobiographical novel about growing up, beside the autobiographies I have just mentioned and the novels of Forrest Reid and Stephen Gilbert, it is clear that exit from childhood is a curiously appropriate allegory for the decline of the Victorian middle-class and upper middle-class orders and for the way vestiges of these orders lingered into the first decades of the twentieth century. When childhood and the society in which it was spent are seen through rose-tinted mists of memory, it is easy for both to assume overtones of paradise. The Paradise theme in Protestant middle-class writers is analogous to but different from the theme in Catholic writers. In the latter, paradise springs from the dreams of a dispossessed peasantry, dreams of racial and national greatness and oneness in remote times. The paradise we glimpse in Cary, Reid, Gilbert, Janet McNeill and Buchanan springs from a more obvious and recent social reality. Perhaps because of this, the Paradise theme in these writers develops in very personal and eccentric directions. Cary, Gilbert and Reid all tend to equate their childhood with the twilight of a social 'paradise' but they have very different conceptions of where the 'original' paradise is located. For Cary it is in the gracious eighteenth century, for Gilbert it is in the Victorian Empire, for Reid in Ancient Greece.

(2)

Neither *Castle Corner* (1938) nor *A House of Children* (1941) is regarded by critics as among Joyce Cary's important novels, yet the latter strikes me as a fine achievement, superior to *Castle Corner,* whose scope, bustle and energy it nevertheless lacks. *Castle Corner,* while a fascinating chronicle of the decline of a

5. MacNeice's sister, who annotated her brother's posthumously published autobiography, expresses the opinion in one footnote that his childhood in Carrickfergus was much happier than he claimed or remembered, *The Strings Are False,* London 1965, 49n.

Big House, an Ascendancy family, an Irish social system and an empire, fails to reach Cary's own high standards in a way that could not have been reversed by either of the sequels Cary originally planned for it. It fails not simply because it creakingly supports too many characters (Irish peasants, African natives, emancipated women, Oxford fashionables, *nouveaux riches,* empire-builders and empire-breakers, to name a few) and is spread too thinly over too many locations (Donegal, Oxford and Nigeria), but because the synthetic principle uniting them is never discernible. The novel is like an immense mural begun at various places and with no clear evidence as to how and where the parts might conjoin. By contrast, the consistency of tone and point of view which is missing in *Castle Corner* gives unity to *A House of Children,* a novel that records in a very different manner the decline of the Corner family and, by implication, the Protestant gentry in Ireland. Although it captures *en route,* in the curious figure of Pinto, the tawdrier and more provincial side of *fin-de-siècle* aestheticism, it has little of the social spread of *Castle Corner.* More modestly, *A House of Children* begins with the English narrator's recollection of fuchsia hedges in Donegal and goes on to compose a semi-chronological, semi-impressionistic picture of his childhood in north-west Ireland.

The narrator is Evelyn Corner (a thin disguise for Cary himself, and like the author sporting a feminine first name) and he remembers from the vantage-point of the 1940s a nineties world of debutantes, private tutors and garden parties, a world from which the noisy peasant Foys of *Castle Corner* are excluded. All is beautifully recalled for us, filtered through the narrator's mature sensibility. Especially good is Cary's evocation of the role of the sea in Evelyn's boyhood—passage on the Liverpool-Derry steamer, the sea journey across Lough Foyle, family trips by scow around the coast with 'the stormy pressure of the air, the brown sail leaning overhead, the arching spray, the swag-bellied clouds rolling down' upon them. The sea and the rain dominate the novel but not in the depressing way in which they dominate rural Ulster fiction. Cary's sea and rain stirred the imagination and shattered his childhood world into colour :

Whenever the clouds broke into rain, the sunlight shone down through their rags, which became as blue as pigeons, floating in a yellow, diffused brightness, so pale and luminous that it seemed to be a pure white light, and to have no colour at all, except in contrast with the pale intense blues, and the glittering foam. Between this thick, confused sky and the charging seas which looked as regular as household cavalry, the far shore of the lough, five miles off, in bright sunshine, came so near that the raindrops, just fallen on the bright leaves, seemed to be sparkling under your eye. But the drops were probably white cottages, or rushing streams, the leaves were whole woods and the trees separate mountain-sides. (pp. 124–5)

Delightful characters animate the recollections—the touchy, disingenuous Pinto, the beneficent Aunt Hersey, Anketel, Frances's suitors (Dingbat, Captain Scoop and Moonlight), Mrs Fee and the volatile, ingenuous Delia. Unlike Joyce in the opening pages of *A Portrait,* Cary makes no pretence of refining his adult sensibility out of existence, and while *A House of Children* conjures up the magical and incantatory quality of childhood, it is also full of a mature man's reflections on childhood, many of which seem almost proverbial in their terse wisdom : e.g. 'Small children are thought happy, but for most of the time they do not even live consciously, they exist.' The reader, thinking his own childhood experiences unique, is often pleasurably shocked by recognition : 'All day one would live in the sense of something to come; it would be with one during lessons, bathing, digging, meals, until at last, getting into bed, one would notice it particularly and say : "But what am I expecting." Then one would discover that it had been doughnuts for tea, already eaten, but without any sense of fulfilment.' (p. 28)

The impressions and reflections are woven around the 'plot' of the novel—the growth of the Corner children out of childhood. There are three moments in the novel which precipitate Evelyn farther along the barbed route to adolescence : the party at the Maylins (at which he discovers the silliness of children's games), the aftermath of the disastrous play the Corner children mount (which affects Evelyn's brother Harry more than it does him), and Pinto's production of *The Tempest* (which for Evelyn gives meaning to words like 'beauty' and 'love' and to real things in nature such as mountains, thunder, stars and boats). The boy's response to the chief images of *The Tempest* con-

Of his bones are coral made; it was a chord of strings, a sextet, each singing quietly in the ear of my soul; not only with music but souls of their own. A tune of lonely spirits, the sober and upright bone with his bass voice and rather austere character at one end, and the glimmering sea treasure, living jewel, rolling its merman's song at the other, in perpetual little curling waves of sound, which fell for ever on the bright sea floor, made of itself the voice of creation. (p. 234)

summates the motif of the sea that flows through *A House of Children* :

These quotations may give the erroneous impression that *A House of Children* is as precious as much of the literature of the decade it evokes. The novel has the motifs and cadences of a musical composition, but it also has the sinewy toughness of all shrewd perception. In addition, it has movement. For Evelyn Corner the transition from childhood to imminent adolescence is one from freedom to the gates of constraint. The narrator sees the childhood exploits of his brother and cousins as 'romantic' and 'revolutionary' and continually compares the lives of children with those of 'savages'. Childhood is that time before the dawning of moral involvement : hence the doubts which the narrator entertains about the justice of the social system in nineteenth-century Ireland are not permitted to distort the memories of boyhood. Childhood is also a kind of borrowed time before social responsibility swiftly ends it : hence Frances is one moment carelessly joining in the childish games and is the next a responsible married woman.

The highly structured social system into which the Corner children are, through their eventual loss of freedom, initiated, is itself under siege because of social and political developments in Ireland, Britain and the Western world. Ironically, it is as if the novel's social universe is reverting to a state of 'childhood', to the anarchy or at least democracy of childhood. Pinto, the children's tutor who plays with his charges and is a spoilt child of the nineties, throws childish tantrums, rails against formal education and finally elopes with Evelyn's cousin Delia, a symbolic blow, one feels, against the values, integrity and history of the Corner family. Moreover, the reader can with benefit of historical hindsight see the childlike peasants of the novel as the last generation of Irishmen who will consciously accept their subservience to the

rich landlords and their henchmen. Part of the novelistic tension
of *A House of Children* originates with the contradiction between
Evelyn's growth (or decline) from freedom to constraint, and the
decline (or growth) from constraint to freedom of the larger
society around him.

This counterpoint could on another level be regarded as
illusory, in keeping with the essentially deceptive nature of the
novel's texture. Whereas the narrator writes as one who has lost
the freedom of childhood, it is possible to see him as the free man
and the child as the captive. For is it not a devaluation of
language for the narrator to describe his childhood exploits as
'romantic' and 'revolutionary'? How socially circumscribed were
those exploits in reality, and how narrow and artificially maintained the social space in which they took place. The families of
the Ascendancy were insulated from the real, peasant, spacious
and impoverished Ireland around them. And in those families
social relationships were conceived in the very terms of constraint:
Evelyn Corner remembers relationships around him as con-
frontations between superiors and inferiors, masters and servants,
and he indulges unself-consciously in the colonialist use of team
sports as a didactic model of virtuous behaviour among gentlemen. Even among the 'romantic' and 'revolutionary' Corner
children relationships are essentially agonistic, expressed in
terms of tyranny, leadership, subservience, disgrace, boycott. And
the high degree of unhappiness must not be overlooked either
(e.g. Robert at boarding-school), for it was a world of square
psychological pegs in round social holes.

It is because of his basically agonistic view of human
relationships that the narrator can permit himself—amid his
fitful awareness of the rank injustice of nineteenth-century Ireland
and his evocations of childhood 'freedom'—a nostalgic nod in
the direction of an even more highly structured and surely more
unjust time, the eighteenth century. Recalling his father confronting the shiftless Pinto, Evelyn remarks :

We were equally astonished by my father's compliments and by
Pinto's surliness. We could not know that in my father's special
politeness, we were seeing a last fragment of the eighteenth century;
perhaps the very bend and smile with which a gentleman of the
grand tour saluted an artist, any painter, or actor or singer or
ballerina; and in Pinto, the first symptoms of the early twentieth,

with its suspicious reaction from anything like a grand manner. Not that my father was eighteenth century. In idea, he belonged to his own time. But from his father and through him from his great-grandfather, as I knew from a great-aunt, born in 1810, he had certain courtesies which belonged to the great age of polite forms and social ease. (p. 186)

It is as if beneath the ostensible nostalgia for the 'revolutionary' freedom of childhood is a nostalgia for the kind of social and class security that was no longer possible during the narrator's own boyhood. The curious figure of Pinto, focus of the novel, embodies the ambivalence. In the above quotation he appears as a prototype of twentieth-century emancipated man; elsewhere he is a decadent child of the tired and yellow nineties. Andrew Wright chooses to see him as the former and claims that Pinto is a recurring Cary character-type we can label 'the free man'.[6] Pinto's real name in *A House of Children* is indeed Freeman, yet it would be sentimental to see him as free in any romantic or revolutionary sense. Surely the most truthful sketch of Pinto is this one in which the notion of decline and the magisterial simile deny freedom :

I read now about the men of the nineties, their bohemianism and disillusionment, and their figures seem romantic. In Pinto, as I realised long afterwards, I knew one of those men, or at least one of the provincials who were affected by the same movement of the time spirit; but he did not seem romantic to us. He was either a shabby, depressed little man in a bad suit, or a lively and amusing companion or sometimes, when he was dealing with plays or poetry or music, masterful and positive, as little romantic as any of the local magistrates, laying down the law. (p. 184)

Truly emancipated men, one feels, lurk just beyond the confines of Cary's novel, but they are radically different from the exiled and decadent Englishman, Pinto.

In deciding whether *A House of Children* celebrates lost freedom or lost captivity, it is hard not to be swayed by the poignancy of the novel's conclusion. 'The quality of our living experience', Evelyn Corner writes when recalling his unfinished childhood poems, 'could be translated only into the experience of poetry which people would not read. They prefer, I suppose, to live it,

6. Wright, 77–91.

if they live, in any true sense of the word, real lives: and that is even easier today than it was when we were children.' The underlying notion in the novel (and one we shall meet again in Forrest Reid) is of childhood as a kind of orphanhood, a state of incompleteness and longing rather than of buoyant fulfilment. Childhood, superficially happy and free, is at once a decline and a thraldom. Perhaps appropriately in the fictionalised autobiography of a writer who spent much of his literary energy in the exploration of freedom, *A House of Children*, a work of joyously free and iridescent surfaces, nevertheless summons from the narrator's recollections the spirit of personal and curious bondage.

(3)

As an autobiographical yet novelistic re-creation of childhood, *A House of Children* might be compared with Forrest Reid's *Apostate*. Both are wistful, sensuous books with a tonal edge of irony and a backdrop of social decline. Both are nostalgic about childhood but present it as a falling-off from a prior state of beauty, order and graciousness. Unlike Cary, Reid was dominated by this notion throughout his entire career. There is another difference. In terms of social background and theme, Reid's work can be more profitably compared with that of Stephen Gilbert, George Buchanan and Janet McNeill, writers who set their novels[7] in the 'better' parts of Belfast—the business centre and the wealthier suburbs of the Lagan Valley and Belfast Lough. No less than Joyce Cary, these novelists portray a traumatic social decline, but in their case it is the decline of nineteenth-century *nouveau riche,* mercantile and professional families of the Protestant North-east. Two of the group, McNeill and Buchanan, have imaged the decline in terms of marriage and the vicissitudes of love; the other two, Reid and Gilbert, have imaged it in a comparable way to Cary through their nostalgia for childhood.

In the first paragraph of *Apostate* (1926), several years before he began his best-known work, the Tom Barber trilogy, Forrest Reid left no doubt as to what he considered the wellspring of his art to be: 'The primary impulse of the artist springs, I fancy, from discontent, and his art is a kind of crying for Elysium.' The

7. That the Protestant middle-class writers are novelists and none of them short story-writers might be considered significant if we choose to link the social dominance in Ulster of this class with Frank O'Connor's theory that the short story concerns 'submerged population groups'.

artist according to Reid suffers from and labours to express 'that same divine homesickness, that same longing for an Eden from which each one of us is exiled'. This was no mere slogan for Reid. From beginning (*The Kingdom of Twilight*, 1904) to end (*Denis Bracknel*, 1947), during forty years of continual writing, it not only informed but dominated Reid's fiction. To the point of diminishing returns, Reid came back again and again to the theme of paradise lost and rediscovered. Exploring childhood was for him no mere personal exorcism, nor was it simply a means of representing the Childhood of Man with its pre-lapsarian bliss and post-exilic homesickness. Childhood for Reid was also the Childhood of the Race spent in an Ancient Greece of his own imagination. Finally, and much less consciously, the happiness of early childhood seems to be confused in Reid's work with the wealth and long vacations enjoyed by the Victorian middle class in Ulster, the Childhood of the Class one might say.

The adult can only recapture childhood in memory and dream, just as man can only recapture the childhood of the species in myth. The Tom Barber trilogy is an exploration, without benefit of Jung or Freud, of the relationship between myth and dream. At one level, indeed, it reads like a fictionalisation of Mircea Eliade's *Myths, Dreams, and Mysteries*, the premise of which serves as the most succinct summary of the trilogy's theme : 'In the oneiric universe we find again and again the symbols, the images, the figures and the events of which the mythologies are constituted.'[8] The dreamer must nevertheless be taught the meanings of the dreams, as the waking man must learn the myths : hence the importance in Reid's trilogy of hierophany and shamanic election.

I do not wish to overrate Reid's trilogy. In order to challenge *Le Grand Meaulnes* in the fantastic re-creation of childhood, it needed to be honed down considerably, for its verbal and even ethical excesses frequently make it cloy. Furthermore, the middle-class sensibility governing the trilogy is no longer in fashion, nor the Georgian delicacy of form with which it expresses itself in Reid's work. Yet the trilogy is a singular and fluent creation, and one might think, amid Tolkien's popularity and the current

---

8. Mircea Eliade, *Myths, Dreams, and Mysteries*, trans. Philip Mairet. New York 1967, 14.

interest in children's literature and in myth and ritual, that Reid's fiction is ripe for resuscitation. In any event, no Irish writer has written more lucidly or stylishly than Forrest Reid. *Young Tom* (1944) won for Reid, as *A House of Children* did for Cary, the James Tait Black Memorial Prize. It was the last written but chronologically initial novel in the trilogy which Reid composed 'backwards' over a period of years. Little happens in the novel—Tom dreams and gambols his way through summer holidays, a squirrel is shot, Tom runs away to his grandmother's house and there communes with a dead boy, his friend Pascoe visits him, and the book drifts to a close in visions of a warm beach and a timeless sea. Yet we are given in *Young Tom* a portrait of Eden, the act of betrayal that makes life in a childhood paradise impossible, and the transformation of paradise into a dream-memory and a dream-promise, in which forms we as adults and imperfect beings know it. Until the act of betrayal, eleven-year-old Tom Barber lives an idyllic existence (in which it always seems to be summer vacation and languorous afternoon) in a garden paradise on the outskirts of Belfast that is magically green and fertile and filled with talking animals. The faithfulness Tom values in animals is the chief moral virtue celebrated or mourned throughout the entire trilogy which on one level concerns Reid's favourite theme of friendship. When the minister's son in an act of betrayal kills Tom's tame squirrel, Tom runs away in fear and disgust to his grandmother's house where he encounters the spirit of the past and dedicates himself to what Eliade calls 'the nostalgia for paradise'.

Like the other two novels of the trilogy, *Young Tom* has ethical, psychological and mythical levels of meaning. The killing of the squirrel and its repercussions is for Tom an ethical awakening, a rude initiation into the faithlessness of men and the pain involved in relationships. Yet instead of being dispelled by the events of the novel, the notion of paradise is reinforced and in being transformed from supposed reality into dream is made intact and impregnable. Psychologically, Tom's solitary pursuit of paradise seems related to his being an only child, and to the remoteness of his scientifically-minded father and aloofness of his mother. Tom relies for warmth and security upon mother-surrogates (Phemie and Granny) and for a model lifestyle upon father-surrogates (James-Arthur and Dr McCrory). It is not surprising to learn that Tom is similar in many respects to the young Reid depicted in *Apostate*. Phemie and Granny represent two aspects of Emma, Reid's first nurse early torn from him, and the most decisive influence on his boyhood; Reid's parents, too, were remote and estranged from him and the boy spent long hours alone with his wistful imagination. Moreover, Tom's dream-vision of paradise as children playing on a yellow beach is a faithful transcription of the dreams Reid had until he was sixteen, dreams that were elaborately narrative and even chronological in the sense that the chief character, a boy, grew older as the dreamer himself aged. Such dreams are a form of escape from the hard realities and loneliness of waking life, but in the fiction they also become re-creations of the Paradise myth. To dream the dreams, as to know the myths, is to re-live the Good Time before the traumatic departure from Eden and from the Mother (or Mother-substitute). It is no coincidence that Reid's first vision of paradise was stimulated by a tale read to him by the motherly Emma, nor that the vision was perpetuated in sleep that recalled the amniotic darkness of the womb. Throughout the trilogy Tom is an Adam-like figure, and the role played by all kinds of animals might recall Eliade's remark that 'friendship with the animals and knowledge of their language belong to the paradisiac syndrome'.[9] Tom's journey to his grandmother's house (partly in bereavement, partly in search of information about a mysterious Uncle Stephen) is the beginning of Tom's journey perilous back to the other kingdom. The first stage of that journey ends in *Young Tom* when the boy mounts the stairs of Tramore House and speaks to the long dead Ralph Seaford. The staircase is a recurring motif in Reid's fiction and symbolises, in Eliade's words, 'passing from one mode of being to another'.[10] For Reid, the magical is located upstairs in the enchanted big house, in those rooms rarely frequented by adults and redolent of childhood spirits. 'To come downstairs', writes Reid, 'was to come at once into a comfortable prosaic world where, if nothing was particularly enthralling, all was safe and familiar.' (p. 213)

The Retreat (1936) gives us the dangerous and unfamiliar side of enchantment. The natural paradise of *Young Tom* has now become the elusive magic garden or enchanted room sought

9. Eliade, *Myths, Dreams, and Mysteries*, 63.
10. Eliade, *Myths, Dreams, and Mysteries*, 116.

by the twelve- or thirteen-year-old Tom. The novel has three sections, the first and last set in Tom's home and dominated by the mysterious black cat Henry. These magical sections frame the dream-section set in Greencastle, Co. Donegal, during summer holidays. There, amid the green sun-soaked landscape, Tom almost recovers his earlier innocent paradise. But now nature is freighted with allegory. Tom falls asleep one day under a hedge in a 'green twilight' and dreams of a straw-haired boy before being awakened by a goat, unnecessary reminder of Tom's pantheism. The boy becomes Tom's guardian angel and appears another night when he accompanies Tom to a dream-Eden in an overdone allegorical sequence involving Tom as an Adam-figure, a serpent, an albatross and a dog. The coherence of the sequence is salvaged in the figure of the old wizard with a black cat as his familiar. This duo appears in the opening dream of the novel and will reappear in the third novel of the trilogy.

Henry the cat dominates *The Retreat*. He is a reincarnation of Blake's tyger and is capable of invoking cosmic powers, as in this schoolroom scene :

There was a sudden rushing noise, a blinding glare, and an explosion that shook the whole building. In the brief pandemonium that followed it was somebody else who screamed, not Tom. The wind whirled through the room, scattering papers, circling in a kind of vortex, as if trying madly to force an outlet through the ceiling. Crash! That was the blackboard—either the wind or Miss Jimpson had knocked it over. Tom sprang to his feet in an ecstasy of excitement. It seemed to him that the darkness was thickening at the centre, concentrating in a spiral twirling column, through which there blazed down two white eyes of fire. He called out something—or a voice called out near to him. Everybody had jumped up : the room was in a tumult. And next minute the whole thing was over, passing as abruptly as it had begun. But the behaviour of Brown was most astonishing of all. He was actually standing on the form, clapping his arms, like wings, against his sides, and making the most extraordinary bird cries. (pp. 71–2)

The motif of fire, associated here with Blake's tyger's eyes, runs through *The Retreat,* and receives its most vivid expression in the bonfire scene that closes the middle section of the novel. The fire which Tom and his friend Pascoe have ignited in the garden of

Pascoe's Aunt Rhoda suddenly burns out of control and is transformed by Reid into a moment of kratophany[11] :

'You're doing nothing !' screamed Pascoe, who was still making desperate and futile efforts to keep the surrounding bushes from catching, though the heat was too intense for him to get near the actual fire. Tom beat out a few sparks, but it was useless, they could do nothing, and he dropped his fork. He retreated a few paces, and then stood still, lost in a rapture that was dreamy yet exultant. Through it, after a while, he became dimly aware of other figures, other voices, than Pascoe's—the wine merchant's, Aunt Rhoda's—and all the voices sounded excited, and the wine merchant's angry. But Tom was only half-conscious of them, like far-off sounds heard in a dream. The growing brambles and furze-bushes had caught now : it looked as if the whole shore would soon be ablaze. And the shifting uncertain wind swayed the fire sometimes towards him, and sometimes away. Through the smooth, rushing sounds there came numerous explosions; blazing fragments fell; and showers of sparks floated far and wide like burning rain. . .
The fire seemed to have divided Tom from the Pascoe family. It had thrust them back to an immense distance; they were no more than gesticulating marionettes. They were outside his world, but the fire was in his world. He heard the seagulls crying, and a startled rabbit ran almost over his feet. The whole world was burning, with bright wings of flame that rushed up the sky, while far above Tom's head, pale and remote and spectral, a white moon hovered like a gigantic moth, appearing and disappearing as the clouds drifted across it. (pp. 237–8)

Tom is protected from the dark and fiery forces of the universe by his guardian angel, who appears three times, and by the white dog that Tom first saw in Donegal and which thereafter invades his dreams and reveries. The dog is aboriginal Dog, the animal that accompanied Tobias and his angel, the agent of daylight ranged against Cat, the agent of fire and darkness. Dog is faithfulness, enchantment and youth and is associated with summer, sunshine and the sea. Cat is fear, sorcery and age and is associated with the moon, winter and the mysterious house that

---

11. I use here Eliade's word *kratophany* (meaning the manifestation of cosmic forces) in contrast to my use in Chapter Four of the Joycean *epiphany* (a word suggesting a more subjective and less alarming experience).

recurs in Tom's dreams. Although at the end of *The Retreat* Tom manages to defeat temporarily the powers of darkness, it is intimated that he will not gain full control over his destiny until he finds the master-magician whose lost apprentice he seems to be. This elusive mentor appears in the novel's opening dream and reappears in the classroom cyclone, in the paper silhouette Tom makes, and in the graveyard dream-sequence towards the end of the novel. He is associated with Blake, but more coherently with Uncle Stephen whose name echoes in the book's final paragraph. In touch with the evil forces unleashed by the fall of the angels and the expulsion from Eden, Uncle Stephen yet holds the keys to the gates of the paradise for which Tom is perpetually searching.

Uncle Stephen (1931) opens with the funeral of Tom's father —his mother has died earlier—and the reader might wonder why Reid never develops the impact of the deaths upon the fifteen-year-old Tom. Actually the traumatic events in the trilogy occur not in the real world but in fantasy. Reid's young heroes are not visited by the emotional crises that shape the heroes of more realistic fiction and, despite their tremendous sensitivity, are self-absorbed to the point of callousness. At the same time, Tom's orphanhood does make explicit an aspect of the theme of lost paradise : namely, the 'search for the father'. This is prefigured in the other two novels of the trilogy in which Tom's father is remote and inaccessible and in which Tom thinks of himself as an unsatisfactory son and wonders what kind of father *would* have found him satisfactory. And now in *Uncle Stephen*, farmed out with his stepmother and his half-brothers and half-sisters, Tom recalls that 'while his father had been alive he had never felt much affection for him : an atmosphere of spiritual remoteness had, as far back as he could remember, surrounded him' (p. 7). Clearly Uncle Stephen (the only living relative of Tom's dead mother) is the boy's spiritual father, and the novel is in part Tom's search for him. The search for the father is a frequent theme in Reid's fiction, most explicitly explored in *Brian Westby* (1934) and given its largely unconscious autobiographical origins in *Apostate*.

The relation between the search for paradise and the state of orphanhood is not hard to understand. The longing for Elysium which preoccupied Reid and his boy-heroes is, in another sense, a longing for parental security, the security of the first and best time—early childhood. Octavio Paz puts it this way: 'Our solitude has the same roots as religious feelings. It is a form of orphanhood, an obscure awareness that we have been torn from the All, and an ardent search: a flight and a return, an effort to re-establish the bonds that unite us with the universe.'[12]

Uncle Stephen, whom Tom discovers after leaving his step-family in Belfast and journeying alone (in the perilous manner of the archetypal hero) to Kilbarron, has been expecting Tom all along. Their introduction recalls the opening dream-sequence of *The Retreat,* with the old man dressed in black and exhibiting the eccentricity of the recluse. He greets Tom as though blessing him and later conducts the boy into his bedroom which is like a shrine, monastically austere and containing a broken statue of Hermes, the guardian of souls, the god of sleep and dream, the watcher over boys. Boyhood initiation is in this novel recalled to its ritual and primitive beginnings as election into the mystery. Uncle Stephen even reveals that he too was pupil to an older man, thus establishing a shamanic succession in which Tom now participates. As befits a shaman, Uncle Stephen is intimate with the dark forces of the universe, although in this novel evil is finally dispelled and the character of the old man is seen at last to be benign. Uncle Stephen is a self-styled custodian of Greek lore and morality who has written a book about Hermes and who worships the boy-god each night before sleep. In return for this homage, Hermes allows Uncle Stephen to re-live youth as a homeless boy (who takes the name Philip Coombe and who becomes Tom's friend when he is not Uncle Stephen). The revelation that Philip is really Uncle Stephen is the dramatic climax of the trilogy, and the rest of *Uncle Stephen* is devoted to Tom's attempts to coax Philip to change voluntarily and for good back into Uncle Stephen. Tom persuades him only after accompanying him to Coombe Bridge, his birthplace, where the young Stephen (Philip) sees he no longer belongs. It is all rather confusing, but we can assume that the youthful Stephen embodies the Reality Principle (the decay of the real world), Uncle Stephen the Dream or Myth Principle. In finally rejecting the youthful but time-haunted Stephen in favour of the aged but timeless

12. Paz, *The Labyrinth of Solitude,* 20.

Uncle Stephen, Tom rejects distasteful reality in favour of dream, time in favour of mythic ideality. At the trilogy's end, Tom's re-entry with Uncle Stephen into paradise is almost complete as they prepare to go on a journey through time and space to 'the shore of the Sicilian sea, far far away from all this, under a bluer sky and a hotter sun'.

Tom's post-Edenic journey back towards the Mythic Centre has also been a metaphoric version of his development of a moral and religious outlook which was Reid's own, a world-view which is Greek (or quasi-Greek), hedonist, supplicatory. The Tom Barber trilogy is therefore a symbolic statement of Reid's philosophy of life and art. Uncle Stephen's paganism consecrates youth, faithfulness and beauty and involves Tom not only as an acolyte but as an intimate. Tom's search for the mentor has also been the 'search for the lover'. The two are easily reconciled in Greek terms. 'Uncle Stephen was his master,' muses Tom, 'and he was Uncle Stephen's pupil. In the old days a pupil had lived with his master. He had that kind of master today.' (p. 268) For the Greeks, the ethical justification of the relationship—'the old man guiding the boy into the paths of virtue' as one scholar puts it— was also a Platonisation of the relationship—'a spiritual relation which the physical act would only spoil'.[13] Still, one feels that disguised within the theme of shamanic election as the apotheosis of friendship was Reid's attempt to explore a theme he dare not explore in more explicit fashion. An earlier attempt to be more explicit incurred the displeasure of, among others, Henry James to whom he had dedicated *The Garden God* (1905), the story of a love-affair between two boys.[14] The same hostile pressures that prevented Reid's close friend, E. M. Forster, from publishing novels such as *Maurice* during his lifetime operated on Reid, though Reid reacted not by withholding publication but by elaborate fictional sublimation in the forms of myth, dream and ritual. Be this as it may, it is not the reserved homosexuality but the passive narcissism which threatens to choke the finer parts of the Tom Barber trilogy. Those guardian angels and statues

13. Antony Andrewes, *The Greeks*, London 1967, 216.
14. For an account of the rift between Reid and Henry James, see Burlingham, *Forrest Reid*, 69–71, E. M. Forster's essay on Reid in *Two Cheers for Democracy* and Reid himself, *Private Road*, 26–31, 65–71.

and boy-companions (with the exception of young Pascoe, the scientist) are projections of Tom himself and he is in love with all of them. Narcissism is the ultimate defence against the pain and complexity inherent in a sexual relationship between two people : if one's image is the other person, the problem is solved. Because narcissism in the Tom Barber trilogy operates from the beginning, it threatens to devalue Reid's notion of paradise into merely the Platonic companionship of one's own dream-image. This devaluation is reflected in the trilogy's opulent prose which makes the three novels, especially *The Retreat* and *Uncle Stephen*, teeter on the brink of decadence. It is no coincidence that the last written, *Young Tom*, is also the best novel of the three; Reid seems to have been yet another victim of the Georgian sensibility from which he awoke too late.

Outside the cabalistic, the precious and the narcissistic, there is a great deal that is enjoyable and valuable in the Tom Barber trilogy. It is, as E. M. Forster claimed, 'a unique chronicle of boyhood'.[15] Despite its professional stylishness, it recaptures the simple joys of discovery that animate boyhood. Reid retained all his days a capacity for such joys : he was the eternal amateur stumbling on new discoveries in old attics and compelled to communicate the charms and fidelities he found there to kindred spirits. Beyond this the trilogy is an ambitious exploration of the theme of paradise lost and regained. As a view of life and of human relationships it was outmoded in its curious Hellenism even in Reid's own day, not to speak of today. Albeit, Reid is a reminder that even amid our industry and technology a solitary and mythic existence, at least in dream-form, is possible.

(4)

Towards the end of *Uncle Stephen* Tom Barber succeeds in persuading Philip Coombe to reassume Uncle Stephen's form only by accompanying him to Philip's birthplace where the ugly and alienating ravages of time are evident. In several poignant scenes Philip is unable to locate any surviving relatives and in the recognition of his orphanhood from community and family he concedes to Tom's desire. On one level these scenes document

15. *Two Cheers for Democracy*, London 1951, 277.

the search for the Mythic Ancestor who, according to Eliade, participates in all Paradise myths.[16] But on another we can discern Reid's distaste for the urban squalor into which his own part of Ireland seemed to be degenerating. There is a distinctly social side to Reid's notion of paradise; we might even say that for him the quest for paradise was in part a search for order, privacy and rather privileged leisure. The search was made against the odds of social reality, and the social decline that is a backdrop to his fiction is a continuing and defining feature of the Protestant middle-class novel written by Reid, Gilbert, McNeill and Buchanan. As his long career progressed it must have become clear to Reid that the kind of paradise he sought resided diminishingly in the real world and increasingly in the world of waking dreams. Such an early sortie into St John Ervine country—the drab, lower middle-class life among Ulster's small shopkeepers—as *At the Door of the Gate* (1915) became improbable later on, as if the author were growing more nostalgic for what was a vanishing social possibility : a spacious and cultured middle class from which the more squalid and demeaning realities of social life could be excluded.

This is not to say that Reid's early ventures into lower middle-class and working-class life in Ulster were any less realistic than those of Ervine or McLaverty. Consider this description of a Belfast slum quoted by Burlingham from Reid's first and rarely encountered novel, *The Kingdom of Twilight* (1904):

Long, narrowly-paved, ill-lit streets of dirty little shops and dwelling-houses succeeded one another with a depressing continuity. An iron urinal, painted green, but looking black in the dull-yellow light of the gas-lamp above it, stood close to the footpath, and formed a centre of attraction for a swarm of ragged children as lending an additional excitement to games of tig. Here and there the gloomy, grimy back of a warehouse, or factory, broke the monotony of the smaller houses. . . At corners, and in doorways, groups of men and boys stood smoking, and spitting, and gazing at the passers-by. From one of the many black, narrow alleys there issued the oaths and obscenity of some drunken quarrel, and now and then the shrill, harsh laugh of a woman, mirthless, horrible, would rise above the gruffer undertone of her companion. Slouching, staggering figures zigzagged along, clawing at the walls, and

16. Eliade, *Myths, Dreams, and Mysteries*, 43–4.

coming every few yards to a standstill. At the door of a public-house the slow, silent invitation of a prostitute was stared into their eyes from a puffed, bloated face.[17]

Even in a much later novel, *Peter Waring,* there is as we saw the occasional flash of harsh realism. But it is hard to escape the suggestion of souped-up travelogue in such scenes; moreover, they are always viewed through the eyes of a young character who is alienated from the ugliness and sordidness. Whereas McLaverty writes of the Belfast slum-dwellers and Ervine of the Belfast lower middle class with love and intimacy and from an inner pressure, Reid's descriptions are there to 'place' ugliness and squalor in his young heroes' moral and aesthetic universe. By the time of the Tom Barber trilogy, Reid's concern for verisimili-tude was reduced by and large to a few quaint sketches of what we are obliged to call 'low-life' characters. James-Arthur, the farm-boy in *Young Tom,* and Deverell, the poacher in *Uncle Stephen,* are really picturesque Noble Savages hardly different from Tom's animals, mere counters in that self-congratulatory game social superiors play when consorting with the salt of the earth.

The 'hankering after things English' that Reid in *Apostate* deplored in well-off Ulster circles informs the Tom Barber trilogy which depicts on the surface an English upper-crust world of full-time gardeners, dinner-gongs and endless summer 'hols'. The dialogue is liberally spiced with 'I say', 'jolly good' and 'you cad'; even the low-life characters tend to speak with an English rather than North of Ireland accent. The trilogy expresses in part a desire for a civilised and Anglicised ideal, but it is also in part a rose-tinted memory of an Ulster middle-class childhood in the late 1870s and early 1880s. Even by then the Protestant middle class that emerged and prospered after the Industrial Revolution, flourishing on mercantile speculation in Ulster and the Empire, had passed its heyday. This class, of which Reid's family was a declining example, tried to align its living standards with those of the English upper class and the Irish Protestant Ascendancy, and dreamed, in the way of any *nouveau riche,* of gentility, culture and leisure, though in reality it spent its days in dull commerce and glumly pious worship. Reid's early realism is

17. Burlingham, *Forrest Reid: A Portrait and a Study,* London 1953, 67.

largely used as a testament to the precarious cultural pretensions of this class and to the truculent boorishness to which it had, for Reid, degenerated. The gloomy portions of such novels as *At the Door of the Gate* (1915) and *The Bracknels* (1911) reflect the dark side of the Ulster Protestant commercial spirit. Later, in the Tom Barber trilogy, Reid chose to replace his distaste for what the middle class had become with a barely camouflaged dream-nostalgia for what it had, or might have, been.

Yet even in the trilogy is there unobtrusive evidence of social decline. Young Tom's family is well-off by today's standards, with a gardener and two maids, but it is noteworthy that his father is a professor rather than a prosperous merchant such as those who must have built the large houses that haunt Tom's imagination. These merchants' houses on the outskirts of Belfast or in the countryside are monuments to a vanishing past, and their occupying families, bereft of large incomes and staffs, have in Reid's later fiction shrunk to leave rooms, even entire floors, uninhabited. Flourishing Derryaghy House in *Peter Waring,* a novel set during the 1880s or 1890s, has become half-empty Tramore in *Young Tom,* a place of pilgrimage for Reid's young hero in his quest for the ghosts of the past. But even from Derryaghy House the breadwinner has disappeared as if (apart from the suggestively oedipal convenience of this for Tom's relationship with Mrs Carroll) the Victorian middle-class system had been somehow 'widowed', the lonely entrepreneurs gone and their fortunes doomed to be divided among the professionals and the bureaucrats, as the large houses themselves were destined to fall prey to the estate-agents and the flat-dwellers of the following generations. The Tom Barber trilogy is at once a paean of joy for the discovery in fantasy of eternal youth and a threnody for a social order whose demise in part provoked the paradise quest. And so the Enchanted Houses in the three novels also happen to be the declining large houses that were as close as the Dissenting Ulster middle class got to the Big Houses of the Ascendancy.

Reid's nostalgia took a more specific form over the disappearance of nineteenth-century Belfast before the inexorable urban sprawl. Though it was lost beauty for which he pined rather than the unobtrusiveness of the lower orders, we can hardly fail to notice the absence of the poor in the Belfast of

Reid's memories. The city he remembers is semi-rustic but civilised, a quasi-Hellenistic halfway house between urbanity and pastoralism, spontaneity and gentility. It is recalled in *Apostate* and favourably compared with what it had become by 1926 :

The whole town was more homely, more unpretentious. A breath of rusticity still sweetened its air; the few horse trams, their destinations indicated by the colour of their curtains, did little to disturb the quiet of the streets; the Malone Road was still an almost rural walk; Molly Ward's cottage, not a vulcanite factory, guarded the approach to the river; and there were no brick works, no mill chimneys, no King's Bridge to make ugly blots on the green landscape of the Lagan Valley. (pp. 51–2)

Reid's sense of decline was doubtless reinforced by the vicissitudes suffered by his own family before his birth. The family sprang on his father's side from 'middle-class, Presbyterian folk living round and about Lurgan and Derry' but his father had left Ireland as a young man and as a shipowner attempted but failed to run the blockade during the American Civil War. Bankrupted, he settled in Belfast and began again as a manager in a local firm. Forrest was born in Mount Charles in a very respectable part of Belfast, though he is at pains in *Apostate* to point out that his mother had to do without a carriage and the large family often had to make do with buttered potatoes and milk for dinner. The decline in the family fortunes seems to have been to some extent behind the note of gradual demise that sounds through Reid's fiction, for Reid in his own fortunes continued the family's slide into modesty and contemporary suburbia. Even more influential, perhaps, was his awareness of the waning aristocratic grandeur of his mother's heredity, for she was a last survivor of the Shropshire Parr family that appeared in *Burke's Peerage* and traced itself as far back as the last wife of Henry VIII. From his mother Reid seems to have inherited that whiff of snobbery that lightly taints the sensibilities of his boy-heroes, the snobbery of decayed gentility.

We must be careful, however, not to be unfair to Reid in discussing the social assumptions embodied in his work. If he plainly disliked the way society was changing in the North of Ireland through industrialisation and urbanisation, he refrained from advocating, even indirectly, the curtailment of personal freedom in order to set the clock back, for the very thrust of his personality and the innocuousness of his pursuits precluded such a thing. A humane concern for personal freedom is an undercurrent in his work, and Tom's attempts to free himself from the pain inflicted by others and his desire in turn never to cause pain to others could be regarded as part of the essential morality of the Tom Barber trilogy. If today it seems a rather *laissez-faire* and negative concern for freedom, it is because Reid was in the main apolitical and came close to a political vision only in his love of a Greek balance between personal freedom ('the greater democracy', as Tom's father humorously terms his son's communion with the animals) and stable social hierarchy based on learning and respect. We might claim to see in this a reflection of the two social strains that seem to have balanced in Reid : planter Presbyterianism from his father's side and the Protestant Ascendancy from his mother's, a liking for self-reliant democracy from the one, a respect for authority and the status quo from the other. The lost ideals of these two strains became blurred images of paradise that played about his imagination. They spoke to Reid of the strange exile that was his adult life in twentieth-century Ulster, orphaned from more congenial times and places. For Reid, as for Wordsworth's Platonic man, the echoes of these times and places were strongest in childhood, and to them he remained faithful all his life.

(5)

Stephen Gilbert is a little-noticed writer whose novels show the influence of Forrest Reid. As a young man he was something of a protégé of Reid's—appropriate enough when we remember that friendship and tutelage are essential themes in Reid—and repaid the encouragement of the older writer by dedicating his first novel, *The Landslide* (1943), to Reid and in his fourth, *The Burnaby Experiments,* by borrowing many details of Reid's life to create the novel's shaman figure, John Burnaby. Gilbert shares Reid's bookishness and otherworldliness, though like Reid he has worked out of the tough city of Belfast. His themes have also been inherited from Reid—boyhood, the magical defeat of space and time, and the decline of the old Victorian middle class. Shed, however, are Reid's sensuousness, pantheism, quasi-Hellenism and, it must be said, his shrewd perception and delicacy of statement. Though always readable and offbeat, Gilbert's work is primarily of interest in advancing the fictional record of middle-class decline in Ulster from Reid's turn-of-the-century shabby gentility to contemporary suburbia.

The Burnaby Experiments (1952) is a competent novel that borrows heavily from Reid, particularly from *Uncle Stephen.* The narrator has become the literary executor of a young man, Marcus Brownlow, whom he knew at boarding-school in England. The narrative purports to be the narrator's fictionalisation of the young man's notebooks describing experiments in psychic translocation and extra-sensory perception conducted under the guidance of an eccentric millionaire, John Burnaby, who lives 'in a sort of castle in one of the wildest parts of Donegal'. The novel documents the friendship of master and pupil until Burnaby's death which climaxes the narrative. Marcus, through psychic translocation, is meant to accompany Burnaby into death, but 'the last experiment' goes awry, Marcus is 'inhabited' by his master's ghost and finally drowns himself in mental agony.

The Burnaby Experiments is a reduction of the Tom Barber trilogy to its dramatic machinery and of Reid's moral and aesthetic philosophy to ESP and spiritualism. In addition, many superficial details from the trilogy and from Reid's life are borrowed. Reid too set his fiction in Donegal when he wanted a wild part of Ireland, though both Gilbert's and Reid's Donegal is symbolic rather than realistic; Marcus' journey from Belfast to the castle in Donegal is the journey perilous to the enchanted spot we recognised in Reid; the boy, like Reid's young heroes, is an inveterate dreamer whose dreams are as real as his waking life. More strikingly, John Burnaby is a composite of Uncle Stephen and Forrest Reid. Burnaby is Marcus' master and friend, as Uncle Stephen is Tom Barber's, and he presents himself to Marcus in the guise of Caldwell, an ex-schoolfriend of Marcus, just as Uncle Stephen assumes the form of Philip Coombe; John Burnaby is a devotee of Henry James, as was Reid, and like the author came from a prosperous shipowning Derry family and, because the family fell upon hard times, was brought up in the 'genteel poverty' we recognise from *Apostate;* Burnaby's mother sprang from an old English, landowning family now reduced to aristocratic pretensions and so recalls

Reid's mother; and if we know that Gilbert is Reid's literary executor as the narrator is Marcus Brownlow's, then *The Burnaby Experiments* reads even more clearly as an act of homage to Forrest Reid five years after the master's death.

The Burnaby Experiments lacks the philosophical and aesthetic significance of the Tom Barber trilogy. It is a more conventionally supernatural novel and, though competently written and constructed, does not advance Reid's play with time and space or his exploration of boyhood. But it does extend in an Ulster context Reid's backdrop of social decline. In a sense, Burnaby is a kind of degenerate Uncle Stephen, for he has used his psychic gifts in order to amass a fortune on the stock exchange and one cannot imagine Uncle Stephen so degrading his magical powers. Elsewhere in the novel are those who cannot afford Burnaby's cultural pretensions and snobbish dilettantism : Caldwell's father has become bankrupt; Marcus' father, a businessman in the wholesale tea-trade (like Reid and several of his characters), has never recovered from the Depression of the early 1930s. *The Burnaby Experiments* portrays the Victorian mercantile middle class, a generation after the Tom Barber trilogy, sunk even farther into shabby commercial pursuits and suburban anonymity. To read an earlier novel of Gilbert's, *Monkeyface,* and his latest, *Ratman's Notebooks,* is to realise how pervasive a theme social decline is in the Protestant middle-class novel.

Monkeyface (1948) combines Reid's themes of childhood and lost paradise, but as a variation on Reid Gilbert substitutes for Reid's boy-heroes a direct specimen of the Childhood of Man. The novel is a freakish allegory about an ape-boy who is captured in an Edenic jungle and brought, improbably, to suburban Belfast where he learns the speech and ways of man and in the end rejects them to return to the forest. I mention the book here because of its implicit social theme that takes up where Reid left off. Whereas Reid was content to lampoon those whom he seemed to regard as middle-class degenerates, Gilbert sees such characters as having fallen so far from any sense of idealism and gentility that they have become positively villainous.

We might in this regard compare a Reid novel such as *Denis Bracknel* with *Monkeyface.* Mr Bracknel is a vicious portrait,

P

almost a caricature, of the philistine and arrogant Presbyterian merchants of Reid's experience. Denis recoils from his father not so much because he distrusts his father's success and competitiveness in themselves as because his father pursues them to the point of boorishness and so offends Denis's aesthetic rather than moral sense. The Bracknels are a late Victorian merchant family living in a large house whose history is much longer than the family's; it is implied, I think, that such families, newcomers to wealth and position, have betrayed and devalued the culture and gentility they usurped through their commercial enterprise in the wake of the Industrial Revolution. The civilised ideals for which Reid and his sensitive, aristocratic boy-heroes pine—those of Ancient Greece and, more mundanely, of the British and Anglo-Irish upper middle class—were erected by the author and his characters in reaction to the commercial and professional middle class into which they were born, and so their nostalgia for these ideals is extremely suspect. Nonetheless, they are the ideals against which behaviour in the novels is measured, and it is possible in the blurred causality of *Denis Bracknel* to see the philistinism of the family (with the bullying father and wastrel son, Alfred) invoking the malignity of the spirit of the house and thereby being partly responsible for Denis's suicide.

Equally, moral responsibility in *Monkeyface* is related to the betrayal of a civilised ideal, in this case that of Empire. The ape-boy Bimbo has been brought by his captor to Beechwood, 'a large suburban house on the outskirts of Belfast' that is owned by the shiftless Sebastian, brother of Bimbo's captor, Dr Theodore Browne, who disappeared on a later expedition. The rot in the Browne family has set in because of the economic problems of the Depression, and Sebastian Browne's evil largely manifests itself in his underhanded and petty attempts to save himself from financial ruin by trying to sell Bimbo for exhibition. But the rot is also due to the fact that Sebastian has inherited his brother's material legacies but neither his expeditionary spirit nor questing mind; that he has, in short, betrayed the imperial ideal. Dr Theodore, though it was presumably he who massacred the hapless inhabitants of those rug-skins and trophy-heads decorating Beechwood, is the novel's offstage hero, the imperial explorer who in a jungle foray stumbled on a hidden Eden

(something young Tom Barber with remarkable foresight maintained existed) and an alternative line of primate evolution.
Sebastian has none of Theodore's virtues; he does not even
possess Mr Bracknel's truculent energy : all he has is the darkest
residue of the Ulster Protestant spirit, a gloomy and groundless
sense of grievance and suspicion. By the novel's end he is living
in a small part of the large house with only one maid (the
estate-agent cometh!), a last survivor of the happy days of easy,
speculative fortunes and uncrowded private enterprise. Dr
Theodore, the middle-class success with the cultural ideals of
Empire, symbolically disappears and gives way to Sebastian
who must learn to accommodate himself to the philistine class
anonymity of the post-Depression era or slide into genteel
poverty. This dilemma lies at the heart of the Protestant middle-
class novel.

Gilbert's most recent novel continues the theme of social decline, extending its psychological repercussions by transforming
Sebastian Browne's sense of grievance into vengeful psychosis.
Ratman's Notebooks (1968) is a melodramatic, Hitchcockian
story sporting many of the formulas we associate with horror
films : the mysterious manuscript (a favourite Gilbert device
employed in *Monkeyface* and *The Burnaby Experiments*), the
peculiar anti-hero inhabiting a half-empty house and, having
become deranged, cultivating terrifying creatures to do his dark
bidding before perishing in the manner of his own most spectacular victim. Ratman is in one sense a Frankenstein who is
destroyed by the monsters—with folly bordering on hubris—
he has unleashed upon the world. The competent and formulaic
nature of the novel has already appealed to American screen-
writers who turned it into a motion picture successful enough
to spawn a sequel. The novel is now 'the book of the film', and
has been reissued in paperback with the Americanised title of
the film, *Willard*. Yet if *Ratman's Notebooks* is more than a
screenplay, it is because of the literary and social contexts in
which we can set the novel, and these contexts are not likely
to be recognised by anyone unfamiliar with Ulster fiction.

Ratman's Notebooks uses a thematic motif also used in
Monkeyface and inherited from Reid : the notion of the innocent
(sometimes an animal) taught the worldly speech and ways of corrupt man and coming to grief because of it. Yet this novel is a

sharp and even perverse variation on Reid's paradise and initiation themes. The animals corrupted are rats, not normally associated with either paradise or innocence; with grim irony the animal paradise of the Tom Barber trilogy has become Ratman's nightmare. Instead of Uncle Stephen's shaman we have a psychopathic pied-piper leading his rodent army against his enemies. And yet Ratman is not a totally unsympathetic character and his notebooks are shot through with humour that is cynical and malicious but endearing because it is directed against the hypocritical, the crass and the boastful. It is as if Sebastian Browne has been given the chance to tell his own story, one of being shunted into the anachronistic sidings of the middle-class business world by the latest and more deadly business types—the time-and-motion men and fire-in-the-belly, Americanised executives from whose forebears Forrest Reid shrank at the close of *Apostate*. In *Ratman's Notebooks* the twentieth-century usurpers and betrayers of the myth of Victorian mercantile gentility (Sebastian Browne, Mr Bracknel, Ratman) have themselves been usurped and betrayed by contemporary executive officialdom, symbolised in the suitably anonymous Mr Jones. It is only for Jones that Ratman feels a murderous hate; until Jones's death Ratman seeks only food for his rats and much-needed money for himself. Jones stands for today's dehumanised society, superficially ordered and rational, and Ratman's psychopathic response is an index of his alienation. In this sense *Ratman's Notebooks* belongs with other first-person novels that involve a psychopathic response to contemporary, suburban, technocratic society such as Joyce Carol Oates's *Expensive People* and Evan Connell's *Diary of a Rapist*.

Ratman's late father was a businessman of the old school whose profits (judging by the family house) were, in the manner of successful Victorian merchants and professional men, inordinately large in relation to the rest of society and who no doubt kidded himself that his was a genteel and cultivated way of life. This delusion seems occasionally to have been inherited by Ratman who contrasts the jiggery-pokery of today's business dealings with the 'honesty' of his father's time. The 'honesty' of old-time business was, of course, simply inefficiency: Jones who now runs the firm is the new breed of businessman—amoral, uncharitable and haunted by the need to be up-to-the-minute.

Jones is snobbish not in the old sense, about breeding or long establishment, but in the modern manner, about the mere possession of wealth. With such a man, business is stripped to the bone, and his calling in of efficiency consultants (who proceed to label Ratman's potential 'nil') is a typical piece of contemporary business acumen without regard for an employee's long association or personal feelings.

Ratman's Notebooks, then, is an allegory about the shift of power and wealth in today's society. More particularly, it is an allegory about the continuing dissolution of the Victorian middle class in Ulster, even though the city in which it takes place is never specified. Once, Ratman writes in his notebook (and thereby reminding us of the maternal families of John Burnaby and Forrest Reid), his mother's family 'kept a cook, a parlourmaid, housemaids; kitchenmaid, bootboy and all the rest of it'. Now his own family, consisting of his mother and himself, has been reduced to his mother's small savings and Ratman's pitiful salary. When his mother dies Ratman shrinks into one small part of the spacious house, like Sebastian Browne and several of the owners of big houses in Reid's fiction. Not content with 'usurping' Ratman's father's firm, Jones covets the family house, even though it is situated on the out-of-fashion, Victorian side of the city.

Ratman is cynical enough not to swallow all of his mother's nostalgic claptrap about the old days. After cataloguing his mother's vanished social advantages, he adds tartly : 'Back to that I suppose would be her idea of heaven. Send up someone from hell to do a bit of scrubbing. But apparently in heaven it's the angels who do the chores, while the few humans who make it just hang about taking it easy, like the Victorian upper classes.' (p. 52) From his mother, nevertheless, Ratman has inherited crippling standards of wealth and behaviour. From her, too, he has inherited the suffocating piety of the Ulster Protestant, that solemn piety which seems to have fitted Victorian commercialism like a spiritual glove and which is caricatured in Ratman : 'I never work in the garden on Sundays,' he notes. 'Mother wouldn't approve.' Furthermore, his binding love for and dependence on his mother has created a mother-fixation that prevents him from marrying the girl in the office who falls for him, an emotional equation we also met in Reid's novels,

notably in *Peter Waring*. It is even possible to think that given
all the wrong circumstances, young Tom Barber might have
grown up to become the disillusioned Ratman. Ratman's sense
of social inheritance, like Tom Barber's, outdistances his actual
position in today's society. Ratman's is the cynicism of a man
without a social identity, suspended between the decline of one
order and the rise of another, between his mother's pious
nostalgia and Jones's insentient moneymaking.

Ratman's fantasies would seem to be a form of escape from
his mother's influence and a form of release for his frustrated
energy. In another sense they are merely sublimations of the
same desire for wealth, position and respectability that motivated
his parents to emulate the landowning class. Ratman encourages,
for instance, a class distinction among his rats between the elite
furry-tails and the proletarian scaly-tails, on the basis of which
he can divide and rule. This leads to a power struggle among
the rats and between the rats and their master in imitation of
the class struggle in human society. Before Ratman leads his
forces against Jones and finally kills him, he inherits a fortune
from an only uncle, proof that the good old days of inherited
wealth are not entirely at an end. Ratman deserts his post as
top rat, becomes director of his father's firm, makes plans to
marry the girl from the office and—in a concession to the new
order of things—renovate the house. At this point his rat army
turns against him in a class coup. The novel's ending might
almost be accounted a motif in revolutionary mythology : the
disenchanted former elite (themselves betrayers of their class
ideals) lead the disfranchised against the usurping classless and
anonymous philistines and are in turn destroyed by their proletarian followers disillusioned with leadership and heady with
new power. The tongue-in-cheek moral of the story is perhaps
that you do not enlist rats to beat the rat-race.

7
ZOO STORIES

CHILDHOOD as a major theme and source of characterisation in the Ulster novel has been successful only in the hands of Forrest Reid. At least two Ulster novelists, Stephen Gilbert and George Buchanan, have had to outgrow Reid's influence and by doing so have acknowledged the limitations of children as central characters. It cannot be said that Gilbert has done more than move into Reid's thematic hinterland, as it were, for even Ratman—superficially so different from any character in Reid—is really a neurotic and spoiled child. George Buchanan, like Gilbert a friend and disciple of Reid's, has been more successful in this regard, and only in his impressionistic autobiography, *Green Seacoast* (1959), has he partially succumbed to the temptation—which he claims originated with Forrest Reid—to present 'the inner murmur of an out-of-date child'. His best novel, *Rose Forbes,* explores in its own curious fashion the territory that was for Reid always beyond the walled garden of his imagination—adult sexuality.

Buchanan has not needed childhood in order to weave into his work the fate of the Protestant middle class. His ostensible theme is change, in particular the social and political convulsions sustained by Britain this century. These convulsions are no more coherently connected than a succession of newspaper headlines, for social and political events in Buchanan are stippled randomly on a social backcloth. From this point of view there is no difference between his novels (e.g. *Rose Forbes* and *A Place to Live*) and his non-fiction (*Passage through the Present, Words for Tonight* and *Green Seacoast*); all of his prose could be called 'fictional journalism' or 'documentary fiction'. Yet it is the social backcloth, a backcloth of middle-class decline, that gives ballast to the lightweight coyness and gnomic affectation that tend to mar his work and lends it a significance by association with the work of Reid, Gilbert and McNeill. As he tells us in *Green Seacoast*, Buchanan 'was born to the academic wife of a country clergyman, who was descended from a line of clergymen, lawyers, army officers, doctors, in Ireland since the seventeenth century' (p. 112); in other words, he came from solid planter middle-class stock. Though his childhood in Kilwaughter Rectory was clearly luxurious when set against the plight of the poor in Ervine and McLaverty, nonetheless *Green Seacoast*, like *Apostate*, plots a downward movement, and as though to accompany the unravelling fabric of Western civilisation (as it endures wars and depression), Kilwaughter Rectory grows steadily more unkempt. Buchanan pictures the rectory with hens and cats jumping on the window-sills and peering into the rooms (as though the humans rather than the animals, as Buchanan remarks, were in the zoo) before his father finally retires to a Belfast suburb. Distant explosions and gentle decay at home characterise not only *Green Seacoast* but also Buchanan's fiction.

Buchanan's novels were written in the 1930s and 1940s. Janet McNeill is a more talented, less showy novelist whose work belongs to the 1950s and 1960s. In her novels the Protestant middle class has sunk into a suburbia at once more familiar and more modest than Ratman's suburbia, and so there remains in her work only vestiges of the Paradise myth we have associated with Ulster middle-class fiction. McNeill's later novels establish a social cross-roads at which the declining post-Victorian middle class and the rising Welfare State working class meet. But while the social background of McNeill's novels grows progressively more anonymous, more generally post-war British and less specifically Irish, the quality of her work seems to me to remain largely dependent on her Ulster settings. Although she was born in Dublin and educated in England and Scotland, Janet McNeill lived her most creative years in Belfast and helped to create the Protestant middle-class novel. Like Reid and Gilbert, she too has been attracted by childhood, and besides her adult fiction has produced a number of successful children's books in addition to plays for stage and radio.

(2)

Janet McNeill's fictional *forte* is the diagnosis of ailing middle-aged marriage and the frigidity of intellectual women;

Buchanan's is the depiction of love in the fatigued manner of Claude in Clough's *Amours de Voyage* who sees it merely as 'juxtaposition'. *Rose Forbes* (1950)[1] is a mannered and dated novel, yet well worth reading. In several respects it might be compared with Moore's *I Am Mary Dunne*;[2] both are narratives presented through the eyes of sexually mobile women rebounding from man to man in a restless quest for emotional and sexual fulfilment. Rose's emotional life is a many-beaded necklace of crises that recalls Mary's—marriage, widowhood, remarriage, adultery, divorce, remarriage. Emotional passage in each novel parallels the movement of the titular character from place to place; moreover, both Rose and Mary begin in the provinces and see their emotional life climax in the impersonal cosmopolis.

From the long list of suitors in her life—Patrick Mullan, Maxwell Smith, Charles, Leaver Trappe, Bodmin Rush, Albert Whitecliffe, Robert, and Luke Macateer ('this value-system in the flesh', as she calls them)—Rose Forbes loves deeply three men. Patrick Mullan is her first husband, a frustrated young journalist knocking his head against the gerrymandering walls of Unionism in west Ulster (where Rose was brought up on a farm) and Belfast of the troubled 1920s. Then there is Maxwell Smith whom she meets in Belfast after Patrick's death, a warm and sympathetic man ('a mountain in her landscape'), but already married and too avuncular for total intimacy. In England, while married to a shopkeeper and suburban councillor, Rose encounters Robert, the revolutionary with whom she commits adultery. After Robert breaks with her, she continues to drift until, her fifteen-year adventure in London among leftists, suburbanites, German refugees and thirties bohemians over, she returns to Northern Ireland and marries her third and presumably last husband, a stuffy schoolmaster ('a dullish figurine') turned wartime meteorologist. Her return is no more successful in fact than Mary Dunne's return to Butchersville in fantasy; it is like the action of a dying animal making its pointless way back to its lair. Nor is Rose's outward and upward social mobility any more a form of emancipation than Mary Dunne's peregrinations. But whereas Mary's

1. A shorter version of this novel appeared in 1937.
2. Both authors, incidentally, were journalists, both were drawn to the big city (Moore to New York, Buchanan to London), both flirted with bohemian intellectualism.

imagined freedom turns out to be an even more terrifying bondage (more terrifying because it so deceptively resembles freedom), Rose's plight does not really alter from start to finish— she really is Rose *Forbes* at the novel's end as Mary is not Mary *Dunne*.

Rose's plight—her inability to give meaning to, let alone derive satisfaction from, her actions and her feelings—is impossible of change because she is at the mercy of incomprehensible social and political events. Mercy is perhaps least tender in 'the callous metropolis', though nowhere is Rose safe from the turbulence of the world. Nor is it tender for a woman who is even less capable than a man of changing the events that oppress the individual. But men, in the act of social and political participation, are diminished sexually and cannot satisfy Rose, whose promiscuity becomes a reflection of particularly troubled times and, like Mary Dunne's, an oblique criticism of society. In the end, of course, even men have no control over events but are toyed with and buffeted by them. Together, Buchanan's men and women form a lost and traumatised generation delivered blow after reeling blow by history—unemployment, depression, world wars. Rather than alleviating the pain, men by their hypocrisy and cant contribute to it, setting in motion structures and institutions in which people are overlooked.

Hypocrisy and cant are everywhere in *Rose Forbes*. They are root and branch of Ulster politics, both in west Ulster where the novel opens and in Belfast to where it swiftly moves. The birthpangs of violence accompanying the creation of Northern Ireland are like muffled applause for the illiterate speeches of the politicians, particularly Unionists who are presented as wholly disingenuous. Rose's boss, for example, gets himself elected to Stormont 'not to benefit the country but to influence contracts towards his firm'. Patrick, who sees through these politicians, nevertheless works for his father's Orange paper, declaring that the system can only be changed from the inside. This turns out not to be true in his case, and his disillusionment upon confronting such corruption is clearly supposed to be a contributing factor in his death-wish. When he drowns while attempting to save a bather, it appears to be a case of suicide, death due to professional as well as physical fatigue.

Soon after Patrick's death, Rose drifts aimlessly to England.

Buchanan's London of the 1930s is recaptured in a trench-coated, English 'B' picture kind of way—all crushed cigarettes, furtive amours and wet afternoons in city cinemas. Rose rebounds from man to man until she meets and marries Albert White-cliffe, a shopkeeper, suburban councillor and future borough mayor. Albert is a minor Babbitt figure for whom, like his American cousin, appearance is all, a principle which even necessitates taking the collection at church because it is good for business. Rose's chance meeting with Robert, the revolutionary who lives—at least during summer holidays—in a commune, precipitates the break-up of her marriage of convenience to Albert. If Albert makes Rose feel like an acquired bargain ('found in the basement of the 1931 Depression'), Robert after a passionate beginning excludes her altogether from his life. Before and after the Spanish Civil War, in which he fights and is wounded, Robert is 'too much afraid . . . of the perils of tender-ness' and subordinates his emotional life, and Rose, to blurred political idealism. Once again Rose is victimised by Europe in turmoil. The Spanish Civil War is succeeded by the Second World War, and when Rose decides at last to return to Ulster it looks like a return to sanctuary, but, of course, in a province where foreign and English airmen are based and her own schoolteacher husband is seconded as a meteorologist, there can be no escape from Europe's afflictions.

Buchanan's vision is apocalyptic, or perhaps one should say entropic. But because he offers no values capable of with-standing their own collapse, his vision is also nihilistic. Mary Dunne moves across North America with an involuntary kind of emotional scorched-earth policy but at least with some kind of direction; Rose Forbes on the other hand is merely a wind-blown leaf. We cannot even describe Rose as a primitive outsider as we did Mary Dunne, for there is nothing substantial or meaningful from which Rose is being excluded, no safe value-system to which she can aspire. Nor is Rose herself in any way substantially per-ceived by the reader. Buchanan sees his theme in *Rose Forbes* as 'the weather of people' as they are swept over the turbulent landscape of political crises and social upheaval. Other images of his theme include 'the emotional storms inside cities and towns', and 'the texture of handclasps, of touching cheeks and glances'. His fiction, in other words, is primarily atmospheric after the manner of impressionist painting. At close range, background and foreground, character and environment, dissolve into each other :

> Trooping the Colour was a pretty, but faintly boring sight. Rose, who had slipped from the shop to see it, was rather frightened by the police who stopped her here, stopped her there, and ordered her down from some railings to which she clung to obtain a better view. She ended by not being sure whether it was desired that she should watch the monarch or not.
>
> For her the event was reduced to bits of red seen in a broken mirror which she held above her head.
>
> She was pleased by a tiny episode : heedless of bands, of red ranks slow-marching, of vast crowds—three pigeons pecked and loitered together on the sanded ground. Pigeons had no feeling for pageantry.
>
> Two hundred yards from the fuss, the lake of St James's Park lay peaceful, almost deserted. Alone, under a tall white umbrella, sat an elderly woman painting clumps of irises by the water. While she jabbed on her greens and her blues, she seemed not to notice the distant strains of the band playing with sentimental precision 'There's Something about a Soldier'. (p. 93)

At times Buchanan seems to be attempting a kind of French pointillism in the service of irony, rather reminiscent of the way Ford Madox Ford, by juxtaposing separate colours and figures in descriptive passages of *The Good Soldier,* manages to suggest a synthesis in the reader's apprehension. Unfortunately, Buchanan does not have Ford's ironic subtlety and his style is inclined to become irritating and affected and to work against the novel's best interests.

Because his characters have only the illusion of solidity, they cannot be said really to change and develop. 'The weather of people' conjures up an aptly barometric image, for Buchanan's characters are finally only instruments for measuring what in *Green Seacoast* he grandiosely calls 'the panorama of the century', by which he means the Troubles in Ireland, the First World War, the General Strike, the Depression, the rise of Nazism, the Spanish Civil War, and the Second World War. *Rose Forbes* is really a journalistic opinion, cast in fictional form, that the jig is more or less up. Yet I think it is marginally something more.

Buchanan's entropic view of society is in one sense nothing else
than the record of Victorian middle-class decline we encountered
in Reid and Gilbert and will encounter in Janet McNeill. While
walking in a crowded London park Rose harks back to a firmer
past she never knew. 'During the early years of the century,
people would walk here,' she muses, 'feeling that there was
nothing more to do, that they all were in a smooth carriage, being
comfortably borne to a well-appointed future. Today they had
been robbed of that facile optimism.' (p. 84) Their optimism was
assuredly shattered for ever by the nightmares of Flanders
and Ypres, but their lifestyle would have passed away in any
event as this short scene argues :

A man with a white beard spoke in a sedate Mayfair square (Rose
overheard him) : 'They were spacious days. They won't come
again.' She saw that a side of the square was being demolished, and
that many vast mansions were already in dusty ruin. Tall, square
blocks of flats, hastily run up by speculative builders, had appeared
at corners of the square. (p. 97)

Rose herself does not spring from the Victorian upper middle
class or even middle class; writing to Maxwell Smith, she says :
'I belong to a rising class who, you may say, have no standards,
except ambition to be secure and to be taken for fine fellows.'
(p. 181) As surely as Jones in *Ratman's Notebooks,* Rose's group
of rising lower middle-class teachers and intellectuals are filling
the social vacuum left by the departing prosperous Victorian
merchants. At the novel's end, Rose and Luke and their friends
the Kells (the central figures in *A Place to Live*) decide to settle
in Ulster and share a large house 'embedded in this landscape'.
They find an old ivied house built by a wealthy merchant 'who
had driven to and fro in a coach with liveried servants'. The
house, once spacious and quiet, is now a 'Victorian symbol of
descending greatness and farewell', and soon, Rose muses,
children would 'dig in the flowerbeds, dance and scream on the
weedy tennis lawn. . . Indoors, the old decorum would vanish.
Men in jerseys and perhaps sandals would argue, where once a
frock-coated gentleman had made his slow, usually courteous,
periphrasis.' (p. 244)

Waiting to move into the house, Rose overhears a woman
speaking of the fate of such mansions : 'What *dreadful* people are

getting these lovely old places!' Yet Rose and her set, unlike Jones, are usurpers not by design but by historical default, and their succession is not without suffering. That suffering is obliquely connected with the loss to the world of Victorian certainty and out of it has come, a generation after, not only Jones and the other mechanical children of the time-and-motion sixties, but today's new Protestant middle class, less privileged and less arrogant than the old.

(3)

If Forrest Reid is the chief Ulster novelist of childhood, and Brian Moore the chief novelist of youth's twilight, Janet McNeill is the novelist nonpareil of middle age. This theme has extracted from Janet McNeill a delicacy and intelligence only equalled among Ulster novelists by Anne Crone. *The Maiden Dinosaur* (1964) is the best novel to come out of Northern Ireland after Moore's *Judith Hearne,* and respectively these two novels of any in Ulster fiction most richly and perceptively explore Protestant and Catholic psychic malaise. Unlike *Judith Hearne,* however, *The Maiden Dinosaur* is imprinted with no special effort and is, in fact, only one of a quiet stream of novels by McNeill turned out with a professional ease bordering on facility. The reader never gets the impression that McNeill is feverishly knocking at the boundary-walls of her talent, and if adverse criticism be justified, we might wish that she would gamble more in the possibility of achieving work of the stature of Doris Lessing whom she sometimes manages to resemble. Withal, her fiction for adults conveys without brouhaha the terrifying vacuum of failure and impotence that can yawn behind the compensating ritual and fantasy of apparently respectable and even successful middle-class lives. And so, even though her characters are incurably middlebrow, this in no way diminishes or dilutes McNeill's fictional vision of life. Even her prose style is undistinguished and unobtrusive, 'Welfare State Functional' we might deem it in contrast to Buchanan's 'Thirties Apocalyptic', yet it enacts perfectly her recurring presentation of the human condition: the skin of cynical calm or precarious fantasy stretched taut over aching hearts and shimmering nerves.

A decaying middle-class milieu is the very stuff of Janet

McNeill's fiction. Whereas Reid occasionally permitted himself dramatic forays into the meaner parts of Belfast, McNeill's fictional context has become a class rather than a religion. For this reason she can effortlessly switch setting from middle-class Northern Ireland to middle-class England within the covers of one novel; for this reason also, the earlier novels, such as *A Child in the House* (1955) are much richer in local colour than *Talk to Me* (1965) or *The Small Widow* (1967). Not unconnected with this, there is in *A Child in the House* an echo of a grander social past, but this shabby gentility gradually fades through the successive novels until it is relegated to the brief Irish scenes in *The Small Widow* in which the descending post-Victorian middle class has blended anonymously with the Welfare State working class.

That her characters are middle-class and middlebrow accords with their also being at the dangerously middle age of declining sexual and intellectual powers and of withering ambition. Menopause is the commonest ostensible crisis among McNeill's chief characters as they pass through the last stirrings of the heart's unaccountable affections into immunity and placidity. Their decline in mind and body has brought an agonising and self-conscious inability to communicate with others, and a neurotic swing between what is, on the one hand, and what was (and what might have been) on the other. They inhabit an emotional and spiritual no man's land between faith and faithlessness, hope and despair, intimacy and isolation. The only light for McNeill's characters at the end of her dramatic tunnels is the promise of sexual and emotional anonymity as though in imitation of their social destiny.

The predicament of bodily and emotional menopause is developed and resolved within two basic situations: firstly, love and marriage gone stale and encased in ritual and fantasy; secondly, a woman coming to terms with her lifelong frigidity. These two situations interconnect to the extent that the intelligent, frigid woman begins in freakishness and exclusion and ends by triumphing over and even assimilating the shipwrecked lovers and spouses, that is if the latter can avoid the snares of illness and suicide that make middle age in McNeill something resembling a minefield.

Q

(4)

Janet McNeill's novels are strewn with marriages at different stages of almost polite dissolution. Over her marital relationships lies a heavy sense of doom generated as much by each partner's awareness that the marriage must pant on as by his or her private acknowledgement of irreversible failure. Because these middle-aged couples have plumped, out of cowardice or lack of motivation, for such small safe lives, McNeill's novels could be misread as mundane or trivial, yet in fact they are tense with unreleased dramatic energy. The very lack of catharsis is McNeill's theme : even the small dramatic explosions occasionally detonated (e.g. the rare suicides and suicide attempts) are muffled and underplayed as though they might embarrass the reader with their melodrama. Whereas Moore in *Judith Hearne* and *The Feast of Lupercal* can afford to create vivid climactic scenes of victimisation, McNeill must constantly remember that her chief characters live in the next flat to her readers, an everyday couple leading a life of continuous anticlimax and denied the wrath of society let alone the wrath of God.

Typically, a McNeill marriage fails because of a mutual lack of passion, even from the beginning. At most one partner had sexual potential, but it is dissipated over the years in grubby, indecisive little amours (like Wilfred's in *The Small Widow*) or more commonly in lifelong sexual fantasy. In such a marriage, contracted for sanctuary or the camouflage of cosy respectability, husband and wife live under the same roof and share the same bed but without real contact or intimacy, like two small boats flashing conventional messages of greeting and information across the darkness. Never does the marriage bring satisfaction and fulfilment (above the animal level represented, for example, by the socially inferior Mrs McNally in *A Child in the House*), and even when there have been children the overall impression is still of infertility. This impression is shared by the characters themselves, and so when she learns that Maurice's wife is expecting a baby, Addie in *The Maiden Dinosaur* remarks to Sarah Vincent in a tone of dark surprise : 'Don't you think it seems out of character for him to be—fruitful?' (p. 36) Appropriately, the grown-up children, Addie's son for instance or Alice's daughter (in *Talk to Me*), are estranged from their parents. Conditioned perhaps by novels of adolescence, we might expect

the children to be the sufferers in this alienation of the generations, but it is invariably the parents who suffer and, in *The
Small Widow,* are positively victimised. The newly widowed
Julia discovers herself in peril from her children's parasitic
demands and only by the end of the novel does she succeed in
emotionally weaning them away from her and in winning, to use
her own term, 'liberation'. Her friend, poor Mildred, is never so
lucky, married as she is to an ageing would-be lecher and tyrannised by wilful and dependent children. When Julia suggests
somewhat playfully that she and Mildred might move into a
home for old ladies together, Mildred's response betrays real
anguish :

'It would be simply marvellous but the girls would never think
of it. And there's Wilfred, of course. But I'll come and help you
look.'
'The girls, the girls! Can't you ever get away from them?'
Something like terror crept in at the back of Mildred's moist
eyes. 'I can't. I don't think I want to.'
'The way they bully you—'
'I know, I know.'
'Then why?'
Mildred stroked her gloves and said : 'Can't you see I have to
be of some use to somebody. Sometimes I'm ashamed, the way I
scheme so that they'll allow me to be involved in their lives—
little things, like fetching their clothes from the cleaners or taking
telephone messages. I'd crawl, Julia, just for the crumbs. If I don't
have this everything just stops.'
'What sort of pleasure do you get out of it?'
'Like when I felt them kindle, Julia. It's like that.'
'Or at the breast,' Julia said . . .
Mildred was tearing her paper napkin into very small shreds
and scattering them on her plate. 'If there was anyone who
needed me—anyone at all.' (pp. 155–6)

Estrangement of the generations in McNeill does not signal a
struggle between the fertile young and the infertile middle-aged
(though Julia seems somehow threatened by the fertility of her
son and daughter) so much as it evidences a breakdown in what
she depicts as precarious at the best of times : communication
between groups of human beings; 'only connect' is not an
admonition in her fiction but a vain plea.

Instead of addressing themselves to their middle-aged problems, McNeill's spouses indulge in elaborate sexual fantasy peopled by the boys or girls they first loved, from a distance, in youth. The unattainability of the loved one maintains the fantasy: Helen's first sweetheart, Oliver (with whom she never slept), was killed over Germany in the Second World War, and Aubrey's girl, Phyllis, in *Talk to Me* (whom he never even kissed) was found dead in a park. If the loss of the first sweetheart was a kind of emotional lobotomy from which they have never recovered, by the same token the dream-memory of the first love makes life liveable and even helps to shape reality. After Rose's death in childbirth, for instance, Maurice in *The Maiden Dinosaur* marries her sister Joyce as though to resurrect her. Or a cosy trio is formed (Madge-Harold-Julia in *The Small Widow*, Sarah-George-Helen in *The Maiden Dinosaur*) which involves fantasy but also acts from day to day as an emotional cushion for those unable to find fulfilment in marriage alone.

McNeill's world is essentially cruel inasmuch as the vibrations of the early traumas and accidents linger on and render ineffectual her characters' entire emotional lives. Yet traumas aside, her characters are still pathetic creatures. Almost without exception McNeill's men are sorry specimens, passionless, impotent or infertile whether or not they are successful broadcasters, lawyers or chemists. Much less differentiated than the women, McNeill's men survive by parasitically deriving from the various women the sustenance they require: from the attractive women they create the models of their fantasy; upon the maternally competent they foist what children their small virility produces; upon the intelligent they patronisingly impose themselves in return for wisdom and reassurance; and finally they live out the tired marital rituals of the evening and of the bed with those who (like Alice and Addie) have a little of everything and all of nothing. McNeill's men are constantly defined in relation to their women and when their male identity exerts an influence (such as Sarah's father in *The Maiden Dinosaur*), it is a restrictive and damaging influence. McNeill's is a world of committee-meetings and tea-parties ruled at the top by career-women and at the bottom by domineering wives. 'In this women's world,' writes McNeill, 'husbands were cardboard.' (*The Maiden Dinosaur*, 27) Even when a man has been the sexually dominant partner, as Wilfred was, he ends up totally dependent upon the wife he always despised a little, a pathetic dumb creature laid out in bed with Julia and Mildred talking heedlessly over his body, their revenge complete.

This portrait of the sex war is itself largely fantasy. In the wider offstage world, McNeill's women are discriminated against in a male chauvinist society that demands they be either brainless housewives or intelligent half-women. The discrimination seems doubly unfair because her women are so much cleverer and stronger than the men : even Helen, a still-attractive flirt, is like a clever female spider devouring the weaker male sex. But in truth, Helen and the rest of McNeill's women secretly yearn for a man to dominate them; it is not so much sexual and intellectual parity these women desire as sexual and intellectual fulfilment in a society where men through commanding strength deserve their exalted position. In the absence of strong men, the energy of the women is turned destructively upon themselves, exercising itself in bitchiness and fantasy. Presumably the strong men exist outside McNeill's small coteries, but even her characters' brief sorties into the 'real' world do not unearth them. Sarah Vincent and Addie, as local writers, participate in a local television interview. The young Belfast interviewer, with an eye, no doubt, on future London assignments, makes patronising remarks about Sarah being a provincial, middle-class poetess out of touch with reality. Addie, a delightfully drawn and droll figure, defends their sheltered background to the interviewer's growing discomfiture, and finally routs him. One gets the impression that Janet McNeill has in this scene cleverly taken the opportunity of pre-empting possible criticism of her own provincial, middle-class femininity, much as Sarah obviates disdain by dressing sloppily. But perhaps like her two characters she protests too much, and in reacting violently to anticipated paternalism prevents an authentic relationship with men (and male readers) from developing. Out of this reaction McNeill's matriarchal coteries have hardened into autonomy and even endogamy.

Within the coteries, men and women are pathetically dependent on each other. Years of sexual potential spent in fantasy, coupled with the sheer repetition of daily events in marriage, have reduced communication to ritual noise, action to mere rote. Through prolonged use, words have become like coins whose dates and values have been gradually erased until they are more like talismans than currency. Yet the effort to communicate, to break fresh ground, must be made, and so when McNeill's characters speak they are flying small flags, not in greeting but in distress. Like the narrator of Stevie Smith's poem, they are 'not waving but drowning' and their eyes (saying 'talk to me') convey silent entreaties. When desolate they indulge in the comforting babble of the nursery. Locked in each other's arms, Addie and Gerald burble 'Booboo' and 'Googoo' while George, rocking his wife, chants 'Pretty Kitty, Pretty Kitty', which noises echo with cruel irony the cackles and squawks from nearby Bellevue Zoo that punctuate *The Maiden Dinosaur*. In his fantasy conversation with the pretty television announcer, Aubrey in *Talk to Me* degenerates into unintelligible panic : 'How he could have talked, but the words choked him. Her small throat bubbled with Oinks and Poos and drivel. He tried to shout her down and heard his own voice—"Blah ! Blah ! Blah !" ' (p. 121)

Out of the collision between hopeful fantasy and hopeless resignation, McNeill's characters synthesise a ritual existence in which the neurotic need for security is satisfied by careful repetition—Helen's and Sarah's annual fortnight at the seaside, Aubrey's and Alice's greeting ceremony each evening. In marriage both partners draw upon a mutual fund of fantasy, not so much to keep their sexless marriage alive as to ensure the survival of each as an individual, on the principle that two vulnerable lives joined in fantasy have a better chance than one of keeping reality at bay. Much of the pathos of *Talk to Me,* for example, arises out of the progress of Aubrey and his blind wife, Alice, towards the mutual acceptance of fantasy over reality. In one poignant and masterly scene Aubrey pretends he has brought home two pears when in fact he has brought one for Alice only. His good-natured attempts to deceive Alice into believing they are sharing the pears (while he himself tries to keep a firm grip on reality) are foiled by Alice's suspicion that she is being pitied (for she too at this stage desires the truth) :

He said he would peel it for her after they had eaten. 'Now let me put it in a dish.'

But her fingers tightened on the fruit and she said, 'Let me feel your pear now.'

'Give me yours then. I'll set it in a safe place.'

'No. Give me yours first. Let me hold it. I want to feel it in my hand.'

'They're both the same, no difference except that yours is the biggest. The best pear for Alice.'

'Give it to me. No—I'll keep my own. I want yours to hold, Aubrey.'

He stood feeling hopeless and defeated, smoothing the paper out between his fingers. At last she said, 'There's only one pear.'

Children were playing in the opposite garden, crying to each other in clear bird cries.

'You only brought one pear, Aubrey.'

The taut paper ripped. 'The man had only one good one left when I got there. It was for you. The others weren't worth buying.'

'You said there were two pears.'

'One pear or two, what does it matter?'

'It wasn't true.'

He tried to keep his voice light and easy. 'If there had been two good pears I would have bought two. But there was only one. I knew you liked pears, so I bought it.'

'And told me there were two.'

'Listen—I simply didn't care whether I had a pear or not. It's you who likes pears.'

'All right—so why tell me there were two?'

'I wanted you to enjoy it, that was why.'

'And what were you going to do while I was enjoying it? Made appropriate noises and told me how sweet your pear was?'

'I only wanted to please you.'

He wanted to shout or yell or weep. He wanted to walk out of the house and have sky above his head. He simply wanted to stop trying. (pp. 63–4)

This painful scene ends at the dinner-table with Aubrey ('munching an almost invisible salad, feeling grateful that he had come safely into harbour at last') unwilling to turn on the light and thus remind Alice that unlike her he inhabits the world of sight. Only at the novel's end do husband and wife come together in mutual acceptance of fantasy. Mary, a neighbour, tries to tell Alice her black cat has been run over but Alice retorts that her cat is white. Aubrey, after a few tense

moments, accedes to his wife's claim. For both of them, pretence
has become what R. D. Laing calls 'collusion', a two-person
game in which each confirms the other in a false position because
it is necessary to the maintenance of the relationship.[3]

If McNeill's characters, particularly her spouses, are trapped in
their unfulfilment, their very bondage permits a kind of mutual
and self-hypnosis that enables them to forget the big failures
and to enjoy the consolation emotions of pity and gratitude. In
a sense their lives are zoo stories: bondage protects them from
the outside world and so ensures survival, while the boredom
of bondage is relieved through the hypnotic repetition of trivial
actions of the type performed by animals in cages. It is the re-
finement in her later novels of this view of the human condition that allows us to speak of Janet McNeill, tentatively, as
Ulster's only existential novelist.

(5)

Yet most of McNeill's people could not be described as outsiders;
outwardly they are remarkably well camouflaged in their middle-
class gregariousness, modest careers and dull lives. It is an index
of Janet McNeill's talent that she has taken such unpromising
characters from the frayed suburban edges of Belfast and engaged
our interest. But among her people there are some who are not,
despite their relatively secure social position, wholly committed
to sexual success and emotional involvement. It is both their
social security and their lack of emotional commitment that
distinguish these particular female characters from Moore's
pathetic triers, Diarmuid Devine and Judith Hearne. Women
like Sarah Vincent in *The Maiden Dinosaur*, Maud in *A Child
in the House* and Alice Garland in *Talk to Me* are altogether
more intelligent than Moore's outsiders, and if they become
resigned to defeat or fantasy, their resignation is the product of
self-perception, even of a triumphant cynicism.

Like Judith Hearne, Sarah, Alice and Maud are unattractive
physically; unlike Judith they are willing to admit the fact. To
Sarah her body seems 'like a badly assembled collection of
breasts and thighs, stomach and shoulders which she carried
round with her in clumsy parcels' (p. 83). Sarah has rarely

3. R. D. Laing, *Self and Others*, Harmondsworth 1971, 108.

experienced sexual passion or maternal emotion, and is constantly amazed at other women's competence and practice in
such feelings, for instance in the casual way Felicity suckles her
baby one-handedly in the garden. Sarah's childhood, like
Alice's, was spent in the secure world of intellectual competition at which she excelled, and her social world began to
collapse once her schoolfriends discovered boys and turned away
from the sexless achievements of the intellect. Islanded as a
woman in a man's world of intellectual endeavour, Sarah dotes
upon the past before she and her girlfriends grew apart; it is a
kind of womb-fantasy about a time of security kept tenuously
alive for Sarah in her poetry and her periodic café meetings
with her old school chums. Although Sarah, like other McNeill
characters, underwent her crippling trauma—in her case as a
child watching a male exhibitionist—one feels that she was
never cut out to be a sexual participant anyway.

Alice was perhaps luckier than Sarah in finding Aubrey to
marry (a poor lover but an attractive man) while Sarah has had
to make do with what little vicarious sexual pleasure she can
get from teaching schoolgirls. Sarah's frigidity ('to share my
body is unthinkable') is a defence not so much against men as
against women, in particular against the expression of her love
for Helen. In honest moments she admits to herself that her
relationship with Helen completes a *ménage-à-trois*, just as Maud
is caught, a passionless buffer, between Henry and Grace, and
Alice between Aubrey and Ellie.

These women are therefore complex characters. In one sense
they are frigid and sexless, and yet in another they are liable to
respond bodily and unstably to men, as Sarah responds to
George's accidental touch. Moreover, they seem to have lesbian
tendencies, though these are repressed and kept just below the
level of consciousness. Repression operates from within and
without : denied full recognition as sexual people and unwilling
to play the expected role of sexual participant, McNeill's women
heroes have instead channelled their energies into preserving
themselves, sexually or emotionally, virginal and intact. This is
achieved through an act of will, a triumph of mind over body
that carries with it the high psychological risk of their becoming
unhinged or of losing their dignity. One of Sarah's cunning
tropisms is to pre-empt the pity and disdain of others by going

out of her way to show that she is not an entrant in the sex or beauty stakes. Getting ready for the gathering of schoolfriends, 'she made her preparations hastily and with purposeful careless-ness, in case it might appear that she had any hope of improving her appearance. This seemed more honest and less effort, and it saved time. No one will be able to say, "Poor old Sarah, how hard she tries." ' (p. 14) When she is tricked by vestigial feminine instinct into trying, she cuts a comic figure as though her femininity were a cruel ruse on the part of nature. But the opposite tack, that of self-denigration, has its own dangers, and during an unexpected visit from Maurice (in typical flight from the reality of his wife's imminent maternity), when they paint their faces with unlikely make-up and enact a childhood fantasy, Sarah tells him of her nickname at school, 'Daddy' Vincent, and runs herself down paranoiacally, to Maurice's acute embar-rassment, in a vivid and painful scene.

Yet Maurice comes to Sarah as George, Helen, Addie and the others come to her, for ironically it is her femininity without sexuality that attracts these lame ducks. Her nickname indicates not only her physical mannishness but her obscure parental warmth, even though she has allowed herself neither husband nor children. She permits herself to be used as a psychiatric oracle, but is cynical enough to realise that the friendship of those who consult her is a damnation with faint praise. Out of fear and revenge she prohibits their intimacy and, as befitting a lifelong and tragic waste of emotion, yearns for the other side of the menopause when she will gain 'pleasurable immunity', just as Maud longs for 'matronly tranquillity'. The companionship without intimacy, privacy without isolation that Sarah seeks are symbolised in the living arrangements of the chief characters in *The Maiden Dinosaur,* Sarah living in her own flat in the centre of a large house and surrounded by flats occupied by Addie and Gerald, and Felicity and Justin, and Helen. Like animals in contiguous cages, they live within hearing of each other but are debarred from total intimacy. It is an unlikely and precarious set-up, and during the novel the arrangement collapses : Helen returns to Hubert in England and Addie is in hospital. Un-apocalyptically, things wind down.

Of all Janet McNeill's characters, Sarah and Alice are best equipped to survive the surrounding entropy in the lives of their friends and coterie. Sarah Vincent (the 'fossilised schoolgirl' and dinosaur of the novel's title) and blind Alice survive because the innermost part of themselves remains untapped, maiden in spirit even when not in fact. Like obelisks they stand relatively un-involved while those around them drift and sink like sand. The brainy schoolgirls, denying the sexual fulfilments of youth and denied the intellectual fulfilments of maturity, have at last a kind of revenge upon the others. Whereas in real life such women might be justly regarded as having run away from reality (Addie tells Sarah she would 'have been a wow in a nunnery'), in McNeill's fiction they become embodiments of the human mind courageously negotiating the assault-course of emotional break-down and physical decline, avoiding the pitfalls of despair and suicide, keeping at arm's length the final, inescapable void.

(6)

The society out of which McNeill and her characters operate is a middle-class one in the process of being reduced to suburban vulgarity and mediocrity. If the novels exploit the universal nightmares of suburbia also exploited by contemporary American novelists such as John Cheever and Joyce Carol Oates, there are specifically Northern Irish aspects of McNeill's suburbia. Favourite locales are the university area of Belfast (the setting of Reid's *Apostate* and Moore's *Judith Hearne*) and the pros-perous northern shores of Belfast Lough (the setting of Gilbert's *Monkeyface*), and in either case the characters occupy the large Victorian houses built by linen-merchants, stockbrokers and ship-builders. The opening of *A Child in the House* shows that the middle-class decay around Queen's University which was under way in *Apostate* has gone on apace; half a century after Reid, McNeill writes : 'Some people might say there was a stagnation about the Crescent, for there are signs that its function has be-come outdated. It no longer houses those whose prosperity allows them to acquire culture, and whose culture instructs them to increase their prosperity. Multiple doorbells and name plates beside them show that most of the houses are now flats.' (p. 7)

No less than the houses themselves, the spacious Victorian gardens have lost their original purpose, and in McNeill have run wild or been paved over. It is useful to remember that

gardens play as important a role as houses in Protestant middle-
class fiction and in the autobiographies of Lewis and MacNiece.
For Reid's young heroes gardens are, at their most mundane,
places of refuge from adults, and at their most magical, re-
creations of the First Garden. Much of the action of the Tom
Barber trilogy takes place in gardens with manicured lawns
(ideal for Reid's beloved croquet) bounded by dense shrubbery
in which the animals of these miniature paradises sport, and
when Tom dreams, often it is of vast magic gardens of miraculous
fecundity and colour. Cared-for gardens also play a large part in
Gilbert's *Monkeyface,* but by *Ratman's Notebooks* the urge to
tend them has, along with the family wealth, almost disappeared.
Indeed, Ratman's machinations originate precisely in his large
back garden, as if its neglect has turned into pestilence like some
blighted paradise :

> Mother says there are rats in the rockery . . .
> The rockery is at the very top of the garden. When Father
> was alive it was a sort of show place—very pretty, rare flowers.
> All that sort of thing. He used to bring along his gardening
> friends to show it them . . .
> I hadn't been in the back garden for ages. The state of it quite
> shocked me. Not that I'll do anything. I'm only surprised Mother
> got as far as the rockery. There are brambles right across the path.
> In one place there's even a tree, quite a sizeable tree, growing out
> of the very middle of the path. . .
> After Father died we couldn't afford a gardener. I suppose we
> should have sold the house and moved somewhere smaller, but
> neither Mother nor I liked the idea. Mother wrote to Uncle in
> Canada and told him how badly-off we were. Uncle's a bachelor,
> and supposed to have money. But he didn't even reply. So we paid
> off the gardener and stayed on, hoping for better times. Uncle
> can't last forever. I kept the front garden looking fairly decent.
> The back's gone wild. (pp. 7–8)

Less dramatically, the running to seed of the large gardens is
also in McNeill a metaphor for the seediness to which the lives
of her characters have been reduced. The green fertility Reid
worshipped and equated with Eden has in McNeill, as in
Ratman's Notebooks, got out of hand and by being *too* fertile
(like the burgeoning lower classes or Gilbert's rats) defeated the
purpose of a garden, which is controlled fertility. 'It must have

been a beautiful garden once,' Sally thinks, walking down Sarah's driveway. 'Everything is overgrown and tangled now. There is a lilac tree fallen sideways because the blossoms on it are so heavy. There is a big straggling bush with flowers on it like plates of cream. Two thrushes are arguing, floundering about in seeded lupins.' (*The Maiden Dinosaur*, 120) Just another legacy of a previous generation, the garden is ignored by the flat-dwellers who have no stake in it beyond its usefulness for airing laundry. As Sarah looks out on a June evening, 'the place has the tattered appearance of a public park near closing time' with deck-chairs and magazines and Felicity's pram; outside the garden, ice-cream vans blare and contrived garages and television masts scar the original beauty of the locality. Rat-like, the rowdy, anonymous public has invaded the green inner sanctums of the Victorian middle class.

We can follow the process of class decline in McNeill as she gradually omits local Ulster colour in her novels on the assumption, no doubt, that middle-class society in Britain and Northern Ireland is becoming increasingly grey and anonymous. But even in *The Small Widow*, set in an undisclosed English suburb, the central character, Julia, has her plight complicated because she originally came from Ireland. If she cannot come to terms with her daughter's post-Aldermaston world of political protest or her son's post-Jimmy Porter sub-bohemianism, neither can she comprehend the Ulster to which she briefly returns after her husband's funeral. At first, the beauty of Belfast Lough seen at dawn from the ferry is like a gentle welcome, with

the exhilaration of standing on the deck as they came up the Lough in the chill of the early morning, purple water, green fields, blue hills, the shape of the Cave Hill remembered a moment before it is seen and coming home to her heart like a bird, the grey sky paling to luminous northern daylight, the houses on the shore watching for her, the gantries, chimneys, steeples, the water calm now, thick like oil with the boat carving its passage through it, the stir on the quayside, the boat shuddering as the rhythm of the engines changed. (p. 182)

But it is illusion. The trip home is a disaster and serves only to remind Julia that she occupies a social limbo almost as anguishing as the emotional readjustments of widowhood and the change of life.

This sense of limbo is increased by an erosion of religious faith : indeed, McNeill's novels present a telescopic view of the recession of belief that accompanied the decline of Victorian wealth and morality. For example, a large part of the complication of *A Child in the House* arises from the stuffy Victorian evangelicalism that pervades the novel, inhibiting Maud's husband Henry in the expression of his love. His sexual repression is of a piece with his tightwad instincts and puritan outlook. 'Physical passion was to him as undesirable as all other forms of extravagance,' though we sense that his righteous tirades against love conceal at once a fear and a longing for its comforts if not joys. Such old-fashioned piety has by *The Small Widow* faded to an agnosticism in which any profession of faith excites outrage or mere embarrassment. The pivotal novel between these two is *The Maiden Dinosaur* which records the religious twilight of a class and a generation. The characters of this novel have allowed the private rituals of the coterie to displace their traditional and historical religious affiliation, leaving them isolated even among the Protestant working class that was once their bulwark and foundation :

For most of them, brought up in Provincial religious homes, faith as they grew older had become an individual solitary relationship, shy, ingrown, a protest against the public emphasis on their Protestantism, against too loud Orange drums and the hysteria of spawning Mission Halls. They were products of their environment and generation who had retained the habit of faith as they had the habit of cleaning their teeth, both learnt in childhood, and recognised that these were private occupations. (p. 175)

Alongside cultural and spiritual shrinkage, social decline is, then, a brilliantly exploited regional metaphor fleshing out McNeill's universal themes. Without inheritors, her people survive like animals from a previous age, dinosaurs in a zoo. They are the last of a species, of a generation and class born around the First World War and who lived through the Second World War. Survivors of these holocausts (unlike pilots Oliver in *The Maiden Dinosaur* and Reggie Baird in *The Small Widow*, whose ghosts haunt the novels like unspoken reproaches), they linger unfashionably and guiltily on, a little shell-shocked, remembering their best years in the 1920s. 'We played tennis on grass courts', recalls Aubrey Garland in *Talk to Me*, 'and thought the Charleston was delightfully abandoned. We made limited love on the dickey seat of our friends' motor cars and in the temples of damp Victorian shrubberies, where our flapping flannels collected green stains. Sometimes we sang round a piano. We closed our eyes and generally our mouths when we kissed. We quoted poetry between kisses. We forgot about the war we'd been too young for and said there wouldn't be another one.' (p. 19)

Towards the conclusion of *The Maiden Dinosaur*, Sarah tries to defend her fellow-survivors: 'I think we've done pretty well, all things considered. We have established a type. Society doesn't recognise a type unless it has some significance.' (p. 177) There is more desperation than certainty in these sentiments, and Addie's mournful questions that prompted Sarah's defence are likely to be the notes we continue to hear when we set down *The Maiden Dinosaur*.

'I am just a little exhausted with emotion and fury at being a provincial lady and not much more time even to be that. What do you suppose happened to us? Modesty and duty, what do you think we expected to get out of that little lot? There used to be something called nobility, too. You only hear about it nowadays in Church. And the emancipation of women going on all around us. Or was it the wars that queered our pitch? Do you remember Miss Alison at school— perpetually in rose beige and we suspected she used a lipstick. "Live boldly and strongly, girls." I used to look at her and wonder if she managed it.' (p. 177)

(7)

Janet McNeill's fiction is characterised by a surface tension which is broken only when a character has a nervous breakdown or commits suicide, and even then the tension is quickly restored, like dangerous water smoothing itself after a stone's entry. Madge takes her own life in *The Small Widow*, and Ellie in *Talk to Me* almost succeeds in doing so. Helen tries to drown herself in *The Maiden Dinosaur*, and in the same novel Kitty commits suicide with an overdose of sleeping-pills, that most suburban of methods. These particular incidents can be explained in terms of profound emotional stress, but because these four characters seem no more distressed than the rest of McNeill's dramatis personae, we are justified in looking for broader reasons, for social as well as psychological factors in their psychic disorder.

A suicidal situation arises in McNeill's novels when emotional stress is set against the social psychology of the middle-aged Protestant who has sprung from well-off late-Victorian parents, who has experienced the recession of his religious belief, and who feels that he subscribes to outmoded social values. The ritual aids of which Solon T. Kimball speaks[4] have fallen away, and are of no help during emotional stress, not only to the individual, as in Judith Hearne's case, but to the entire group, which has resorted to the fantasy-ritual of the coterie. The predicament facing Moore's lonely anti-heroes now afflicts McNeill's whole cast. The ritual content of religious and social values has dried up but has left its permanent marks upon the psyche. And so McNeill's characters may lose their Protestant faith, but a puritan guilt still gnaws at them, encouraging anxiety and neurosis. And while the social relevance of their life-values may have withered before their eyes, her characters still adhere to those values tropistically and *faute de mieux*. The disparity between this class atavism and the social reality around them contributes in no small measure to their psychic distress.

This is the plight too of many of the characters in Reid, Gilbert and Buchanan, so it is not surprising that there is a fairly high incidence of suicide in these novelists as well. Patrick Mullan's death in *Rose Forbes* is a disguised suicide, and so arguably is Ratman's. Then there are the overt suicides of Doreen in *Rose Forbes* and of Denis Bracknel in the novel of that name. Reid's young hero Peter Waring attempts suicide by courting pneumonia; we recall, too, that Reid describes in *Apostate* how he attempted to commit suicide as a boy with an overdose of laudanum. Most of these hypertensive and suicidal situations in Protestant middle-class fiction could be termed, after Durkheim, *anomic* in so far as they involve a breakdown in society's capacity for regulating the aspirations of the individual and in the individual's ability to integrate with society.[5] In Janet McNeill and George Buchanan, this breakdown is imaged in unhappy marriages and love affairs (separation,

4. See Chapter Five above, p.163.

5. Emile Durkheim, *Suicide*, trans. John A. Spaulding and George Simpson, London 1952, ch. 5.

adultery, divorce, widowhood), and in the plight of intelligent, bored, under-employed women in a male chauvinist world. In addition, McNeill has taken the condition of menopause—male and female—to image generational and class decline. And underpinning all action in Reid, Gilbert, Buchanan and McNeill is suburban ennui, the failure of Victorian morality and stability, and the loss of Protestant faith, a coalition of social conditions that fits Durkheim's definition of anomie.

According to sociologists, such a society in evident transition would be likely to produce a higher suicide rate than, say, a Catholic lower-class society. Statistics show that 'suicide rates are higher in the most and the least prestigious occupations', and the most prestigious occupations in Ulster are represented in the middle-class fiction. There is also a tendency for suicide rates to reflect the degree of urbanisation, interesting since middle-class fiction is Belfast-set or Belfast-orientated. But perhaps of more relevance to Ulster fiction than class or social environment, at least as a negative factor, is religion. The sociologist already quoted makes the qualified observation, after Durkheim, that 'Protestants have higher suicide rates than Catholics.'[6] Another writes: 'The lowest suicide rate has been in Roman Catholic countries and among Roman Catholics in any community. Certain characteristics of this denomination point, then, to deterrents against suicide. Among these may be included: the authoritarian attitude against suicide, the threat of punishment, the relief of guilt feelings through the confessional, opportunities of atonement for sins committed, and the unity of the church.'[7] Irish fiction, as well as Irish statistics, would seem to bear out the denominational factor.[8] It is rare to find suicide or suicide

6. Sanford Labovitz, 'Variation in Suicide Rates' in *Suicide,* ed. Jack P. Gibbs, New York 1968, 66–70.
7. Elizabeth Kilpatrick, 'A Psychoanalytic Understanding of Suicide' in *ibid.*, 152.
8. Suicide figures from the overwhelmingly Catholic Republic of Ireland (though possibly not totally reliable) compared with those from mainly Protestant Northern Ireland show a clear disparity. For the years 1962–69 inclusive, numbers for the South were 52–70–58–51–69–72–71–52 and for the North (with half the population of the South) 61–87–79–70–82–98–99–92. For the years 1966–69 inclusive, rates per 100,000 of the Southern population were 2.4 – 2.5 – 2.4 – 1.8 and for Northern Ireland 5.5 – 6.6 – 6.6 – 6.1. See the *Annual Report of the Registrar General* for Northern Ireland statistics and for Southern figures see the Department of Health's *Report on Vital Statistics.*

R

attempts in Irish fiction by Catholic writers. There is the suicide of Leopold Bloom's father in *Ulysses*, of course, but then Bloom's father was Jewish, and the Catholic aversion to suicide is summed up in the hostile reaction and petulant comment of Mr Power : 'The greatest disgrace to have in the family.'[9]

We might have expected suicidal situations in rural fiction, especially among those characters we have called 'primitive outsiders'. Given the highly ritualised and regulated nature of Irish rural society, we would probably have called such suicides *fatalistic*, again after Durkheim.[10] Fatalistic suicide is committed by those living in a society of 'excessive regulation' whose futures are blocked and passions choked. Yet if the fictional transcription of rural Irish society is accurate, outsiders are paradoxically integrated because their estrangement is itself ritually conceived and processed. Irish society accepts eccentrics and oddities and is continually fabricating a thriving corpus of folk legend about them. In life and in fiction this makes for a very primitive psychology of character, but also makes for toleration so long as community morality is not offended against. Such tolerance lies, for instance, at the heart of the comedy of Kiely and Boyle, which is less satirical than celebrative.

The crude reduction of rural character to psychological humour and type—by the novelist as by the real community—may itself be a healthy barrier against total despair, and may help to account for the absence of suicidal anguish in rural fiction. Through tale and gossip and humour (often malicious in themselves, as we have seen), and a balancing kind of obligatory tolerance, the rural community at once distorts and safeguards, victimises and sustains. William Carleton, however, suggests another reason for the rarity of rural suicide, at least among the peasants he knew. According to Carleton, the native Irishman gives vent to his feelings without stint or disguise. 'This constitution of mind is beneficial,' he adds; 'the Irishman seldom or never hangs himself, because he is capable of too much real feeling to permit himself to become the slave of that which is factitious. There is no void in his affections or sentiments which a morbid and depraved sensibility could occupy.'[11]

9. *Ulysses*, London 1960, 120.
10. Durkheim, 276n.
11. 'The Party Fight and Funeral', *Traits and Stories*, 181.

What we interpreted earlier, then, as a kind of manic-depression, an unstable oscillation between grief and joy, is seen by Carleton as a healthy, almost childlike form of catharsis.

Neither in life nor in fiction is there a single, isolable cause of suicide or of its absence, but instead a constellation of factors, among these being, no doubt, the psychology of the Irish race as Carleton saw it, and the tolerant crevices of Irish ritualism as I see it. But these would not explain the absence of suicide in Brian Moore's Belfast novels whose chief characters are inhibited and pent-up, nor in his American novels which depict a de-ritualised society. Judith Hearne, as someone who is sexually frustrated, in the process of losing her Catholic faith, and already bereft of rural roots in a city she finds inhospitable, would seem a prime candidate for suicide; so too would Diarmuid Devine, a thirty-seven-year-old impotent, emotionally crippled by the dogmas of a community from which he is effectively excluded and of a religion in which he no longer believes. Yet the lingering taboos of Catholicism that are an important cause of the suffering of these two characters also seem to prevent them from entertaining suicide as a serious resolution of their problems. An analogous situation obtains in the American novels. The very sense of dislocation that causes distress—the clash between the heroes' provincial Irish past and their cosmopolitan American present—also ensures that enough of their Irishness and Irish Catholicism remains to create a taboo around thoughts of suicide while compelling and protracting sexual guilt. The very nature of Moore's dramatic crises, then, provides a built-in defence against the most desperate human reaction to exclusion and anomie.

It would be wrong, of course, to suggest that life is merely reflected rather than refracted in fiction, and yet it is obvious that the novelist must respond, both consciously and unconsciously, positively and negatively, to pressures from his society. These pressures tend to be heavier and more inhibiting on Catholic than on Protestant novelists, and so the fact that a much weaker taboo surrounds suicide in middle-class Protestant than in Catholic society might encourage novelists like Reid, Buchanan and McNeill to catalyse despair, where dramatically appropriate, into the final destruction of self. (The range of primary emotional situations is, in fact, altogether much greater in Protestant than in Catholic fiction. We have already contrasted Sam Hanna Bell's unabashed use of cohabitation in *December Bride* with the general propriety of McLaverty's plots. In the middle-class Protestant fiction we encounter conditions and situations that are discountenanced in Catholic society—divorce, adultery, homosexuality, lesbianism, impotence, frigidity. Ulster Catholic writers tend either to ignore such things or else present them in a peculiarly 'literary' fashion which conveniently precludes their mature investigation. Even Boyle's *Like Any Other Man,* in one sense about sexuality and personality imbalance, is less serious fictional psychology than medieval allegory. This is not, *ipso facto,* to pass facile critical judgement on the relative *literary* merits of Catholic and Protestant fiction; it is arguable that the best Catholic fiction, where it yields to Protestant fiction in latitude of theme and emotional situation, compensates—perhaps sublimates—by exhibiting superior energy, formal facility and textural wealth.)

In one important respect, however, suicide in Protestant fiction might indicate the writers' recoiling from, instead of their transcription of, Protestant middle-class society. I am thinking of the exaggerated and psychologically destructive influence of the mother on the male characters. In Reid, McNeill, Gilbert and Buchanan, men are frequently fussy, womanish and neurotic, and very often dependent on mother-figures. Reid's fiction, of course, (the 'search for the father' notwithstanding) is soaked in mother-worship. Rose Forbes mothers her men incorrigibly. Ratman is dominated by his mother. McNeill's husbands languish in the bosoms of their sturdier wives. It is true that mother-dominated characters also abound in Catholic fiction (Ned Mason in *In This Thy Day,* Tommy in *Come Day—Go Day,* Fenner in *Red Is the Port Light,* to name but a few), but then the Catholic family, community and religion have traditionally matriarchal aspects,[12] and so we would not expect the Catholic writer to perceive a connection between mother-domination and the sexual passivity and guilt that characterise much Catholic fiction—though I believe the connection is implicitly there—nor to use mother-domination in the

12. Cf. the figure of the mother in fiction and folk tale and the personification of Ireland as such in folk mythology; cf. also mariolatry in Roman Catholicism.

creation of suicidal situations in his plots. On the other hand, a conscious or unconscious reaction away from the male-dominated and father-orientated Protestant milieu, which Reid, Buchanan, McNeill and Gilbert stand outside of as well as in some respects typify, might be expected to carry high risk. George Buchanan, in a parenthetical remark in *Green Seacoast*, claims : 'A turning away from this Protestant aspect to a matrist Hellenism was to form the theme of Forrest Reid's remarkable *Apostate.*' (p. 114) He adds that the label 'weak' is attached to those, like Reid and himself, who 'show a leaning to matrist values'. In the fiction the price is higher than mere name-calling. Denis Bracknel's suicide (like young Reid's attempted suicide) fits Durkheim's definition of *egoistic* suicide as that committed by those (often apathetic or melancholy) weakly integrated into a society by its nature incapable of ensuring their integration in any case, the kind of suicide we associate with artists and writers.[13] However, a Freudian interpretation of suicide as 'the supreme manifestation of the Oedipal stress and of the conflict between Eros and Thanatos'[14] might help to account not only for the suicidal tendencies of Reid's young heroes who are dependent on mother-figures (tendencies that accord well with the languishing pantheism they embrace), but for the generally oedipal cast of emotional crisis in Protestant middle-class fiction. This side of suicide, the reaction of many characters who suffer from sexual inadequacy as well as anomie—the burbling spouses in McNeill, the same writer's frigid women recalling pre-pubescent achievements, Reid's countless boy-heroes—is a longing for childhood and the uterine comforts. Indeed, we might even interpret the recurring image of the walled and fertile garden as something of a womb-symbol as well as an image of middle-class security. For those characters outside Reid's novels for whom the reversion to childhood is no safe sanctuary from the pressures of adulthood, Eros gives way to Thanatos, desire to despair. And so Ratman's mother-complex and abortive love-affairs erupt into psychopathic loathing, the emotional *terminus ad quem* of the Protestant middle-class novel.

13. Durkheim, chs 2 and 3.
14. Austin L. Porterfield. 'The Problem of Suicide' in *Suicide,* ed. Gibbs, 50.

8

FATHERS AND SONS

I HAVE already commented upon the dearth of realism in Irish fiction. Among Ulster fiction writers, only Brian Moore and Janet McNeill could be called realistic writers in the sense that I have been using the term; i.e. they seriously confront, in a relatively unswerving manner, the sexual and spiritual problems of maturity. The rest, realistic in flashes or (as with Reid and Ervine) in an historically generic sense, tend towards outrageous comedy, fantasy, allegory and equally outrageous pathos. The Irish literary tradition militating against realism is self-perpetuating but there are probably social pressures as well, so that it may be possible to regard comedy and fantasy as to some extent sublimations of the Irish writer's realistic desires.

Realism often accompanies a writer's courage to expose unpleasant aspects of society, and this it is hazardous to do in Ireland, North and South. McNeill and Moore, writers who did not feel compelled to stay in Ireland, are writers who have never accepted morally or literarily the co-ordinates of Irish society as the boundaries of their fictional universe. Many of those Ulster writers who elected to remain in Ireland (irrespective of where they published)—Forrest Reid, Patrick Boyle and Benedict Kiely among the best of them—have compensated with elaborate fictional texture and a unique personal vision for their underlying conservative outlook. None of these three writers is a realist, nor can they really be called primarily psychological writers. Psychology has been as badly served in Irish fiction as realism. Outside of Moore and McNeill (and isolated novels by other writers), the psychology of character in Ulster fiction tends to be typological and very much subordinated to other, equally legitimate fictional intentions—dream, allegory, caricature, satire, mock-heroics. Again, there are social pressures persuading the fiction writer not to attempt depth analysis of sexuality or abnormality : censure and censorship in the Republic of Ireland (where several Ulster writers live and work), community puritanism North and South, as well as a basic tribalism —with which the writer is himself afflicted—that forces people into age, party, sexual and sectarian stereotypes.

There are several Ulster fiction writers around or under forty who have begun, with an almost crude vengeance, to make good the lack of serious psychological exploration of social and personality problems. The work of Jack Wilson, Maurice Leitch and John Montague was first published in the 1960s; these writers are therefore still developing. Though they have set their fiction on the land, they exhibit that urban consciousness that is, as we have seen, necessary for liberating rural fiction. Better still, Montague and Leitch are worldly writers, not in the sense of having written Irish fiction for consumption in America but in the sense of having soaked up influences from outside Ireland. They are not 'performers' in the way that so many Irish fiction writers who go in for satire, comedy, anecdotage and fantasy are performers. In the most obvious sense of the word, they are 'serious' writers.

Any fiction writer who wants to illuminate Ulster society has to press realism and psychology into service in the exploration of three things : sex, violence and sectarianism. Sexual relationships are still too grotesque in Leitch and Wilson, in part because of the persistent Irish tradition of the grotesque and in part because Wilson and Leitch, like Kiely and Boyle, see the land as a grotesque place : sexual grotesquerie is a literary reflection of, and a metaphor for, life outside the city. The difference between Boyle and Kiely on the one hand and Leitch and Wilson on the other is that the former use abnormal sexuality as an atmospheric and textural part of a blackly comic vision of the land whereas Leitch and Wilson use it as evidence of psychic disorder brought about by the inhibitive and perverse forces of rural life. Unfortunately, we can still only catch a glimpse of the beauty and tenderness of love and sex in the writing of Leitch and Wilson, but I suspect that this is due less to the kind of fiction to which they are committed than to the kind of society they want to portray truthfully. The desire on the one hand to characterise the stunted sexuality of Ulster society and on the other to explore love and sex in their fullness is a dilemma that no novelist writing about Ulster, outside of Anthony C. West, has been able to resolve. Moore resolved it only by setting novels such as *An Answer from Limbo* and *I Am Mary Dunne* in America. In the unself-conscious treatment of sex and love, Ulster writers have still a long way to go.

There has never been a shortage of violence in Ulster fiction, though until recently Ulster was not, outside of sectarian eruptions, a particularly violent place. Violence is simply part of the fictional vision of Ulster, and perhaps, too, an easier dramatic catalyst to handle than the more sensitive mysteries of sex. Yet in the fiction, violence is sometimes associated with sexuality. If sex is violent, there is the suggestion that violence is in turn sexual and can be imaged in sexual terms. Brian Friel's story 'Ginger Hero', for example, is climaxed by a cockfight presented in sexual terms. The linking of sex and violence is an ironic commentary on the love Annie's husband cannot give her and which she violently demands from Tom, the narrator, while the cockfight is in progress. But the cockfight—between a bird owned by Tom and Annie's husband (who work on Lord Downside's estate) and one owned by the English Captain Robson— also invokes the conflict between the English landowners and the Irish peasantry. Embedded in 'Ginger Hero' is the idea that in terms of racial psychology the violence between the Irish and the English can illuminatingly be given sexual overtones. When this notion is taken up by Leitch and Wilson and applied to the conflict between the Planter and the Gael, we have the germ of a genuine fictional insight.

Sex, violence and sectarianism are interrelated in the fiction of Leitch and Wilson. Sectarianism is a primary fact of life in Ulster and takes both a positive and a negative form : positive in the direction of violence, negative in the direction of self-segregation. Fiction that imitates negative sectarianism by choosing its characters, settings and dramatic complications from one side only must in the end itself be accounted sectarian. When we say that Friel, Kiely, Moore and McLaverty are Catholic writers, we are not saying that Catholicism is either their faith as private individuals or their theme as writers, but that in the main their fictional material is drawn from Catholic experience in Ulster. We make a similar assumption when we call Reid,

McNeill and Ervine Protestant writers. That the terms 'Catholic writer' and 'Protestant writer' are still meaningful is an indictment of the community but also of the writers who, rather than being 'antennae of the race', in Pound's phrase, have done no more than keep pace with any intelligent and compassionate Ulsterman in the encouragement of mutual knowledge between Protestant and Catholic. On the other hand, little of the fiction that has tried to confront positive sectarianism has been enlightening. Lynn Doyle turns it into knockabout comedy with results that are more comic than illuminating. Sectarianism in its crudely violent aspect has, of course, attracted all kinds of adventure and thriller writers. Such fiction ranges from the morally motivated adventure of F. L. Green's *Odd Man Out* (1945) through George Birmingham's satirical adventure, *The Red Hand of Ulster* (1912), and W. A. Ballinger's American-style 'blockbuster', *The Green Grassy Slopes* (1969), to the popular and often contemptible and pseudonymous efforts that have cynically flooded the paperback shops since 1969. The exploration of sectarian psychology remains very much a low priority in all of these books.

Until recently no fiction writer has brought Carleton's courage to the theme of sectarianism and its racial and sectarian wellsprings. With less compassion than Carleton and only a fraction of his talent, Montague, Leitch and Wilson have nonetheless tried to explore, not simply 'tour' 'the other side' so that the mutual knowledge so desperately lacking in real life between Protestant and Catholic has begun to exist at least between the covers of a book. They have tried to be realistic and psychological writers but have not been able to avoid allegory. This is hardly surprising since the first step in the exploration of sectarianism must be an examination of sectarian stereotypes. In the United States clamour for racial equality and integration was followed by violence which was in turn followed by a mutual and frank confrontation of the differences between the races, and the same thing seems to be happening in Northern Ireland. Only after psychological understanding has gone beyond sectarian stereotype will the groundwork for mutual acceptance and dependence be laid.

Leitch, Wilson and Montague, then, are writers whose work has a realistic surface and a good deal of psychological intention but which is also a kind of racial or sectarian allegory. In this context we can add to these three the name of Victor Price who, in *The Death of Achilles* (1963), has written a good novel about the Cyprus Emergency that bears an uncanny resemblance to what is sometimes called the Ulster Emergency. Price's novel is in part a racial allegory that can, without too much interpretative violence being done to it, be made to illuminate the Northern Ireland situation. As a result of the allegories being written by these writers, insights are being wrested from the very obduracy of caricature, stereotype and folk myth that could help us liberate ourselves, not necessarily from the falsehood of these things (they may well turn out to be true) but from their relevance and necessity. It is still an elementary, almost adolescent task facing these writers, but only when it has been accomplished will writers be in a position to transcend the divisions in Ulster society from which they themselves suffer.

All three writers, Leitch, Wilson and Montague, have gone back to the 'lost fields' for their vision in the awareness that the land is the crucible in which the Northern character, Protestant and Catholic, has been forged. The land, they have discovered, has lost none of its violence, its perversity, its blight. The land still sustains with one hand, divides the sects and rebuffs the exile with the other. But the land is under seige now like never before and the city, having drained the land of its manpower, has begun to spill back into the countryside in the alien and irreversible form of suburbia. The return to the land by fiction writers and by poets (Mahon, Montague, Heaney) has a particular urgency in Ireland and at the same time is part of a general trend of return to the land by the urbanised throughout the Western world. If the Ulster poets are archaeologists, the novelists with less urgency are anthropologists. In both genres the past is being revaluated : many of the novels and stories discussed in this chapter involve sons confronting fathers from whom they are alienated, as the writers themselves are like sons confronting the ancestral sins of the land. The encounter with the father is, as Campbell shows, a stage in initiatory trial, and we can equate it with return to the land if we regard the urban experience (explored in Chapters Four to Seven) as the initiation of an originally rural people. My scenario, in other words, re-enacts the separation-initiation-return sequence followed by van

Gennep's initiate and Campbell's monomythic hero. In Chapters
One to Three the land (symbolised by those of its people who
left) was seen as a child seduced by the mature city; in this last
chapter those who have lived in the city have returned to confront the land (symbolised by the father) that never submitted
to the outside world. Those who return to the land discover, like
Peter Douglas in Montague's 'The Cry', that their maturity in
the city has been an illusion and that coming to terms with the
father and with the dark land is in fact their last initiation into
manhood.

One Ulster fiction writer alone, it seems to me, has already
completed the fictional task facing Leitch, Wilson and Montague.
Perhaps he has been able to do so because for him the land is
not a father but a woman—mother and sweetheart—to be loved,
and it is only through love that the divisions that rend Ulster
society can be transcended. Anthony C. West's career has all the
necessary credentials : he was born in rural Cavan, travelled
widely abroad, periodically returning to Ireland, always trying to
set the record straight. His work supplies most of what I have
felt to be missing, in combination, in Ulster fiction : seriousness,
psychological perception, poetry, a variety of modes (including
realism), an unabashed and evocative celebration of love and
sexuality and an ability to straddle the sectarian divide. West's
novel *As Towns with Fire* may not be the Great Ulster Novel,
but in the brilliance, poetry and cultural span of its ultimate
failure, it is the nearest an Ulster writer has come to that unlikely phenomenon.

(2)

I have deferred discussion of West's fiction until now because
the exuberance and exorbitance of his talent make it difficult
to classify him. West's fiction first appeared in book-form in
the 1960s but he is a rather older writer than Leitch, Wilson
and Montague. The settings of his work include his native
Cavan, Belfast, England and North America where he has
travelled and lived. There have been three novels and a volume
of stories, *River's End* (1960), many of which were originally
published in *Esquire* magazine. West is the most strapping talent
in contemporary Ulster, perhaps Irish, fiction, a writer who has
created a unique and personal style that combines acute realism

with poetic impressionism. His prose, lavish and zestful, is rich and tactile and seethes with images as a carcase seethes with maggots. The simile is advised, for West's rural Cavan between the two world wars is a place of great rankness, decay and fevered energy, of contention, brutality and raw sexuality. Yet even when his subject is violence or decay, West is a lyrical writer. Here, for instance, is his description of dead rats floating down the river after the rat-hunt in *The Ferret Fancier:*

Three big dead rats came turling down the river, tied together by a single strand of current and drowned in their own fear, the waterflow making them deathlessly alive as they floated over each other's backs, bowing to each other in a happy kind of mime, swirling and dancing invitingly before him like three old pirates fresh from Davy Jones, bobbing about as if laughing, suddenly darting away and as suddenly returning. (p. 74)

The delicacy of West's observation could be both evidenced and metaphorised in his image of 'a little tobacco-brown wild-duck that's so light it can sit on the water without breaking the skin'. But his descriptions are never without sap or strength. Here is a passage from *As Towns with Fire:*

A big hare with a roan-red back and creamy flanks steps softly across the breeze, rooks take wing as their sentries warn my approach, swirling the wind to drift them to a safe field; a silver shroud of gulls up from the sea for the worms drowned by recent floods, a choir of larks and modest primrose banks, chaffinch and chiff-chaff and sky of bluebells with white clouds of ramsons, a few last windflowers and the whirring of a wren, grey stone outcrops engraved with lichens, new bracken rising out of the old, a kestrel standing on its topless tower of air, young nestling rabbits almost fearless while their policeman parents drum my trespass through the warren : faces and facets of beauty and fear, the trace of beauty and the stain of fear everywhere, one with the other like water and wetness. (pp. 54–5)

Alone among Ulster fiction writers, West is a poet and a life-lover, someone whose celebration of life is not elegy in disguise. Several writers come to mind when I read West. There is in him D. H. Lawrence's poetic vision of the sexual rhythms of the land, Lawrence's race-consciousness and Lawrence's idolatry of animal and flower. There is something of Hopkins's word-invention (an author West frequently alludes to in *As Towns with Fire*) and the lyricism of Dylan Thomas's nature poems. In *As Towns with Fire* I detect too the influence of J. P. Donleavy, with his fragmentary poems and Mr Skimpole naïvety crossed with a cynical gingerman paranoia. West is a hugely eclectic writer whose prose, piled page on page, yet manages to be unmistakably his.

The Ferret Fancier (1963) is set barely over the Northern Ireland border, probably in Cavan, just after partition and the Irish Civil War. Young Simon Green, of a Church of Ireland family, attends a Protestant country school also attended by Roman Catholics because the nearest Catholic school is four miles away. The school is presided over by Rainey, the slovenly and tyrannical headmaster, only Nonconformist teacher in the big Episcopalian parish. Everything we have associated in the rural naturalists with the blighted land and bad blood is there in Simon's world—the family squabbles ('As he learned more about the parish, he found there was hardly a house in it that didn't roof some kind of domestic contention'); the community unease ('These folk weren't kindly gregarious as sheep, they were suspiciously communal as rats'); the poverty (for some 'the breadth of a crust and the depth of a bailiff's whim away from straight destitution'); the shrunken libidos and malformed egos, the simmering sectarian hatred. Through the tumult of rural life Simon, the adolescent hero, has to make his hazardous pilgrimage towards adulthood in a novel that is unusual firstly in being a genuine novel of rural adolescence that does not involve the city, and secondly in depicting a border community where, if sectarianism abounds, Protestant and Catholic are nonetheless thrown together much more than anywhere else in Ireland.

What dominates *The Ferret Fancier* is the land's brutal, perverted yet curiously innocent sexuality and its unlimited, not wholly salutary fecundity. Almost everything, and not merely in Simon's adolescent fever, is sexual. Ferreting for rabbits, for instance, becomes a violent series of sexual acts : 'every hole a female one and every tuft of moss a tuft of pubic hair, the ferret a kind of cock which they shoved into the holes to rape the waiting rabbits' (p. 38). The jackass and Mrs Rainey's mare blithely couple in the school playground while Mrs Rainey, herself pregnant, tries to separate them; the schoolboys handle the

hens to encourage the rooster to tread; Simon watches through a
hedge as Agnes Jameson is mated by a tinker's lurcher. More
often than not, sex has an edge of menace and violence to it and
Simon's predicament is his sensitivity amid the brutishness of
life and death in the parish. His foil in this regard is Thubby
Knight, a clubfooted youth so obsessed with sex in all its possible
guises that we rightly sense he is doomed to loneliness and failure once the obsession wears off. Others accuse Simon of weakness and his anguish arises from his suspicion that this is true.
His father 'often accused him of lacking guts. That may have
been so, but his courage was such a small thing that it always
had to be wrung tight as a greasy dishcloth to give it any appearance of solidity at all and when he did come to any sort of a
decision he had to abide by it since he was too poor to risk any
further loss of integrity.' (pp. 19-20) Like Gavin Burke, Simon
needs to be galvanised out of his adolescent faintheartedness into
action and will. But Simon's is the less enviable task because
his sexual tumult becomes confused with the forces of death
around him : when ferreting, 'every time a rabbit was hounded
up and down an unknown maze of burrows and caught and
killed in some awful blind corner in screaming darkness, he
endured a hot and tooth-edged lawless ecstasy that had all the
power, fear and pity of the subterranean terror of dreams' (p. 38).
Occasionally Simon seems himself like a rabbit, transfixed and
helpless in the face of such brutality, and this suggestion is reinforced when almost unwillingly he accepts the gift of a ferret
named Jill. Ferrets, says West, are 'huge animals in small disguise, made so by the mercy of God. Were they even big as cats
nothing on earth would be safe.' (p. 85) Jill is evil, ruthless,
blindly fearless, pure will : everything Simon is not. She is a
death-dispenser (illustrated graphically in West's account of a
rat-hunt on Simon's farm) and at the same time, despite her
femaleness, a lithe, phallic principle that excludes love. Simon
becomes tyrannised by the ferret, even giving her a live rabbit
that sits transfixed, arousing Simon's fascinated disgust because
it is 'giving itself to death like a whore'.

The ferret is a brilliant Freudian symbol of Simon's projected
adolescent fears and also a more obvious symbol of the brutality
of life and death, of the interrelation of sex and violence on the
land. To escape from adolescence into manhood, to find release

S

from the land's enslavement, Simon must clearly throw off the tyranny of the ferret. His hope of emancipation lies in his ability to come to terms with the land—a sign of imminent maturity—by participating in its rhythms of life without succumbing to its violence and decay and destitution. Different kinds of love assail him. There is the pure pubescent love for Miss Gibson, the assistant teacher, shattered when she marries. There is a kind of love for Mrs Jameson, the poor Catholic married to a Protestant now ostracised among the Orange parish for his folly and transgression. Mrs Jameson in Simon's imagination is his 'mother-lover, womb-dam, breast-mistress, hearth-whore'. She is not merely a product of adolescent fantasy, for big-breasted older women abound in West's fiction and symbolise the earth. Watching Mrs Jameson suckle, Simon experiences a 'single loneliness of yearning for lost comfort', a womb-longing that is indistinguishable (as in Reid) from the pantheism of West's vision. More particularly, Mrs Jameson can be taken to represent the slovenly fecundity of native Catholic Ireland at whose breast the Protestant has never, to his half-chagrin, been suckled. Either way, Simon's love is no mere futility but is consummated in the spectacle of Ireland's natural beauty, in the image-laden re-creation of which no fiction writer or poet has surpassed West. Simon finds a more conventionally consummated and fleeting love with Mrs Jameson's daughter Agnes by whom he is initiated into sex in a tender scene enhanced by the imagery of the nearby salmon river and marred by the heavy symbolism of the graveyard in which intercourse takes place. While making love Simon is visited by sexuo-violent thoughts of stoat and rabbit and haunted by his dead grandfather commemorated on the neighbouring headstone. Out of violence and death springs life. Agnes becomes pregnant but marries a farm-labourer of her own faith when the Jameson family slide into the terminal destitution of the travelling people.

Simon finally escapes the ferret's despotism by starving her to death. It is something of a coward's victory, the attainment of freedom within a larger captivity. Simon may now be privy to the mysteries of elemental life, but he has yet to learn understanding and to transcend understanding in idealism. It is a daunting task symbolised in the beckoning peak of Knockbawn, the mountain he has yet to scale and which has overlooked the novel's entire action. There is too the blurred offstage figure of Paul Noble, an odd character (is he alive or dead?) who lived in a tent apart from the parish. Mountain and mentor damage the novel, I think, in the obviousness of their referents. Noble represents nobility, solitude, the understanding of beauty and love, all conspicuously absent from the sensual, here-and-now parish. Knockbawn, a 'constant spire' and at the end of the novel 'a prophetic white in a bridal dress of Christmas snow', represents idealism and the kind of purity Simon's love for Miss Gibson (whom, significantly, the children refuse to call by her married name) exhibited. At the novel's end Simon feels trapped in a world whose mystery he has penetrated : 'The shoddy town's mean buildings seemed to close round him like a nightmare, his own desire to see the world's far places becoming weak and frightened.' After burning the hutch and ferret, he sets out for Knockbawn but has to turn back in the deep snow, his journey into manhood complete but his journey into knowledge and virtue, which manhood alone cannot guarantee, only begun.

Simon has achieved guts but as yet neither heart nor head. The pilgrimage in search of these is continued, within a new persona, in *As Towns with Fire* (1968). He is now Christopher MacMannan but still a border child who finds himself at the age of thirty embroiled in the Second World War. Even more explicitly in this novel, West—*rara avis* indeed—bestrides the various social and cultural traditions available to the Ulster Protestant : Orangeism, nationalism, Gaelic culture, English culture, the British military tradition. Considered purely as a novel, *As Towns with Fire* is a lesser work than *The Ferret Fancier* but is still the most ambitious Protestant novel yet written and one that happily makes the description 'Protestant novel' seem clumsy and out-of-place.

As Towns with Fire opens on the outbreak of the Second World War with Christopher MacMannan writing poetry and ekeing out a living in London. In a forty-page flashback (written in the first person unlike the rest of the third-person narrative), MacMannan recalls his childhood in Kilainey (Co. Cavan?) in Ireland; the narrative returns to the London present and MacMannan's nomadic movements from flat to flat during which a flatmate with whom he has a brief affair kills herself when he flits without telling her. He marries an English girl, Molly

Chester, and after a brief stint in the ARP he moves to Dublin and from there to Belfast where he becomes a fire-watcher and then joins 'a kind of para-military supply organisation'. Soon after the Belfast blitz, MacMannan returns to England where he joins a pathfinder squadron of the RAF; at the end of the novel, having safely weathered the war until VE day, he apparently crashes during his last operation, in peacetime.

The lengthy flashback summons up for us the rural North of *The Ferret Fancier,* brutal and superstitious and racked by border sectarianism made worse during MacMannan's childhood by the Great War and the contemporary Troubles when rural life was polluted by 'Orange propaganda about Rome and its popes, mixed up with garbled versions of old Irish myths'. 'The whole atmosphere of the parish, the parish soul, never at any time snow-white, was infected by a kind of unleashed, subconscious malevolence that was real as the awful confusion of the Trenches.' (p. 27) Through the land flows the River Bannim from which his mentor, friend and nurse, the simple Dilemma Doake, keeps young Christopher away, afraid as she is of 'the swirling indigo depths that held, she claimed, water-snakes, her name for eels for which she had a horror, saying that they came out on the banks at night and would destroy unsuspecting women—how destroy, she never told' (p. 31). In the poisoning of the river ('like a sewer, fouled with tea-dark water from the dozens of retting-holes') we are given an apt image of the blighted land. Of this land, nevertheless, MacMannan considers himself an unseverable part. His father is a 'black-haired Milesian celt', his mother a MacDonald, 'oddly enough a sprout off the same old Scotto-Gaelic stock of the MacMannans'. MacMannan, we are told, 'was out of a lost people and culture': the name 'MacMannan' comes from 'Manannan son of Lir, the Danann king of the devachanic seas'. Part of West's originality is his ability to synthesise the two strains of Gaelic Irishry and Scots Protestantism into one Irishness. When young Simon in *The Ferret Fancier* confronts Catholic nationalism it is a jolt for him to discover its exclusiveness: 'It was the first time Simon had come up against catholic nationalism and it made him uncomfortable. He had always taken it that his birth guaranteed his Irishry even though [his father] saw himself as a protestant loyalist and no more than an Anglo-Irishman whereas [his mother] looked on herself only as a protestant and would remain one were she floating in the ocean on an ice-floe.' (p. 41) If MacMannan rejects Catholic nationalism, he is equally opposed to King Karson ('first Fuehrer of this twentieth century') and what he considers Orange fascism. He even denies that he belongs to the Scots-Irish planters, 'a Cain-cursed afflicted post-Tudor nation'.

The question of race with which MacMannan is preoccupied throughout the novel is essential to the plot in so far as Mac-Mannan's predicament is the conflict between his nomadic indecisiveness on the one hand (a mature version of Simon's adolescent bewilderment) and on the other his sense of civic and moral responsibility; this conflict can also be seen as that between his neutral Irishness in the war and the growing pressure on him to fight. This is good, but I think West takes McMannan's race-consciousness too far and focuses too much attention on it. In London MacMannan meets people (e.g. Sommer the Swiss Nazi) who pervert race for ideological purposes, and of course the Second World War is to some extent a race war. Yet no one is more conscious of race than MacMannan, no one readier to ascertain the racial origins of every acquaintance. For all of MacMannan's coy disavowals when taxed about his Irish pride, I think the reader's difficulty in distinguishing the novel's rampant political race-consciousness from MacMannan's race-consciousness (however healthy this is in a purely Irish context) hurts *As Towns with Fire*. This difficulty renders suspect West's handling of human beings on the land. MacMannan and West are too ready romantically to identify farmers and cottiers with the soil on which they live, in a kind of Lawrentian racist pathetic fallacy. There is in West a pastoral mock-naïvety that he can well do without.

Withal, West is eager to show the universality of the land and in doing so exposes, intentionally or unintentionally, the humbug in MacMannan's race preoccupation : 'The land : still there and its old hungers, sowing, growing; land had no nationality, soil was soil under the international sun.' (p. 137) When Mac-Mannan's consciousness does not get in the way, the oneness of the land operates beneath and against the divisiveness and polemics of the city from where the war-effort is directed. Wherever MacMannan finds himself, he turns from men, from the city and from the war to find solace in the landscape. West is good at re-creating the savage and menacing beauty of the wilder Irish landscape, but he is even better at capturing the pastoral beauty of old rural England whose plants and herbs have quaint, strong, no-nonsense Anglo-Saxon names. Such a land will, one feels, remain when the superficial chatter of war ceases. Even in the city a little of the land's bounty is for MacMannan embodied in the countless large-breasted older women he encounters. The English landscape and the female gender with which West endows it at once frees and exacts humility : the cottier's wife to whom he makes love is appropriately, if heavily, called Modesty Liberty.

   MacMannan drifts between the city and the land. The city is successively London and Belfast, the latter evoked during the blitz in scenes that use some of the same historical incidents Moore uses in *The Emperor of Ice-Cream.* MacMannan is also trapped between war and peace, between his Irish neutrality and his European commitment, between moral anarchy and moral responsibility. Indecisively he drifts into the RAF and with hindsight we can see that this is a fatal surrender to everything that is wrong with the world. Yet his protracted indecisiveness and awareness of the issues involved have themselves robbed him of the qualifications to make a moral decision about the war. The very ambiguity of his nationality and of his racial allegiance seem to have decided his fate, along with the fact that the land he sprang from was not this pleasant English landscape but a darker, more blighted land. Certainly joining the RAF has been no resolution of the conflict within him. When he is apparently to die at the novel's end, his name acquires a halo of martyrdom : he is Christopher MacMannan, saint and mythic Irish hero, but also Dylan Thomas's Jack Christ, Son of Everyman. His 'sacrifice' proves that our deferment of the choice between freedom and responsibility means that the choice has already been made, that the indecisive middle ground is itself a kind of thraldom. Like Simon Green, MacMannan wishes to be instinctive man at one with nature but in his self-consciousness and in his race-consciousness is alienated from the land : and so it is Modesty Liberty and not he who is privy to the old names and healing properties of the plants and herbs. MacMannan (in a way not so very different from the hubristic heroes of Bullock and McLaverty) suffers from a surfeit of knowledge and worldliness.

In MacMannan's case, knowledge lacks direction, coherence, and objective; he dies to redeem himself from knowledge as Christ died to redeem us from the sin that knowledge brought.

By a curious irony, *As Towns with Fire* in its sprawling form and diffuse style enacts MacMannan's 'sin' but is without its own means of redemption. Against a kaleidoscopic background of pastoral and polemics, it has been impossible for West to keep MacMannan in focus. As an embodiment of the racially and nationally ambiguous Ulster Protestant, MacMannan's lack of clarity is effective. Indeed, when he joins the RAF and is thereby given a more sharply defined context, MacMannan loses force as a character. MacMannan in the RAF is an ordinary mortal, a possible analogy being with Christ who con-descended to become a man before dying and ascending once more (Mac-Mannan ironically ascends in life and descends in death). It is hard to reconcile this uniformed MacMannan with MacMannan in civvy street and in mufti. West works best with unfocused characters barely glimpsed through the foliage of the narrator's consciousness, but the price he pays for this is loss of novelistic structure.

In order to harness the prodigality of his imagery and insights, West substitutes a crude kind of irony and weighty symbolism for the normal organic exigencies of plot. MacMannan patiently rears a duckling given to him by Mrs Liberty and towards the end of the novel his own twin children kill it. Modesty Liberty, whose elderly husband is impotent, asks MacMannan to give her a child in a scene that is beautifully handled. Clearly Mrs Liberty, 'breast-mistress' and 'womb-dam', will conceive, but she and her husband are killed the following night by a wandering German fighter whose pilot spots their innocently un-blacked-out window. And of course the supreme irony of the novel is Mac-Mannan's survival of missions over Germany only to die while on meteorological duty during his last operation.

The virility of West's writing bridles against these feminine literary ploys. The novel's title is from Berowne's lines in *Love's Labour's Lost*:

> So study evermore is overshot :
> While it doth study to have what it would,
> It doth forget to do the thing it should;

> And when it hath the thing it hunteth most,
> 'Tis won as towns with fire; so won, so lost.

Since West's novel takes place during the Second World War and involves MacMannan in bombing missions, Shakespeare's simile is especially apt. The simile is also illuminating if by 'study' is meant MacMannan's surfeit of love and knowledge that consume their own objects. Cruelly, the simile also ironically rebounds upon the consuming fire of West's inventive, image-rife prose. In the end the objective of the novel is obscured amid West's brilliant efforts to attain it; from the blurred issues of war, race, land, love, morality, knowledge and poetry it is difficult to discern permanent contours and perspectives. To restate this more positively, West can been seen as the most fertile and originative fiction writer the North has produced since Carleton; his fiction, like the fecund and untidy border landscape he comes from, outstrips his novelist's attempts to shape and husband it (a not un-West-like metaphor). Leitch, Wilson and Montague, all of considerably less talent, have had to opt for the shapelier compensations of fictional husbandry.

(3)

Maurice Leitch is a writer whose honesty and forthrightness, judging by his first two novels, compensate in fair measure for his sometimes costive lack of fluency and flair. The common thematic denominator of *The Liberty Lad* and *Poor Lazarus* is homosexuality, an index of Leitch's courage as an Irish writer. *The Liberty Lad*, Leitch's *Bildungsroman*, was published in 1965, the same year that saw the publication of *The Emperor of Ice-Cream*. Comparison is by no means to Leitch's obvious detriment. Frank Glass, 'the liberty lad', is a twenty-four-year-old schoolteacher. He lives in Kildargan, a small industrial village in Antrim that sprang up with that most Ulster Protestant of enterprises, the linen trade, and began to suffer when the trade receded. In the course of the novel Glass is initiated into the dark realities of power when he becomes involved with a Unionist MP in the course of seeking the headmastership of his school. He is also initiated into the bitter-sweet joys of sexual love. Lastly, through his father's experiences at the mill where he works, Frank is initiated into the meaning of decline and loss. In each of the novel's dramatic matrices, Frank loses out : he fails to secure the headmastership, his father dies and he does not find the right girl. It is in loss rather than in fulfilment that Frank Glass becomes a man.

To the extent that Leitch shows the victimisation of Kildargan by the corrupt city, *The Liberty Lad* is a novel in the tradition of local naturalism. But in other respects this is an urban novel, just as Kildargan is really an industrial suburb of Belfast. In the tradition of the *Bildungsromane* we discussed in Chapter Four, Frank Glass has to 'penetrate' the city before achieving manhood. He does so by entering Belfast's homosexual underworld, the kind of purgatory we also noted in the novels of Chapter Four. Frank's homosexual friend, Terry, nevertheless comes across as a sympathetic character, someone who simply never outgrew the sexual ambivalence of adolescence. Not so Bradley the MP who in a fairly blunt scene tries to seduce Glass when the latter goes to canvass him about the headmastership. Perhaps too facilely, homosexuality is in this context a metaphor for, or agency of, corrupt power. Leitch's vicious portrait of Unionist politicians totters on the edge of caricature (Bradley's dogs are called Carson and Craigavon) but is salvaged by an interesting twist that makes Bradley the son of a lapsed Catholic and former gombeen man, an example of Castle Catholicism that is the mirror opposite of Protestant 'reversion' and which allows Leitch to flay both sides of the political fence in Northern Ireland.

In a larger sense, homosexuality seems to be a metaphor for the stunted sexuality of the Irish, an obstacle in Frank's progression towards sexual fulfilment. Perhaps Frank Glass is a more sexually ambiguous character than Leitch intends. He is apparently virgin when the novel opens and during the novel's course fails to make it with a married girl, Mona. The scene in which he meets Jack and Mona Purdy in a pub and drunkenly fails to capitalise on a situation in which he finds himself alone with Mona is coincidentally similar to the Plaza scene in *The Emperor of Ice-Cream*. Frank is happier in Terry's company and he humours Terry's feminine wiles to the point of connivance; only at the very last moment does Frank break away from Bradley's physical overtures; and throughout, Leitch gives Frank an over-hearty manner of speaking that suggests sexual uncertainty. My impression is that Leitch in his desire for honesty has misplaced his psychological emphasis and made Frank Glass not so much enigmatic as passive and vulnerable, thereby letting his novel lapse into the sentimentality that traps Tomelty in *The Apprentice* and that Moore, by a positive ending, avoids in *The Emperor of Ice-Cream.*

Poor Lazarus (1969, and winner of *The Guardian* Annual Fiction Prize) is a novel without any of the gauche charm of *The Liberty Lad* and which instead throbs with tenebrous anger. Even more uncompromisingly, this novel explores the loneliness and misogyny that seem to lurk beneath the male camaraderie of the time-haunted Irish. In addition, Leitch confronts sectarianism in an allegorical but unwaveringly realistic fashion. At one point in *The Liberty Lad,* Frank Glass confesses his ignorance of Catholics. In *Poor Lazarus* Leitch tries to make up for Frank's ignorance by presenting a view of Catholics through the (admittedly paranoid) eyes of his chief character, the Protestant Albert Yarr. But he also gives us a picture of Protestants through the (admittedly Catholic) eyes of the 'returned Canadian', Edward P. Quigley. *Poor Lazarus* is set in South Armagh and also over the border in Monaghan; the time of the action is 1967, supposedly not long after an IRA campaign. Yarr is a Protestant shopkeeper in the overwhelmingly Catholic village of Ballyboe and he receives a visit from Quigley, a Canadian who is in Ireland to make a film about 'the old country'. The relationship between the two men during the succeeding month is the novel's drama.

Thirty-six-year-old Yarr is a strapping, loud man whose wife Ruby would appear—Yarr never confronts the fact—to be expecting their first child. His once powerful sex drive has, partly because of his slovenly and shrewish wife, partly because of failing powers, become perverted into impotent fantasies alternating with sexual disgust. In addition, he has a history of mental imbalance and has apparently received electro-shock treatment in hospital. Quigley himself is not without his difficulties. His movie work has recently been poor and this assignment is in the nature of a last chance to redeem himself in the eyes of his Toronto boss. While in Ireland Quigley keeps a diary and first-person extracts alternate with a third-person narrative seen mainly from Yarr's viewpoint. In one diary entry Quigley speaks of having at a precise time and on a precise assignment lost his nerve. His loss of nerve is an ironic complement to Yarr's own lurch towards nervous breakdown. In mutual bereavement—Yarr of his sexual creativity, Quigley of his artistic creativity—these two impoverished men cross paths at a highly critical stage in their lives.

Quigley asks Yarr to show him around so that he can gather ideas and material for shooting his documentary. No shooting actually gets done, however, and more and more it appears as though Quigley is instead living his film through Yarr. He becomes increasingly dependent upon Yarr until at the end of the novel, unaware that Yarr has taken a paranoiac seizure, he nets the idea for the documentary which he has stalked all novel long—'A Day in the Life of Yarr'. If Quigley the artist feeds parasitically on the inartistic Yarr, the sexually obsessed Yarr feeds parasitically on the sexually modest Quigley. He manoeuvres young girls into Quigley's half-willing grasp in order to derive vicarious pleasure and to achieve over Quigley the power which he impotently lacks in home and community. Quigley and Yarr develop a symbiotic relationship that is latently homosexual. There are rumours abroad that Yarr had an 'affair' with a young Catholic, Joe Donnelly, a rumour given substance in Yarr's fitful and recurring memory of Joe's death in a car-crash—'wee darling Joe—the only man he ever loved'. He begins to suspect his feelings for Quigley and to suspect that Quigley himself may not be straight. Quigley for his part describes the relationship in his diary as a marriage, and though he means this figuratively, the novel is in a way the story of a doomed love-affair between two rejects whose mutual sense of failure is a powerfully binding emotion.

On the most concrete level Yarr and Quigley are unique and solitary individuals with specific problems. On another level they symbolise, respectively, Ireland and the outsider's concept of Ireland. The outsider humours the Irish, pretends to take them at face-value but in the diary of his secret thoughts despises and fears them : 'Yes, the Irish are feared abroad,' Quigley scribbles, 'and rightly so. The smell of madness hangs about them. A bell should be rung before them.' (p. 21) The Canadian's attitude towards the Irish swings between love and hate. In turn, Yarr is a desperately Irish figure reminiscent of Patrick Boyle's Simpson.

But the very media of his swaggering self-expression—the drinking, the pub camaraderie, the roaring—conceal the opposite and complementary traits the Irishman fears or is ignorant of : his terror of time, his contempt for women, his melancholia ('the Irish malady', Quigley calls it). The struggle to camouflage these things is a factor in Yarr's mental distress. The final seizure is precipitated when surreptitiously he reads an entry in Quigley's diary that speaks of 'some creeping horror' eating Yarr from the inside out. Yarr's response to this unwanted self-revelation is as outrageous as his lifestyle and when he plunges into a bog, croaking like a demented crow, we might think of the equally apocalyptic conclusion to *Like Any Other Man.*

On a third level, the love-hate relationship between Quigley and Yarr images the sectarian relationship. Quigley, after all, is not just a Canadian but the son of an immigrant Irish Catholic, one of the people by whom Yarr sees himself victimised. A Protestant surrounded by Catholics, an Ulsterman living close to the border, Yarr *affects* rather than *feels* the political supremacy that is technically his. 'Popeheads. But his derision could never quite ease away his hatred. You could laugh at them, fine, but you couldn't ignore them, no, by christ, you couldn't.' (pp. 66–7) 'He lived his life in an ant-hill, a tolerated guest, ignored, as they moved about skirting him carefully, day to day, but one false move and they could turn on him, picking his bones white any afternoon they chose. God, there were times when he'd felt so tired handling them with the kid-gloves never off.' (p. 149) In this novel the hubris of Bullock's Protestants becomes Yarr's paranoiac madness; Yarr's paranoia is that of the Ulster Protestants, victims of their own sombre imaginings that have just the fatal modicum of justification. At the end of the novel, however, Yarr's madness is really an inspired attempt to lift the siege against his Protestant survival. He is already a fish out of water and so decides to embrace his piscean nature by swimming away. Wondrously liberated from his lifelong garrison psychology, he becomes one with the elements—he is fish and animal and bird :

Then he begins to run, bounding across the heather, leaping turf rows in his path. He feels blank inside, scoured. He flaps his arms in the air as he runs, feeling the sun on his bare shoulders.

Run and swim, float and run. His jumps become higher, wilder, and he calls out to the sky and the moorland—a cry like the wild-fowl flying distressed far above his head. He mimics the curlews and a solitary lark like a palpitating dot high in the heavens. (p. 203)

Alas, the terminal irony of his flight translates his freedom back into madness. There is no place to where the Ulster Protestant can escape: he is trapped forever on an alien island. When Yarr plunges into the bog, it is 'the brown obliterating depths' of native Ireland that claim him.

Leitch sees Catholic Quigley and Protestant Yarr as separately impotent, mutually doomed but engaged nonetheless upon an inescapable and infertile relationship. As a sectarian allegory, *Poor Lazarus* is a brave and exciting novel. It is blemished by the fact that Quigley never comes alive. It is true that he is a good vehicle for Leitch to depict the contemporary rural Ireland that might surprise returning Americans—a place of transistor radios, pub television and showbands. This post-Kennedy Ireland lies uneasily on top of the older Ireland with its ancient privations and sullenness. If Quigley sees this new Ireland, it is Yarr who is paranoiacally tuned into the Ireland that affords Leitch such scenes as that in which Yarr drunkenly tries to buy some poteen from evasive, slightly sinister mountainy men. Less paranoid, Quigley too sees things in Ireland not to his liking and makes some trenchant entries in his diary: 'A country sagging under its weight of place-names. . . A nation of myopics.' (p. 154); 'Funerals. It was the obituary column in his newspaper my old man read first. An Irish thing.' (p. 57); 'First signs of human inadequacy to cope in all this natural perfection. Ruined cottages—roofless, yellow fudgy crumbling walls, doors plastered with auction posters, old bedsteads taking the place of gates.' (p. 73); 'I never witnessed such a mania for physical contact. Hand-shaking is always an embarrassingly long drawn-out affair and, with a few drinks, the hugging, the shoulder and arm squeezing.' (p. 159) What does not convince, however, is Quigley as a North American—he is clearly the creation of someone not really intimate with Americans or the American mind and speech. Yarr, upon whom the novel stands or falls, is a far more considerable creation, and a comparison with Boyle's

Simpson evidences once again the recurring difference between Protestant and Catholic fiction in Ulster. Yarr is a more interesting and faceted personality than Simpson, a potentially larger fictional achievement, but Boyle by some distance is the better prose stylist and image-maker of the two writers. It is lack of sheer writing ability more than a defect in conception that prevents Leitch creating in Yarr a truly tragic figure. Simpson on the other hand has only the merest pretence at tragedy and is instead a brilliantly rendered clown.

(4)

At one point in his diary Quigley notes: 'The Protestant ruling minority. An ugly race. In-breeding? No poet will ever sing for them—of them.' Similar sentiments have recently been voiced in real life; Protestants have been called 'mongrels', 'a collectively petty people' and 'a peculiarly unattractive people'. Such sentiments reinforce the Protestants' unflattering self-concept and make them strengthen the psychic walls that not only protect but also confine and inhibit. For the Ulster Protestant who is conscious of his heritage and is not merely a peripheral Englishman, this self-consciousness is creatively crippling. The meaning and implications of being an Ulster Protestant have to be investigated before the siege can be lifted, and this involves the writer's confronting the less pleasant aspects of Ulster Protestantism, which Leitch and Wilson—and in a different way West —have been prepared to do. Their chief Protestant heroes exhibit that perversity caricatured in *Hudibras* when Samuel Butler writes of 'true blue' Presbyterians:

> Still so perverse and opposite,
> As if they worshipped God for spite.

When Leitch and Wilson show us the dark face of Ulster Protestantism, they are rectifying one of the Protestant Ulsterman's defects: the inability to know himself. Recognition of this dark face is something Leitch and Wilson share with their chief characters to whom it is revealed—after the tragic manner —brutally and too late for their redemption. And so it is possible to see the Ulster Protestants, beneath the simple perversity, as tragic people and therefore prime material for the fiction writer. They are tragic in the classical senses of having wasted their creative potential, misused their power and failed to recognise their character flaw of overweening pride that has rendered their power brittle and their outlook myopic.

Ulster Catholics, on the other hand, seem much less tragic; they have a solid sense of their Irishness forged over the centuries by the oppression and suffering endured by all Irish Catholics. Their experience is matter not for tragedy but for pathos and, paradoxically, comedy, twin dominant modes in Ulster fiction written by Catholics. Perhaps this view of Ulster Catholics will seem facile when they come to realise how indissolubly their fate is coupled with that of the Ulster Protestants; in conceiving the sectarian relationship in dramatic terms, I tend to think of the manner in which Creon and Antigone are locked together in Sophocles' play. Antigone is the obvious sufferer whose side time is on and whose dilemma—to submit or not—is easily and early resolved. Creon, however, is the more tragic figure who is short-sighted, proud and inflexible and whose fate plots all the co-ordinates of the tragic curve.

In a blurred and inchoate way, Shan Bullock sensed the tragic, 'Creontic' nature of the Protestant psyche and his novels are gropings towards tragedy; and we have seen how *Poor Lazarus* is Leitch's attempt to create a central character invested with tragic stature. Perhaps even more consciously, Jack Wilson has aimed for tragedy. For Wilson Ulster Protestants are doomed to tragic unhappiness because of the original 'sin' of dispossession and maltreatment of the native Irish. Having won a victory of sorts in the Plantation, the Protestants have been paradoxically enslaved by that victory ever since, never secure, nerve-torn through the need for constant vigilance, guilt-racked, garrisoned in what remains an alien country.

In Wilson's *The Tomorrow Country* and *Dark Eden* the setting is a Protestant farm or settlement ringed by hostile forces. The land is rich and beautiful, Edenically so, but there is no tranquillity in which to enjoy it; besides, there is a canker working from the inside : the violence by which the land was appropriated and which has thereafter been endemic to the land, and a puritan guilt that continually seeks to atone for that violence. Here then is a third version of the Paradise myth in Ulster fiction and one which is associated with, but different from, the Catholic folk myth of the lost pre-Plantation paradise. Wilson's paradise, wrested from the Catholic peasantry, has been lost in the act of its appropriation and in the hubris of the planters' notion that the natural paradise could be improved by being 'Protestantised'. Unfortunately Wilson's vision of planted Ulster as a green fertile valley stained indelibly with blood errs on the side of melodrama. What looks like Eden is in reality for Wilson Sodom and Gomorrah or Golgotha, favourite biblical analogies that we can set beside Leitch's Lazarus and West's Cain in the mythicising of Protestant Ulster and its people.

Violence and guilt are self-perpetuating. Leitch's Yarr and Wilson's Protestants destroy themselves without too much help from the forces that ring them, waiting. For this reason sectarianism is of secondary rather than primary importance in their fiction. For this reason, too, Leitch chooses to make Yarr semi-impotent and Wilson uses incest literally to show a family in distress and symbolically to represent the autistic self-destructiveness of the Ulster Protestants. Wilson's dramatic context is a long-established Protestant family suffering, in a fairly literal sense, from bad blood. In *The Tomorrow Country* and *Dark Eden* the central character is a son of the family whose innocence is lost when he discovers the nature of the sin or crime committed by his father. The sin of the father is also the sins of the ancestors : if the father is Oedipus, Oedipus is in turn Adam.

Ex-boxer Wilson is a spunky writer whose writing has, from his first novel, *The Wild Summer* (1963), always had a high adrenalin flow, prodigal of simile and image. *The Tomorrow Country* (1967) demonstrates what happens when his raw talent is not harnessed by rewriting and careful editing, for it is a novel marred by a slapdash approach and unintended illiteracies. Only in the sense of telling us something about the narrator, Ken Cameron, is the breathless, vulgar language effective. Cameron is the eighteen-year-old son of a farmer who took the boy away from school to work on the farm when the eldest son, Ray, took off for faraway places. Ken Cameron seethes with hatred and frustration and he tells the story in bursts of colloquial Ulster speech that on occasions resemble a combination of punches delivered by a boxer whose tenacity exceeds his agility. Here he is describing the hired female help at dinner :

Yet here by tradition and habit the respectfully awed and subdued women in curlers and cardigans were invited to dine, to sit in prim silence or incline heads to whisper, so that in the awkward moments of waiting between sitting and eating they seemed more like a congregation in church with the whispering like the furtive brief rustlings of hymn-books or Bibles, and me sat there at the foot of the table up-pricked in massive frigidity on account of every glance I let slip down the length of that table towards the still-empty and conspicuous place at the head of it had to run the gauntlet of eyes and faces and never got far before the suspicious attention it got turned it aside to retreat in confusion via the salt-cellar and milk jug back to my plate. (p. 85)

On a five-hundred-acre Ulster farm called Sunridge live Ken, his father, his simple, hulking brother Sebastian, a hired help James Henry, and Katherine, whose relationship to the Camerons is at first obscure. A development company wants to buy the farm and is prepared to offer up to half a million pounds for it. Ken, who loathes life on the farm, urges his father to sell but the old man, dying of cancer, is proud and recalcitrant. Soon after the novel opens Ray, the prodigal son long estranged from his father, returns to claim his share of the farm. At first Ken believes that Ray is after only money, but it transpires that the latter's desire to inherit and work the farm in the face of development threats is genuine. Ken for his part wants immediate cash without strings and when his father wills him the farm he offers it to Ray in exchange for a small cheque, his lust to escape the farm exceeding his material desires.

A secondary theme in *The Tomorrow Country* is, then, the besieging of the land by the city, in the guise of planners and developers. The land is resilient, however : significantly the new farm machinery keeps breaking down and the family has to revert to its old implements, the old order reasserting itself beneath the veneer of modernity. Ken wants the land opened up to the new and the urban, but he is not the villainous or hubristic character he would be in McLaverty or Bullock : hubris for Wilson resides in those who wish to maintain at all costs the land's integrity and who resist change. This pride in the land is inseparable from the arrogance and violent mentality with which the land was secured in the beginning. Ken Cameron sees the curse of Sunridge—the novel's primary theme—dating

T

back to 1627, when the land was stolen from the native Irish
and its original Irish name changed :

> Every time I stop working this place long enough to take a good
> look at it I think in awe of the blood that was spilled to secure it,
> the centuries of sacrifice it has taken to sustain it, and I find myself
> wondering what there is about it that enslaved each one of my
> ancestors in turn, why none had the sense to repudiate the cross
> that was bequeathed them and escape from the curse that came
> with it, why each succeeding generation seems to have felt obliged
> to take on its shoulders the guilt of the past and strive to atone
> for it. (pp. 10–11)

The curse had been revived by Ken's father who, it turns out,
is Katherine's father by a woman other than Ken's mother.
Ignorant of their real relationship, Ray and Katherine made
love (watched surreptitiously by Ken) and their growing affection
for each other was the cause of Ray's being driven off the land.
Such happenings recall the fiction of the American South and
Wilson is aware of the resemblance when he introduces a black
Southerner as an employee of the development company and has
Ken describe the Camerons as similar to the declining Southern
gentry. Sebastian too might put us in mind of Steinbeck's Lennie
Small or Faulkner's Benjy.

Ken is torn between two aspects of the Ulster Protestant
character : one, violent, sinful and vengeful (represented by Ray
and various Cameron ancestors), the other proud, puritanical
and atoning (represented by Ken's father in his later years). The
two aspects are incestuously related, feeding off and perpetuating
each other. Ken's task in the novel is to flee his poisoned roots
and the Camerons' 'incestuous hypocrisy'. The only way he
can do this is by finding love and intimacy untainted by
abnormality and vested interest; he seems to find these with
young Mrs Ingraham and at the novel's conclusion is preparing
to go away with her after his father's funeral. One doubts, however, if even Ken can escape the curse he imagines to be upon
the Cameron family. Meanwhile it appears as though Katherine
is going to remain at Sunridge and perhaps even marry Ray. The
Protestant garrison, faced with real and imagined hostility, re-
tracts even more incestuously.

Wilson is a pulpish and pulpitish writer but he has a good

deal of reckless courage. In *Dark Eden* (1969) he seeks to dramatise how the curse upon the Ulster Protestants originated. This has involved him in a very free historical re-creation of the early years of the Plantation and—such being Wilson's *métier*—a lot of blood and thunder. Behind the rodomontade is a new dimension to the sectarian stereotypes. The obvious comparison is with Marshall's *Planted by a River,* set about seventy years later than *Dark Eden.* Marshall's is the more authentic and circumspect of the two, but *Dark Eden* gambles and wins a trifle more.

Dark Eden takes the form of dramatised entries from a diary kept during the early years of the Ulster Plantation (1616–18) by the significantly named Ansil Adams. The narrator, who introduces and occasionally interrupts the dramatised entries, is a descendant of Ansil's and claims that the diary 'shattered the smug illusions of a comfortable lifetime, turned the false pride of three centuries to dust and put for me the final stamp on the hypocrisy of people I had held for so long in awe and respect' (p. 4). Reading his ancestor's diary has been the narrator's recognition of his inherited guilt, just as the revelation to Ansil of the identity of his father is the near-tragic climax to the diary's events.

Young Ansil Adams, reared in a border village near Berwick, loses his parents to disease, and journeys to Ulster to be looked after by his father's brother Joel. He finds an Ulster in the process of being planted and at a time, as the narrator puts it, 'of massacre, of rape and murder, of witch-burning, a time when the people prayed to God but had an even greater faith in ghosts' (p. 2). Ansil's father was a stiff, puritanical man, but Joel is a brash and lawless leader of a band of virtual brigands who live in a defended settlement from which they make forays for booty into the wild forested land around them. Throughout the novel Ansil—in a way reminiscent of Ken Cameron—is divided between these two characters, his dead, apparently honourable father and his outlaw uncle, very much alive. The dead father would seem to represent the true Scot, laconic, virtuous, frugally productive. Joel on the other hand has reverted to the unproductive, clan-like ways of the native Irish. Joel, however, appears thoroughly evil because, having been castrated by a 'vengefule Irishe Tribe', he has turned his sexual frustrations into perversion and war. He has a common law wife,

Rachel (whom he renamed after capturing her from the Irish), and because he cannot have her, he derives vicarious satisfaction from watching selected men from his band take her. Joel's impotence works on two levels. In one sense it is the price he has paid for his reversion (turning his reversion into a mockery), the price for losing that vigilant and puritan application that created the Plantation Joel has betrayed. In a larger sense it represents the inability of the Ulster Protestant ever to defeat or subdue the Irish. Joel owns Rachel from whom he exacts obedience but he cannot, literally and metaphorically, penetrate her innermost self. Joel calls Rachel 'a most passionate martyr' and hates her because her very martyrdom (in a similar but more highly charged manner to that of Mary in Bullock's *Dan the Dollar*) renders her impregnable—she does not, in fact, bear a child despite repeated ravishing. Taxed by Ansil about the passivity that meekly allowed Ansil, under the bloodshot commanding eye of Joel, to assault her, Rachel replies : 'Lie down, Ansil. Lie down quickly. Let them do what they want with your body. Tramp on it, spit on it, kick it and soil it, but don't let them know of the feeling inside. They will tear out that feeling, they will destroy it. They fear it.' (p. 109)

As a homicidal extremist, Joel is matched by McQuilballa, a bloodthirsty Irish patriarch. In contrast Rachel and Ansil are compassionate human beings who must renounce the potential for violence they have inherited in order to come together in love and understanding. Ansil's is the more difficult task since he carries a double cross. Rachel has her Catholicism but the puritan heritage to which Ansil has cleaved throughout the novel and used as a shield against Joel's corrupt influence turns out to be a hypocritical hoax. He discovers that Joel is his real father, that his 'father' stole his mother's affections from Joel and subsequently inhibited her love with his puritan dictates. Ansil's Scots blood is therefore poisoned by hypocrisy, while his Irishness derives from Joel's violent reversion. Ansil Adams, in a way the aboriginal Scots-Irish Planter, is the Cain-cursed 'son' of two men whose respective qualities together create the tragic character he has inherited. The only way he can escape his inherited guilt is by going into exile. Having been pardoned by the commanding officer of the soldiers who capture the brigands and who hang Joel, Ansil prepares to leave for America with Rachel : only in a neutral country can Protestant and Catholic come together as human beings instead of as warring foes.

Wilson's notion of the Protestants' original 'sin' is facile; equally simplistic is the idea that the Protestant must make a choice solely between violence and hypocritical puritanism. Yet these notions do, in their allegorical way, say something about the Protestant character, and the metaphorising of sectarianism through sexuality is crudely effective. Perhaps others with subtler literary equipment will benefit from Wilson's pioneering, machete-wielding forays into the Protestant heart of darkness.

(5)

John Montague is a poet of sizeable reputation with one volume of stories to his credit. *Death of a Chieftain and Other Stories* (1964) contains a couple of stories that are typically Irish in their nostalgic re-creation of a rural childhood in Co. Tyrone, but on the whole Montague does not belong to the Irish short story tradition. Perhaps it is the power of suggestion, given that Montague has lived for long periods in Paris, which makes one detect in his stories the influence of the French *nouveau roman*. On first impression he seems to lack the touch of the genuine storyteller : he has few flashes of brilliance and his stories tend to be for the eye rather than the ear. His style however has its own rewards and he has painstakingly hammered out his own kind of coherence. His favourite technique is a slow, reluctant approach towards the core of the story. Scene is built upon scene architecturally rather than organically until the narrative—typically novella more than short story—is completed.

The titular story of the collection has perhaps the most bizarre setting possible for an allegorical journey into the Ulster psyche : the jungle of Central America. The 'chieftain' is Bernard Corunna Coote, a renegade from life's cause, who visits the town of San Antonio on a guided tour from Boston, engages in conversation over a bottle of tequila with the town drunk, Hautmoc, and elects to stay rather than continue his vacation with Sunlite Tours. Coote moves in permanently to the Hotel Darien where he drinks, plays cards and exchanges sparing intimacies with three other permanent guests—Mitchell Witchbourne, 'a cadaverous Iowan', once manager of a chain of mid-western hotels; Jean Tarrou, once in the French consular service and who served under the Vichy regime; and Carlos Turbida, black sheep of a wealthy Mexican merchant family. These four men, alienated from their past and even, during festivals, from the local inhabitants, live a drugged and purgatorial existence, constituting a small universe in which no questions are asked, no judgements passed and personal revelations received with the nonchalance of forwarding an empty glass for refilling. The Hotel Darien is an end-of-the-line reception lounge for the spiritually bankrupt. The setting is similar to that of Tennessee Williams's *The Night of the Iguana,* with Coote playing Williams's defrocked minister. Coote is in fact by his own confession 'a renegade Protestant'. When the others receive the news politely, Coote exclaims : 'You do not understand. . . I am a renegade Ulster Protestant. . . I am a renegade Ulster Presbyterian; an Orangeman !' (p. 142) The story opens with Coote engaged on a search in the jungle, backtracks to tell Coote's life-story (including the above revelations of spiritual and sectarian dereliction) up until the jungle search which then continues, the story thus concocting a 'flashback sandwich'.

Coote, we learn, sprang from a proud Ulster family that over the centuries distinguished itself in British military campaigns and engagements—Corunna, Waterloo, the Somme. As a young man Coote became enamoured of Irish history and archaeology and after Oxford dedicated himself to discovering the burial places of the chieftains of Uladh, a search interrupted by his mandatory spell in the British Army during the Second World War. While in the army he refused a decoration 'on the grounds that he did not recognize the present king of England' and also campaigned for the use of Gaelic in Irish regiments. Invalided out of the army he lived in Dublin before disappearing to America. Montague presents Coote's interest in Irish history and archaeology as 'a demonstration of the principle of cultural reversion, i.e. the invasion of the conqueror by the culture of the conquered' (pp. 143–4). He has never lost this interest, for it is when Hautmoc tells him that the pure race of Indians who founded American civilisation lived beyond the neighbouring mountains that he decides to remain in San Antonio.

At first Coote is content to live a limbo existence in the

Hotel Darien; what lies the other side of limbo is hinted at in Montague's observation on the daily card-playing: though their skills are roughly equal they keep a tally of their impossible debts 'to keep an edge on the game' and because in order to continue they find it necessary 'to believe in some apocalyptic day of reckoning'. After an unpleasant incident with Tarrou who infringes the fragile unspoken rules holding the sad quartet together, Coote disappears into the jungle in an attempt to locate the graves of the Indian chieftains of which Hautmoc had told him. He is convinced that the burial places will resemble those of the Ulster chieftains, thus proving—in corroboration of his belief that Saint Brendan discovered America—that the entire Western hemisphere is at base a Celtic civilisation. His fellow-guests at the hotel, afraid for his sanity and wishing him back, conspire with Hautmoc to fake an Indian burial place beyond the mountains. Coote accompanies Hautmoc there, detects the hoax but is mollified when Hautmoc explains why he partici-pated in the conspiracy: 'because if the place you are searching does not exist, then it should. Your dream and mine have much in common.' (p. 160) As though to authenticate the hoax and prove his theory, Coote enters the burial place to die like an Indian chieftain but also like a military chieftain of the Irish and British military traditions. 'Softly on fields of history, Ramillies and El Alamein, Cremona and the Somme, the war-pipes began to grieve. Closing ranks silent regiments listened, Connaught Rangers and Clare's Dragoons, Dublin and Innis-killing Fusiliers, North Irish Horse and Sarsfield's Brigade.'

In a straight reading of 'Death of a Chieftain', Coote is gradually transformed from a family dropout into a slightly demonic figure (passing whom the local American women would make gestures of expiation) and thence into a mythic hero. He begins as a renegade provincial aristocrat in whom Dona Anna, madam of the local brothel, sees unmistakable signs of social distinction. Engaged in his jungle search for the burial places, he is then likened variously to a mountain, Excalibur (rising from a lake), a grey mammoth and a whale. When he steps into the grave passage his exaltation into mythic hero is at hand. He is a giant sacrificed in the cause of racial union and harmony. Not only straddling Old and New Worlds, he manages—even more miraculously!—to combine Protestant Orangeism, British imperialism and native Irishry in a way only West's Christopher MacMannan (also a suggestively symbolic hero) has equalled. Indeed, Coote's search for the lost Indian race and for the lost Ulster chieftains might put us in mind of the 'lost people and culture' from which MacMannan claims to derive.

However, Montague's ponderous style in 'Death of a Chieftain' signals a satiric undertow. If Coote is unlikely as an heroic figure, he is equally unlikely as a mere Ulsterman. When he claims descent from the oldest civilisation in Europe he is guilty of self-delusion, similarly when he asserts that 'we are the secret mother race of Europe'. He is descended, after all, merely from Captain William Coote 'who was rewarded for skilful butchery in the Cromwellian campaign with a large grant of Papish land'. No doubt Captain William brought to the subjugation of the land and its people the same 'alien discipline' his descendant Bernard visits upon the resilient American jungle in his search for the burial places. Like Leitch's Yarr and Wilson's young Protestants, Coote tries and fails to escape his roots. Reversion can never be identification, and over-zealous reversion is matter for ridicule. When we are given a picture of young Coote during his Oxford vacations striding Irish hills in kilt and with wolfhound, he becomes a comic figure. In this light, the descriptions of Coote as a whale, mammoth and mountain become tongue-in-cheek. If Montague intends us to see the story's final scene only from Coote's point of view, then his transmogrification into a mythic chieftain is his own mere delusion. When we are told that in his face as he awaits death is 'provincial crudity refined to a patrician elegance', we are reminded of what Coote is in reality—a demented Ulster Orangeman far from home and easily turned into a mock-heroic figure.

Save it be guilty of self-parody, 'Death of a Chieftain' only works seriously as satire. It satirises the zeal of converts and, in particular, of those who try to become *Hiberniores Hibernicis ipsis*. But finally the target is the bemused Ulster Protestant, a figure close to mock-tragedy even in Leitch and Wilson. The Ulster Protestant, half-caricatured in Montague, is Ulsterman, Irishman and Briton all at once and yet truly none of these. Coote's sequence of names spans the confusion : the first commonly Irish, the second commemorating a British military engagement, the third Anglo-Irish. The Ulster Protestant has no mythology, no deities or saints, few heroes and martyrs. In Bernard Corunna Coote he is given a deity; in Coote's death he is given a founding martyrdom; in Coote's story a mythology. And yet, despite the pseudo-epic march of the story, the impression persists that perhaps satire is not Montague's real intention.

Satire or no, Montague is a courageous writer conscious of the deep and irreversible interdependence of Protestant and Catholic in Northern Ireland. He chooses for a reconciliatory epigraph to *Death of a Chieftain* lines (that generate added poignancy because of events since 1969) from an Ulster Protestant poet, John Hewitt, with whom he was later to co-operate in a poem sequence for recital and publication, *The Planter and the Gael:*

> I wrestled with my father in my dream,
> and in that dream remembered who we were
> and why we should not struggle, he and I . . .

The Ulster Protestant cannot escape his Irishness, neither can he wholly segregate himself from his Catholic fellow-Northerners. But if he wishes instead to embrace his Irishness, he has no call like Coote to become more Irish than the Irish themselves. For his part, the Northern Catholic cannot escape the Protestant colouring that has been given to Ulster by the planters, neither can he pretend he lives in a purely native Ireland which the Protestant must either revert to or depart from. The mutuality that traps both sides also defines them : to this extent, both labour under a false identity when they deny that mutuality. But their respective real identities reside not in the different stocks from which they spring, no longer recoverable (and a racist illusion), but rather in the union that still eludes them. With Leitch, Wilson and Montague, the first and superficially divisive steps in the long trek towards synthesis have been taken. In Montague's long story 'The Cry'—set like *Poor Lazarus* not long after the IRA border campaign—the coupling of Protestant and Catholic is as private and exclusive as any mating, something which has been learned during the current troubles by all manner of carpet-bagging politicians, do-gooders and alien ideologues. 'The Cry' (first published as 'Le Cri' in *Les Lettres Nouvelles*) assumes added interest because it was written several years before the civil rights movement it prefigures.

Peter Douglas who works for an English newspaper returns

home for a visit to his parents' small town in Northern Ireland. One night in bed he hears the sounds of someone crying for help and when he investigates finds a group of B Specials roughing up a man on the way to the police barracks. Outraged as a liberal, he also reverts momentarily to a sectarian hatred of the Protestant police. His father, a man of extreme republican sympathies, calls him gutless when, instead of joining the IRA, Douglas determines to write a muckraking article on the North for his newspaper. If his father supports the argument of force (and so is really no different from violent Protestants) and Peter the force of argument, his mother believes in strict neutrality for fear of stirring up 'bad blood'. Of the B Specials and the police, she says with unassailable martyr's logic : 'We have to live with them—why else did God put them there?'

When he begins his investigation into the incident, Douglas finds the visiting County Inspector of police politely dismissive and impregnable in a manner born of decades of colonial-type administration. The town clerk, presumably a Protestant, supports the Specials. The Catholic neighbours who witnessed the incident refuse to deepen their involvement. In desperation, Douglas accompanied by his father visits the victim in his mother's upland cottage. No archetypal Irish peasant he, dressed in jeans and studded belt (a bit of a Teddy Boy, the Inspector had said); but his reticence and apparent passivity are only too typical and Douglas cannot persuade him to consider action against the police. Returning to his parents' house, Peter Douglas looks out of the bedroom window and sees Joe Doom, the village idiot, holding up 'so that Peter—or anyone else in the street who was watching—could read' a piece of cardboard inscribed : 'Nosy Parker go home'.

Peter Douglas is an outsider unwanted by either side because in order to get his views across he employs alien methods—investigation, argument, moral protest, publicity. It is implied in the menacing scene with Joe Doom that ends the story that such methods are in Ulster only temporarily peaceful and must lead eventually to violence, an implication unhappily borne out since 1969. Violence lies in wait beneath a fragile mutual agreement by Protestant and Catholic to maintain the status quo. The status quo is of course to the disadvantage of the Catholics, and in 1968 young, newly educated Catholics broke the agreement in

order to effect reforms. On one level, 'The Cry' prophesies what
the reformers discovered : that until the tribal realities of Ulster
life are broken down, liberalism must either fall into self-travesty
or else abandon reform for revolution.

Peter Douglas is also an outsider because he went away and
thereby forfeited his right to speak for or to either side. He does
not have to live in Northern Ireland, unlike those whose help
he seeks. Besides, Protestant and Catholic are more alike and
more mutually dependent than Douglas realises. Montague
establishes this in fairly subtle ways. Douglas's father, for all his
republicanism, was in the British Army and when Peter first
returns home the family drink a welcome to him in Coronation
mugs : just as the republicanism of Burke Senior in *The Emperor
of Ice-Cream* is sabotaged by external events, that of Douglas
Senior is sabotaged by internal ironies. Moreover, everyone,
Protestant or Catholic, is given a Protestant name—Wilson,
Douglas, Ferguson. And what Peter Douglas diagnoses as
Catholic passivity is in another sense an ability to adapt, to
manoeuvre and to survive. Characteristically, the champion of
the downtrodden paints a picture of his people's plight that is
black instead of subtle shades of grey.

In the end, Peter Douglas is rejected because he attempts to
rewrite the rules of a sectarian game played so long that its
players not only know their opponents intimately but even
harbour a kind of love for them. The reader feels that once the
foreign body has been removed, the native tissue of fear and
deceit (but also of organic-like equilibrium) will close again as
though nothing had ever disturbed its cancer.

It is fitting that the author of 'The Cry' should be a Catholic
from the Carleton country in Tyrone where the scenario of this
study opened. Carleton also from his vantage-point in the city
found the land dark and obtuse and peculiarly self-sustaining
(for good and ill) despite the pull of the outside world. There is
reason to believe, though, that 'The Cry' marks the end of one
strain of rural Ulster fiction that began with Carleton. The composition of the native tissue of sectarian relationships has probably altered for all time since 1968. As Montague himself has
written : 'Old moulds are broken in the North.' A new fiction
will emerge in response to the new situation. One would expect it
to be written mainly by those whose parents were workers or

small farmers and who have been educated in the city—the 'new educated' who are supplanting the middle-class 'new rich' as opinion-shapers in Ulster. The city and the outside world can no longer be resisted by the land. Neither in city nor upon the land can enlarged understanding of sectarianism be halted. The land's beauties and disabilities will remain, but Protestant and Catholic —with time and good fortune—will transcend their respective solitudes into mature and uncharted conciliation.

SELECT BIBLIOGRAPHY

PRIMARY SOURCES

Sam Hanna Bell, *December Bride*, **London 1951,** New York 1951.
George A. Birmingham (pseud.), *The Red Hand of Ulster*, London 1912.
Patrick Boyle, *Like Any Other Man*, London 1966, New York 1968.
    At Night All Cats Are Grey and Other Stories, London 1966, New York 1969.
    All Looks Yellow to the Jaundiced Eye, **London 1969,** London 1971.
George Buchanan, *Rose Forbes*, London 1950. (Extended version of the edition of London 1937.)
    A Place to Live, London 1952.
Shan F. Bullock, *The Squireen*, London 1903.
    Dan the Dollar, Dublin 1906.
    The Loughsiders, London 1924.
William Carleton, *Traits and Stories of the Irish Peasantry*, **London 1893,** London 1896; reissued in a multi-volume paperback edition, edited by Maurice Harmon, Cork 1973.
    Carleton's Stories of Irish Life, ed. Darrell Figgis, London 1918.
    Fardorougha the Miser, Dublin 1839, London 1848.
    Valentine M'Clutchy, Dublin 1845, Dublin 1847.
    The Black Prophet, London 1847, facs. of 1st ed, Shannon 1972.
    The Emigrants of Ahadarra, Dublin 1847, **London 1857.**
    The Evil Eye, Dublin 1860.
Joyce Cary, *Castle Corner*, London 1938, London 1952.
    A House of Children, London 1941, **London 1951.**
Anne Crone, *Bridie Steen*, New York 1948, London 1949.
    This Pleasant Lea, New York 1951, London 1952.
    My Heart and I, London 1955.
Lynn Doyle (pseud.), *Ballygullion*, Dublin 1908, London 1967.
    A Bowl of Broth, London 1945.
    Back to Ballygullion, London 1953.
St John Ervine, *Mrs Martin's Man*, Dublin 1914.
    The St John Ervine Omnibus (*The Foolish Lovers*, *The Wayward Man*, *The First Mrs Fraser*), London 1933.

Brian Friel, *The Saucer of Larks*, London 1969. (Contains most of the stories published in Friel's earlier collections, *The Saucer of Larks*, London 1962, and *The Gold in the Sea*, London 1966.)

Stephen Gilbert, *Monkeyface*, London 1948.
The Burnaby Experiments, London 1952.
Ratman's Notebooks, **London 1968**; repr. as *Willard*, London 1971.

F. L. Green, *Odd Man Out*, London 1945, Harmondsworth 1948, Glasgow 1967.

Benedict Kiely, *Honey Seems Bitter*, London 1954.
There Was an Ancient House, London 1955.
The Captain with the Whiskers, London 1960, New York 1961.
A Journey to the Seven Streams, London 1963.
Dogs Enjoy the Morning, London 1968.

Maurice Leitch, *The Liberty Lad*, London 1965.
Poor Lazarus, London 1969, **London 1970.**

Patrick MacGill, *Children of the Dead End*, London 1914, **London 1972.**
The Rat-Pit, **London 1915,** London 1971.

Michael McLaverty, *Call My Brother Back*, London 1939, Dublin 1970.
Lost Fields, New York 1941, **London 1942.**
The White Mare and Other Stories, Newcastle, Co. Down 1943.
In This Thy Day, London 1945.
The Game Cock and Other Stories, London 1949.
Truth in the Night, London 1952.
The Choice, **London 1958,** New York 1958.

Janet McNeill, *A Child in the House*, London 1955.
The Maiden Dinosaur, **London 1964;** repr. as *The Belfast Friends*, Boston 1966.
Talk to Me, London 1965.
The Small Widow, London 1967.

W. F. Marshall, *Planted by a River*, Belfast 1948.

John Montague, *Death of a Chieftain and Other Stories*, London 1964.

Brian Moore, *Judith Hearne*, London 1955, Toronto 1964; repr. as *The Lonely Passion of Miss Judith Hearne*, Harmondsworth 1959; repr. as *The Lonely Passion of Judith Hearne*, New York 1964, **London 1965.**
The Feast of Lupercal, Boston 1957, **London 1958;** repr. as *A Moment of Love*, London 1965.
The Luck of Ginger Coffey, Boston 1960, London 1960, **Harmondsworth 1965.**
An Answer from Limbo, Boston 1962, New York 1963, **London 1963,** Harmondsworth 1965.

The Emperor of Ice-Cream, New York 1965, **London 1966,** London 1967.
I Am Mary Dunne, New York 1968, **London 1968.**
Fergus, London 1971.
The Revolution Script, London 1972.
Catholics, London 1972.
John O'Connor, *Come Day—Go Day*, Dublin 1948.
Victor Price, *The Death of Achilles*, London 1963.
Hubert Quinn, *The Soil and the Stars*, Belfast 1943.
The Land Remains, Belfast 1944.
Forrest Reid, *The Kingdom of Twilight*, London 1904.
The Bracknels, London 1911.
At the Door of the Gate, London 1915.
Uncle Stephen, London 1931.
Brian Westby, London 1934.
The Retreat, **London 1936,** London 1946.
Peter Waring, London 1937, **London 1939,** Harmondsworth 1946. (Rewritten version of *Following Darkness*, London 1912.)
Young Tom, London 1944, **London 1946.**
Denis Bracknel, London 1947. (Rewritten version of *The Bracknels*.)
Joseph Tomelty, *Red Is the Port Light*, London 1948.
The Apprentice: The Story of a Nonentity, London 1953.
Anthony C. West, *River's End and Other Stories*, London 1960, London 1966.
The Ferret Fancier, London 1963.
As Towns with Fire, London 1968.
Jack Wilson, *The Wild Summer*, London 1963, London 1964.
The Tomorrow Country, London 1967.
Dark Eden, London 1969.

SECONDARY SOURCES

W. F. Adams, *Ireland and Irish Emigration to the New World from 1815 to the Famine*, New Haven, Conn. 1932.
Walter Allen, *The English Novel*, Harmondsworth 1958.
Conrad M. Arensberg, *The Irish Countryman*, London 1937, Gloucester, Mass. 1959, New York 1968.
Conrad M. Arensberg and Solon T. Kimball, *Family and Community in Ireland*, London 1968.
Michael Banton, ed., *The Social Anthropology of Complex Societies*, London 1968.
J. C. Beckett and R. E. Glasscock, ed., *Belfast: The Origin and Growth of an Industrial City*, London 1967.

Sam Hanna Bell, *Erin's Orange Lily*, London 1956.

John Boyd, 'Ulster Prose' in *The Arts in Ulster*, ed. Sam Hanna Bell, Nesca A. Robb and John Hewitt, London 1951.

George Buchanan, *Passage through the Present*, London 1932.

Green Seacoast, London 1959.

Russell Burlingham, *Forrest Reid*, London 1953. (Includes virtually complete Reid bibliography.)

Joseph Campbell, *The Hero with a Thousand Faces*, Cleveland 1970.

T. P. Coogan, *Ireland since the Rising*, London 1966, New York 1966.

John Cronin, 'Prose' in *Causeway: The Arts in Ulster*, ed. Michael Longley, Belfast 1971.

Edmund Curtis, *A History of Ireland*, 6th ed., London 1950; reiss. 1961, 1964.

Hallvard Dahlie, *Brian Moore*, Toronto 1969.

R. J. Dickson, *Ulster Emigration to Colonial America, 1718–1775*, London 1966.

Émile Durkheim, *Suicide*, trans. John A. Spaulding and George Simpson, London 1952, New York 1966.

Mircea Eliade, *The Myth of the Eternal Return*, trans. Willard R. Trask, New York 1954, London 1955.

Myths, Dreams, and Mysteries, trans. Philip Mairet, London 1960, New York 1967.

Myth and Reality, trans. Willard R. Trask, New York 1968.

E. Estyn Evans, *Irish Folk Ways*, London 1957, London 1967.

Thomas Flanagan, *The Irish Novelists, 1800–1850*, New York 1959.

E. M. Forster, *Abinger Harvest*, London 1936, London 1953.

Two Cheers for Democracy, London 1951, Harmondsworth 1965.

John Wilson Foster, 'Crisis and Ritual in Brian Moore's Belfast Novels', *Éire-Ireland* III (Autumn 1968), 66–74.

'Dog Among the Moles: The Fictional World of Benedict Kiely', *The Dublin Magazine* VIII (Winter 1970–71), 24–31.

'McLaverty's People', *Éire-Ireland* IV (Fall 1971), 92–105.

'Separation and Return in the Fiction of Brian Moore, Michael McLaverty and Benedict Kiely'. (Unpublished doctoral dissertation, University of Oregon 1970.)

'Passage through Limbo: Brian Moore's North American Novels', *Critique: Studies in Modern Fiction*, Atlanta, XIII, 1, 5–18.

Jack Gibbs, ed., *Suicide*, New York 1968.

Rosemary Harris, *Prejudice and Tolerance in Ulster: A Study of Neighbours and 'Strangers' in a Border Community*, Manchester 1972.

Benedict Kiely, *Poor Scholar: A Study of the Works and Days of William Carleton*, London 1947, Dublin 1972.

Modern Irish Fiction—A Critique, Dublin 1950.

R. D. Laing, *Self and Others*, Harmondsworth 1971.

C. S. Lewis, *Surprised by Joy: The Shape of my Early Life*, London 1955, London 1959.

Jack Ludwig, 'Brian Moore: Ireland's Loss, Canada's Novelist', *Critique: Studies in Modern Fiction*, Minneapolis, V (Spring-Summer 1962), 5–13.

Louis MacNeice, *The Strings Are False*, London 1965, New York 1966.

Jack Matthews, 'An Interview with Patrick Boyle', *Malahat Review*, Victoria, B.C., Oct. 1970, 85–90.

Vivian Mercier, *The Irish Comic Tradition*, Oxford 1962, New York 1969.

T. W. Moody and J. C. Beckett, ed., *Ulster since 1800*, London 1957.

Brian Moore, 'Bloody Ulster', *Atlantic Monthly* (Sep. 1970); repr. as 'Now and Then', *Threshold*, Belfast, 23 (Sep. 1970), 29–37.

Frank O'Connor, *The Lonely Voice: A Study of the Short Story*, London 1963.

David J. O'Donoghue, *The Life of William Carleton*, London 1896.

Sean O'Faolain, *The Irish*, Harmondsworth 1969.

Octavio Paz, *The Labyrinth of Solitude: Life and Thought in Mexico*, trans. Lysander Kemp, New York 1961.

Forrest Reid, *Apostate*, London 1926.
Private Road, London 1940.

Philip Stevick, ed., *The Theory of the Novel*, New York 1967.

Rosita Sweetman, *'On Our Knees'*, London 1972.

Arnold van Gennep, *The Rites of Passage*, trans. Monika B. Vizedom and Gabrielle L. Caffee, Chicago 1961.

Cecil Woodham-Smith, *The Great Hunger*, London 1968.

Andrew Wright, *Joyce Cary: A Preface to His Novels*, London 1958.

INDEX

Major references to authors and works are indicated by bold type